THE
MYSTERIES
OF EGYPT
Secret Rites and Traditions

LEWIS SPENCE

ILLUSTRATED

DOVER PUBLICATIONS, INC.
Mineola, New York

Bibliographical Note

This Dover edition, first published in 2005, is an unabridged republication of the work originally published in 1929 by Rider & Co., London, under the title *The Mysteries of Egypt, or The Secret Rites and Traditions of the Nile.*

Library of Congress Cataloging-in-Publication Data

Spence, Lewis, 1874–1955.
    The mysteries of Egypt : secret rites and traditions / Lewis Spence.
        p. cm.
    Originally published: London : Rider & Co., 1929.
    ISBN 0-486-44369-8 (pbk.)
        1. Mysteries, Religious—Egypt. 2. Rites and ceremonies—Egypt. I. Title.

BL2450.M9S64 2005
299'.31—dc22

                                                                        2005051969

Manufactured in the United States of America
Dover Publications, Inc., 31 East 2nd Street, Mineola, N.Y. 11501

PREFACE

THE quest of the hidden things contained in the Sovereign Mysteries of Egypt and the comprehension and restoration of their secrets have engaged my close attention for nearly forty years, but it was only recently that I felt it possible to arrange my ideas concerning them in anything approaching logical form. Not only is the subject obscured and shadowed as few others can be, but the searcher has perforce to penetrate the sacred silences of one of the most obstinately unvocal fraternities in the whole history of arcane philosophy.

The two clear lamps which may guide us in such a quest are inspiration and analogy. For that school of Archæology which, uninspired itself, denies and abhors inspiration, I can only profess that serene amusement with which the archæologists of the future will assuredly regard it. Indeed, is not the "Tape-measure" School the most empirical of all, unconsciously forming its conclusions in the event by the aid of that long-discredited Philosophy of Numbers by which Pythagoras distorted the Eastern wisdom he but partially understood ? If there be virtue in absolute standards then is there much value in that Archæology which exists by rule and theodolite. But absolute standards and a fixed ritual have always been the insignia and the bane of the Magic of the lower cultus !

If certain intricacies appear in the succeeding pages

I must crave indulgence on that score as having essayed the first book in English on a theme as confused as chaos itself. To travel the realms of ancient night and attempt to chart its geography is a task, I suggest, at least equal to mapping a new-found Continent. Gleams here and there twinkle and glimmer. But if we study those arcane systems of which we possess at least the outlines and apply them to the Mysteries of the Nileland shall we be altogether at fault, especially when it is admitted that the sources from which we draw were themselves inspired and perhaps actually founded by Egyptian colonists or hierophants ?

As regards the ultimate secrets of the Mysteries of Egypt, I have naturally been unable to convey more in mere words than my predecessors in the task, for the pure and simple reason that, as in any other arcane system of a genuine character, it is only possible to convey them by apprehension and not by language, which utterly fails man in the attempt to impart information respecting the Absolute. I say nothing regarding the propriety of doing so had I possessed the power, which, by the way, no man possesses, for the reason just given. Initiation into any of the Mysteries of the Secret Tradition and comprehension of the same are, in reality, acts of the spirit, separated by a whole heaven from the crudities of vocal exposition. But I have, I believe, restored the ritual of the Egyptian Mysteries, in its general structure at least, and prepared the way for those genuinely desirous of approaching those arcane schools which in all times and countries have attempted to lead the soul of man along one and the same path—toward reunion with the Divine.

More than my predecessors, I have employed the

Anthropological method of proof, a method much too neglected by mystics, who are as prone to despise it as the anthropologist is to despise the inspirational. But I feel I have not divested my subject of that sovereign charm of wonder which is to the true mystic what the craving for things elfin is to the poet, what the hunger for the sea is to the sailor, or that I have dispersed altogether these lofty and noble shadows which stand like pillars before the great secrets of the Soul. To know all, were it given to us, would be to be old, blasé, satiated. But God in his goodness has elected that, strive as we may, mount as we can, there still remain for our continued wonder and rejuvenation in the illimitable space of His universe forests and wildernesses, secret cities and mansions of marvel, which will secure to us an eternity of quest, of initiation, of exploration, an everlasting satisfaction of that curiosity which is so human, but which lies at the basis of the godlike virtues.

L. S.

CONTENTS

CHAPTER I

CHAPTER IV

CHAPTER V

CHAPTER VI

CHAPTER XI

CHAPTER XII

CHAPTER XIII

CHAPTER XIV

CHAPTER XV

LIST OF ILLUSTRATIONS

THE MYSTERIES OF EGYPT

CHAPTER I

INTRODUCTORY

NO land can lay claim to such a chronicle of mystical and occult thought as Egypt, the mother of magic. Herself a mystery, she brought forth the Mysteries, laying the foundations of arcane science and philosophy for the future, and seeming thus like some dark cavern of issue and origin, whence have emerged those shadowy sorceries and that philosophy of the higher wisdom which have proved the amazement of the succeeding ages.

But even to their profoundest seekers the Mysteries of Egypt too long remained merely a name—a word of conjury, perhaps, still a verbal skeleton unfleshed with reality, for no man could with certainty speak of the rites and marvels enacted within the walls of her temples, the initiations, the tests and trials of her wise priesthood.

Light, however, is slowly breaking in upon the dark places of the Egyptian philosophy, as the golden finger of the sun pierces the recesses of a dungeon. Although we can never know all with certainty, the valuable instrument of analogy gives us power to choose resemblances and argue from their premises. We know that the Hellenic Mysteries, Eleusinian,

Bacchic, and Cabiric were merely the offspring of those of Egypt, and, judging from their details and adding to these the evidences from paintings and monuments, we have been enabled to reconstruct in a large measure the process of the Osirian and Isiac rites of initiation, the dramatic representations enacted at the Mysteries, and to more than guess even at the most profound of their secrets, so that the fabric of the Egyptian arcana may be rebuilt at last as an ancient temple, the stones of which were buried, is later excavated and reassembled.

The actual significance and purpose of the Mysteries of Egypt was a preparation for the higher life, for a more exalted spiritual existence after death. It is beside the point that in their ritual origin and inception they had a less elevated intention, the early form of them being designed more to the material well-being of the astral body on the next plane and protection through identification with deity than with any desire for a higher spiritual communion with the gods. The early Egyptians, like other primitive peoples, believed that the success of existence after death was chiefly associated with the amount of food and liquor the ghost or Ka of the dead man received from his family. Did they fail to succour him with constant offerings of pabulum and libation he would unquestionably become a haunting danger, possibly, like the vampire of the Balkans, preying on his own relatives in order to obtain the necessary nourishment to keep him " alive " in the other world.

Later belief refined this barbarous notion, although the idea that the dead must have nourishment obtained until the end. But the ideas of survival in a specialized paradise and the means of winning one's way there by magic were introduced side by side with it. Just as the religion of Egypt was solely devoted to the proper manner of reaching the paradise sphere of Aalu past the numerous dangers which beset the road thereto, so the Mysteries seem expressly to have been created for the purpose of higher instruction in the manner of reaching the Otherworld and in preparation for the life beyond.

The precise process by which the soul of the dead man was enabled to reach the Fields of the Blessed, and the nature of the journey will be found outlined further on. In this preliminary place it is necessary to describe more the general nature and significance of the Mysteries than to deal separately with their minutiæ. Reasons for the secrecy which surrounded them have been advanced by many writers. Perhaps the least probable is that suggested by Jevons in dealing with the Greek Eleusinian Mysteries, that any who unwittingly partook of them would suffer from " the infection of holiness "—fear of the danger which contact between the holy and the unclean would bring upon both.[1]

Such an " explanation " is typical of the most meretricious kind of argument too frequently advanced by the Anthropological school. Not only is it far too intellectualistic, but actually too fantastic. The passage in which it occurs is worthy of consideration because it puts the " scientific " point of view so typically.

Dealing with the conversion of the cult of the Grecian and Eleusinian Demeter into a " mystery," Jevons remarks that modern scholars have paid little attention to the point :

" That little regard has been paid to this important

[1] *Introduction to the History of Religion*, pp. 62–65.

point is probably due to the long prevailing but now slowly dissolving view that the chief characteristic of the mysteries was secrecy, and that the most important problem was to discover their secrets. Hidden wisdom and esoteric doctrines were supposed to have been handed down from priest to priest, and by them communicated under a vow of secrecy to the initiated.   But the mysteries were not secret societies : they were open to all without distinction ; and all could be initiated into every grade, even the last and the highest.[1]   The priests, again, formed no secret order, but were plain citizens, having no such superiority in education or political or social position that they could be in exclusive possession of any sublime religious knowledge—and, as we have said, the whole Greek world was at liberty to learn the whole of what they had to teach.   But the priests were not preachers or teachers : their official duties consisted simply in knowing and performing the traditional ritual.   About the doctrine of immortality and the future blessedness of those who partook in the mysteries, there was no concealment whatever : Pindar, Æschylus, and Sophocles openly refer to it ; Aristophanes parodies it ; the Homeric Hymn to Demeter, which was an official publication, so to speak, states it expressly and explicitly.   It is therefore not surprising to find that no oath of secrecy was required of the candidate for initiation.''

The real reason for secrecy, Jevons proceeds, was not a desire to keep the Mysteries a secret, but '' fear of the danger which contact between the holy and the unclean would bring upon both.''   The silence observed after initiation was not for the sake of

---

[1] This is not so, as will be seen further on. The neophytes were most carefully selected.

concealment, " but in order to prevent pollution and its consequent dangers." The secrecy which shrouded the celebration of the Mysteries was " accidental and not deliberately designed for purposes of concealment."[1]

But that the very reverse is true is clear from the statements of many writers who themselves had been initiated into the Mysteries. Herodotus expressly mentions that " it would be impious " for him to divulge the arcana, and " upon these Mysteries, all of which, without exception, are known to me, let my lips guard a religious silence." Let the word " religious " be expressly noted. It does not necessarily imply a danger of pollution. It evidently refers to something much more terrible in its results—the dread of drawing down the wrath of the gods by the exposure of secrets which they chose to unveil only to the prepared and the advanced in religious science and faith, and not indiscriminately to the multitude at large. To this has to be added the popular indignation directed against Æschylus and Aristophanes for divulging secrets connected with the Greek Mysteries in their works.

Some years ago the priests who conserve the Mysteries of the Jurupari cult on the shores of the Uapès River in Brazil were so scandalized at the public display of the relics of that deity by two French missionaries that they decreed the massacre of every tenth woman in the tribe—the secrets of Jurupari being withheld from women. The reason they gave was that Jurupari was " angry." There was no question of taint. The arcane symbols of the god had been revealed, and " naturally " he was wroth thereat, because it was unmeet that those not destined to

[1] *Introduction to the History of Religion,* pp. 360 ff.

behold the sacred symbols of his shrine should have done so.[1]

Mystery, as the very name reveals, must be observed because the truth must not be defiled or made a public show. To make common the holy of holies was to reduce it to the level of an everyday thing, and, furthermore, to give its mere symbolical significance a greater importance than its real or arcane significance, a very actual crime, a sin against the Holy Spirit, a debasement of it by the assumption that that which materially represents it is actually the same as the intangible essence itself. The inability of crude or debased minds to recognize the essential difference between the symbol and the truth it typifies is one of the actual reasons for the concealment of the Mysteries.[2]

It is precisely for the above reasons that wise men in all ages have sought to veil from the corrupt and the ignorant those lofty truths and serene ideals the consideration of which alone raises mankind above the level of things terrestrial. Few indeed have penetrated to the knowledge of these matters unaided or by virtue of their own studies and contemplation, although in every generation men are born who by reason of superior intelligence and spirituality have approached within measurable distance of the gates which guard the arcanum and even beyond them. But the genius of such knowledge is unquestionably associational, for, just as no one man can with success take for his province the entire field of science, whether theoretical or experimental, so none can gain more than a general cognizance of that far loftier

[1] See my article " Jurupari " in Hasting's *Encyclopedia of Religion and Ethics.*

[2] The apprehension of the arcane sense of the symbol is, indeed, essential to true initiation as will be seen.

science which is embraced for lack of a better term by the expression Magic, or the Great Art.

That this Art actually entered into the rites and ceremonies of the Mysteries of Egypt who can doubt save those who, blinded by their own conceit and folly, confound microcosm with macrocosm, the genius of spirit with its terrestrial manifestation ? Just as in the world of everyday, men in their thousands are to be encountered who wilfully and impiously abuse and decry the supernatural gifts of music, poetry, and the artistic sense, holding ribald language to their ministers and debasing these sacred things to their own vile and paltry uses, so in the much loftier sphere of Magic, of which these arts are but the shadows and emanations, we find the false priests of a shoddy modern science abandoning themselves to the examination of material things alone and totally disregarding superior and spiritual things, which, indeed, they contemn and hate because of their own native inhibitions. When the history of the past century comes to be written no patch of chronology, perhaps, will loom so darkly in the pages of the world's story as that among its passages when men, in blasphemous folly, turned aside from the consideration of the Universe as mystery and resolved to regard it in terms of matter alone. But the reaction from this heresy, cannot be far distant, and already the heralds of a brighter age of understanding and a larger humility are challenging the walls of the crumbling fortress of a Science built on the sands of that tangible which of all things is the most unsubstantial.

Into such a pit of error the priesthood of Egypt could not fall for the reason that it combined science with a true knowledge of and understanding of the

supernatural. Nor did it make the mistake in which
so many modern mystics indulge, in altogether
neglecting science, knowing as it did that science
is the handmaid of Magic, its concomitant and
necessity.

But with a pure mind alone could the neophyte
approach the Mysteries. Indeed, Thomas Taylor, the
Platonist, makes this abundantly clear when he says :
" I shall . . . prove that the different purifications
exhibited in these rites, in conjunction with initiation and inspection, were symbols of the gradation of
virtues requisite to the reascent of the soul. And the
first part, indeed, of this proposition respecting the
purifications, immediately follows from the testimony
of Plato in the passage already adduced, in which he
asserts, that the ultimate design of the Mysteries was
to lead us back to the principles from which we
originally fell. For if the Mysteries were symbolical,
as is universally acknowledged, this must likewise be
true of the purifications as a part of the mysteries ;
and as inward purity of which the external is symbolical, can only be attained by the exercise of the
virtues, it evidently follows that the purifications were
symbols of the purifying moral virtues. And the
latter part of the proposition may be easily inferred,
from the passage already cited from the Phædrus of
Plato, in which he compares initiation and inspection
to the blessed vision of intelligible natures, an employment which can alone belong to the energies of
contemplative virtue."[1]

This is, indeed, rendered indisputable by the
language of Olympiodorus in his commentary on the
Phædo of Plato, in which he says : " Popular purifications are in the first place brought forth, and after

[1] *Dissertation on the Eleusinian and Bacchic Mysteries*, pp. 78–80.

these such as are more arcane. But in the third place, collections of various things into one are received ; after which follows inspection. The ethical and political virtues therefore are analogous to the apparent (or popular) purifications. But such of the cathartic virtues as banish all external impressions, correspond to the more occult purifications. The theoretical energies about intelligibles are analogous to the collections ; but the contraction of these energies into an indivisible nature corresponds to initiation. And the simple self-inspection of simple forms is analogous to epoptic vision."

It is obvious that the above requires some explanation, owing to the obscurity of the language employed. It is plain that the first kind of purification alluded to, the " popular," was merely directed to the ceremonial cleansing of the body, whereas the later kind had reference to the " arcane," or secret cleansing of the soul, by the elimination of evil thoughts and ideas. The " collection of various things into one " is merely a rather clumsy philosophical term such as the Greek thinkers frequently employed in a desire for simplicity, meaning that all the ceremonial and rite which had gone before was now recapitulated and reviewed, and generally inspected with a view to discovering its efficacy in the case of the individual, that is, whether he had profited by it or not.

We are also informed that " the ethical and political virtues are analogous to the popular purification." That is as much as to say that the cleansing of the mind and soul was carried out in the same manner as that of the body, except that it was naturally on a higher plane, and symbolical. The " collections," that is, the philosophical grouping of ideas,[1] are

---

[1] And the display of arcane symbols.

analogous to the review and comprehension of the
sublime, in that reason must be employed in understanding both, although a higher reason is naturally
essential to the comprehension of the more lofty.
The contraction or epitomizing of these ideas into one
corresponds to initiation, that is, the whole task of
the initiate was the proper apprehension of one great
truth. For the one great truth embraces all truth,
all understanding, and, once revealed, the whole
apparatus of divine wisdom becomes the possession
of the initiate.

The masters of the Egyptian Mysteries were,
indeed, fortunate in one thing, that their theology
was much better accommodated to a perfect comprehension of the sublime than those which have emanated from the schools of Europe during the last five
hundred years. For, being in touch with the simpli-
cities of an earlier form of religion or divine knowledge, they were the better able to discern the direct
and unpolluted principles of communication between
mankind and the Deity. Indeed the modern student
of Comparative Religion is, by the nature of his study,
in a much more fortunate position for appreciating
the whole question of divine communion than the
pure theologian, who is frequently insufficiently
acquainted with the earlier processes of religious
thought. From the consideration of even the earliest
religious notions we often perceive the veridical
meaning and significance of all religion much more
truly than from the speculations of a more advanced
theology, stale, quasi-profound and dialectical. Indeed
religious science defeats itself and denies all truly
scientific method when it proceeds to the consideration of its subject from the basis of modern religious
experience and pseudo-philosophy alone rather than

from a review of the actual ascertained facts of primitive religion.

Of such an error the Egyptian priests were incapable, not only because they were innocent of modern sophistry, but because their experience and usage had not so far outgrown these simpler, truer, and more direct methods of divine communication of which we glean the broken lights from our own sacred Scriptures, especially as described in patriarchal practice. To early man God was much more real than to his successors. The modern ignorance of things divine is entirely owing to the confusion of thought which has regarded theology as necessarily a " science " capable of advancement and progression in knowledge, as well as to a neglect of the forgotten and disused methods of antiquity in apprehending, approaching, and communicating with deity. The outrageous confusion, social and ethical, to be observed in the modern world is, indeed, the consequence of the ignorance of and disbelief in that divine communion and personal fellowship with the Creator of which the early world was so conscious as affording mankind a much more certain foundation of thought and conduct than anything else.

If one circumstance is more clear than another it is that early man not only valued personal communion with his Creator, but made full use of it in his daily life. It governed all his actions and considerations, conscious and subconscious. After the first chaotic ages of groping, he developed for himself quite a clear understanding of the fact that the spiritual or higher universe in its different phases, so far from being outwith the material, interpenetrates it and is merely a higher manifestation of it though it is not to be confounded with it. Of the fatherhood of God he was

convinced. The late Andrew Lang showed conclusively that, apart altogether from and behind the
superstitions and fancies of animism and totemism
and the ideas of the lower cultus, primitive peoples
had and have a clear, distinct, and perfectly natural
conception of " a magnified non-natural man " whom
they regarded as their divine Creator, " a god behind
the gods."

And that this native conception was founded on
instinct and inherent apprehension is the truth which
lies at the root of all religious knowledge and marvel,
at the foundation of Christianity itself. For God *is*
" man," just as man partakes of the nature of God,
the twain are one and indivisible in essence, major
and minor, condensed and dissipated instances and
emanations of that great all-pervading Spirit which
interpenetrates all matter, of which, indeed, matter
itself is merely the palpable and visible type. For as
heat is to fire, growing less and even less as it sends
out its influence from the central flame, so is man
to God.

These simple truths—so much more grand and
impressive than the contortions of theology, because
so simple—were well understood by the sincere and
truly learned priesthood of Egypt, as many a text and
inscription proves. It was only when they became
degraded by the needless and fruitless elaboration of
pseudo-philosophers that they were forgotten or were
cynically set aside as the childish imaginings of a more
primitive age. The whole force and revelation of
Christianity was an endeavour to restore them. I
wholly believe it to have been a direct intervention
from the Great Intelligence to bring man to a realiza-
tion of his folly in breaking and setting at naught these
instinctive and divinely inspired means of personal

communion with God which the men of a happier age had enjoyed. The whole of Christian mythology, if so it may reverently be described, makes this inevitably clear. The allegory of man's fall, the primal necessity for spiritual rebirth, the need of constant communion are legendary not only of the break in divine communication, but also illustrative of the necessity of the restoration of those very processes which the Mysteries revealed and inculcated —the esoteric processes by which man communicated spiritually and personally with his Creator and archetype and by the power of which he hoped at last to dwell with Him after the separation caused by material barriers was brok⟨ ⟩ by death.

This is as much as to say that in its higher aspect Christianity is actually the restoration and continuation of the Mysteries. And are these not actually illustrated in the Christian allegory ? Are not descent into Hell, the resurrection and the divine rebirth of the soul the most powerful restatements and corroborations of the Mysteries which the mind can conceive ? It is entirely vain to describe the Mysteries, Egyptian or Greek, as " pagan," for the Christian faith, in its mystical sense, is in direct line of descent and development from the types so described. That it instituted a much loftier and more practical system of conduct and ethics is admitted, but let it be remembered that while casting aside the worst superstitions of the religions which had preceded it, these were, after all, of popular origin and had little connection with the sublime ideas inculcated by the pious priesthood of Egypt.

That M. Moret, the French Egyptologist, recognizes the true nature of the process by which the mysticism of Egypt affected that of Christianity is proved by a

striking passage in his *Kings and Gods of Egypt*,[1]
wherein he says : " The Isiac creed appealed forcibly
to men by its direct call to the individual.   The
Roman religion, cold and formal, a State sacerdotal
office, associating man with God only through the
intermediary of the priest, had failed to touch the
heart, stir imagination, or move the depths of
enthusiasm.   The votary of Isis, wrapt in ecstasy at
the feet of the goddess, interpreted the revelation
not in the word, but in the spirit, according to the
need of his heart, in the glow of his faith.   From that
day Mysticism has lived.   The Isiac became his own
priest ; the god, no longer a far-distant entity, a
remote State providence, deigns to converse with him,
becomes his tutelary friend, and, as it were, ' a thing
of beauty and a joy for ever.'   Each man ' possesses '
the God who is father of all, and keeps on in doing
good in his own way.

" The Isiac mystics are at the same time ascetics.
To know God, man must live soberly, chastely, and
die to the things of this world.   Greek philosophy, on
the contrary, taught man ' to live his life ' (*carpe
diem*), and to seek the supreme good on this earth by
the light of reason, wisdom, righteousness.   The
Oriental Mysteries may also have conferred upon
Cicero and other initiates an eagerness to live to relish
all the joys of life.   Isis promises to Lucius that he
shall enjoy a lengthy earthly happiness.   But supreme
happiness is a boon of the next world ; it is the hope
held out to the initiated, as, later, to the Christians.
By the influence of Eastern religions, a new character
is imparted to the aspirations of men.   Life is
desirable, yet, in the confines of this perishable body,
it is only a preparation, a stage upon the road to

[1] Pages 197-8.

THE WINGED ISIS
From a statuette.

death. Man has vanquished for ever his terror of the unknown. One step further, and he will despise all earthly joys, his eyes fixed upon the vision of eternal bliss promised by Christ ! ''

By the unwisdom of modernity the divine Magic—the true and ineffable comprehension of deity—has been partly, though not wholly, lost to mankind. Yet there has always existed a remnant who, by reason of the possession of the supernatural and instinctive knowledge and belief in the power of man to communicate with deity, have not only enjoyed this privilege, but have eagerly sought to restore it to the world. Like men seeking to found a new art or novel law where there was no foundation save their own belief and trust, these have perforce been obliged to struggle on through the darkness and bleakness of the dead and soulless centuries, guided only by the star of their own hopes and the chart of their own intuition.

But the rays of a new lamp have of recent years been cast upon the path. New light now shines upon the world's older faiths from the labours of students of Comparative Religion, Egyptologists, historians gifted with insight, archæologists and excavators, who have discovered and interpreted lost manuscripts and inscriptions. Too often, indeed, these cannot be regarded but as the mere instruments of Divinity in its intention to restore to the world the ancient wisdom so long buried and neglected. Too seldom have they appreciated the true nature and significance of that which they brought forth from the darkness or laboured to make plain from the customs and beliefs of those primitive peoples who in some cases still possessed the germs of the great secret.

It is, then, through the frequently undiscerning

efforts of modern workers in the vineyard of Folklore
and the allied sciences that the veridical nature of
religion and the true root and origin of the Mysteries
have been unveiled—not that they were in most
cases capable of realizing the nature of their dis-
coveries nor have they possessed the insight to refer
them to the vital needs of humanity or accept them
as clues to the lost wisdoms of the past. But no
longer has the man of faith and intuition need to
grope on his way by the aid of these torches alone, for
the systematized mass of modern discovery and the
results of scholarship have placed at his disposal a
quite ponderable amount of data concerning the
beginnings and the practice of that Magia which he
formerly apprehended almost by instinct alone.

At the period when Herodotus was initiated into
the Mysteries of Egypt a very considerable change
had obviously taken place in the practice of their
guardians and in the ritual by which they were surrounded in comparison with that which had obtained
in earlier times. Indeed this is partly rendered clear
from a comparison of his description of them and
that of the Egyptian official Ikhernofret, some
centuries earlier, as we shall see. The truth is, that,
as it has been made clear by modern observers and
students, Magia tends to descend, like religion, into
formula and ritual. Once a certain formula of
invocation, a prayer, a spell has been found to be
efficacious on one occasion, it is assumed that it must
be efficacious on every occasion. Nay, more, for the
very tone of voice in which it is spoken, the very
gestures which accompany it must be arbitrarily
repeated, or the act, petition, or spell will surely fail
of its purpose.

Man is by no means an original being, and falls only

too readily into the error of vain repetition. In all likelihood the early masters insisted that their disciples should employ the selfsame formulæ, the very words and actions which they had found to be of virtue and efficacy. This proceeding had, of course, its natural consequence. It instituted a formal ritual which in time was bound to grow lifeless and even meaningless, and from which the spirit which had animated the original appeal had vanished and escaped.

I believe it to be, if not heretical, at least unintelligent to suppose—and it is merely a supposition —that a fixed ritual is absolutely essential to the efficacy of magical or religious appeal or undertaking. To regard it as essential is to place Magia on the selfsame footing as science, where the same causes are known to produce the same results. But in my belief it has no such experimental—shall I say empirical— significance. It is even blasphemous, as implying a tendency to enforce the divine power to a certain prescribed action. In any event, I believe the blind acceptance of this theory—and theory is the stigma and bane of the lower Magia—to have been certainly a contributory cause, if not the only one, to the loss and official disappearance of the Mysteries from the supernatural life of humanity. Their ritual grew outworn, it degenerated into gibberish, the language in which it was couched became archaic and obscure ; its theatric side—a most important one—grew meaningless, it sank into squalor and disrepute as the hocus-pocus of the itinerant sorcerer.

Let me not be mistaken. I do not mean to infer that where ripe experience has blazed a trail that the same should not be beaten into a well-trodden path. Symbolism, too, is at least as lasting as the profound ideas which give it birth, if its allegory be just and if it conveys an idea sufficiently true and profound. It is, indeed, the one and only method of conveying profound ideas. But room must be left for individuality in Magia. Just as in the world of letters we say " the style is the man," so in Magia a certain spice and flavour of personality must inevitably enter into the act, appeal or rite in order to be effective. Nay, more, the whole individual soul of the prac- titioner must enter into the act.

It is thought, intention, which moves the Absolute to act in conformity with the desires of man, not acts, tones, or gestures. But here again I must not be mistaken, and indeed, no mystic of experience will mistake me, knowing, as he will, the supreme value of the theatric gesture, the correct tone, *to himself*. The ritual of the Lower Mysteries was rich in this species of dramatic action and ceremony, which has its own peculiar mental and physical preparatory value, and that this should be unchangeable was inevitable. Man should not cast aside the stereotyped for the merely allegorical and less essential, for the good reason that it is impossible to cast it aside because of the very circumstances of its uniqueness.

But, as I maintain, it is thought, purpose, intention which count in the truly and inherently mystical, the essentially magical. In the event, Magia yields nothing out of its merely rhetorical and dramatic expressions alone, which are, indeed, as the fume and the colour of the wine, but not the divine draught itself. For the agitation and reaction of the Absolute in its favour, if such terms may be employed of pure spirit, eternal and omnipotent, the moving essence, so to speak, must, in some measure, resemble the Absolute, partake of the cardinal qualities and

virtues and might of that which it desires to attract
or involve. Mistake not this for enforcement, however,
as did the impious among the sorcerers of the past,
and as do the foolish among living pseudo-mystics.
For, in reality, the Absolute requires no attractive
influence to render it cognisant of the necessities of
its part or creature ; it demands, rather, that that
creature should symbolically apprise it, approach it
with obvious feeling, in order that the material
circumstances in which he exists shall sufficiently be
borne in upon him and that it shall react to his call.
The gesture, the tone, to these the Absolute cannot
respond, simply because they are the concomitants of
the material, constant reminders to him who employs
them that such puny apparatus must be surmounted
if he is to rise in time to the plane of that which he
supplicates.

But, if in time the wise priests of Egypt fell into
the error of employing pure ritual predominantly,
as, indeed, did those of Babylon, Yucatan, and of all
countries and religions, there is ample evidence that
they retained in a measure the true spirit of the
ancient Mysteries until almost the last days of the
Egyptian faith. Many texts exhibit the extraordinary
reverence they had for the sacred, a reverence which,
indeed, all wise men in all times have shown, for it
is the levity of fools which misapprehends the true
character of these outward shows and circumstances,
casting ribald opprobrium on that which it can never
understand. Just as men to-day, in domestic or
workaday life, scoff at those very tones and gestures
which they applaud lustily on the political platform,
or in the theatre, so did the cynical Greeks and the
light-minded Syrians laugh at what they took to be
" Egyptian jugglery." We find even the Christian

apologist Arnobius jeering in a manner unfitting a
wise man at the " antics " of the hierophants of the
Mysteries as something childish and even depraved,
and failing to apprehend the secret behind the act or
symbol because of an inherent inability to plumb
such spiritual depths.

To the Egyptian priests the temples were not so
much the residences of the gods as their resting-places
on earth, and the images of divine beings not these
beings themselves, but the shapes and vessels into
which at times and seasons they might pour their
essence and commune with man. Inexpressibly lofty
was the life and communion experienced in these
shrines ; perhaps never before or since in the
history of mankind has a sense of such holiness
pervaded any dedicated fanes. No spot or stain
of uncleanness or evil was tolerated within their
enclosures. Such places were fitting sites for the
performance of Mysteries the object of which was
the introduction of a human soul to fellowship with
its Creator.

In these lofty shrines of immense silences which
seemed to borrow their vastness from the eternal
quiet of the surrounding desert, was found the
appropriate atmosphere and environment for the evocation of the Divine, for communion and the
sublimities of comprehension. Not that this may
be unaccomplished even in the market-place, but
wisdom, that rare growth of the quiet and lofty spirit,
admits that for the first steps of the uninitiated into
the spaces of the mysterious, silence and shadow are
necessities as fundamental for contemplation in its
beginnings as sun and rain to the plant. Silence and
gloom are, indeed, the light and life of arcane existence, the shutting out and cloaking from the material

world of the growing spirit, which, like a child in the
womb of its mother, must experience absolute
immunity from the disturbance of outward things if
it is to arrive at healthy birth and survival.

So the silent chambers of initiation were indeed the
matrices or alembics of those initiate souls who offered
themselves for the divine rebirth which was the end
and purpose of the Mysteries. There the neophyte
waited until, apprised inwardly by the voice of the
god Himself, he admitted his perfect readiness for the
ordeal. But the enormous impressiveness and self-
searching of this experience in preliminary were alone
an ordeal, steeling the heart and soul of the searcher
for that which was to come. Perhaps the reader,
sitting in some ancient cathedral where sacred
traditions cluster among its bright shadows, has
gradually experienced an awe of the surroundings
which by degrees environed and uplifted him. Then,
as water is to wine, is such a passing feeling of veneration compared to that which descended upon the
neophyte consciously dedicating himself to the
service of the god on the greatly more exalted plane
soon to be revealed to him.

God gives each age its separate revelation, fitting
its circumstances. But who shall say that ancient
Egypt was not vouchsafed the highest and noblest
revelation of any this star has known ? For where,
as all men agree, has a profounder holiness and loftier
sublimity been displayed ?

The relationship of the Egyptian Mysteries to those
of Eleusis and the Orphic cult is as that of mother to
daughter, and, indeed, it is chiefly by virtue of what
we can glean of the circumstances of the latter that
we can check our knowledge of that of the former.

But the associations of the Egyptian Mysteries with

the Hellenic are fully set forth elsewhere in this book. It remains, however, to examine generally the Greek attitude to things mystical. At the beginnings of Greek history we find the Orphic Mysteries flourishing, and these, according to Herodotus and others, were actually of Egyptian origin. From this cult the great mystical school of Pythagoras borrowed its ideas of the wanderings of the soul and its essential purifications. In the philosophy of Heraclitus[1] we find, perhaps, the clearest account of the allegorical ideas behind the Mysteries, a species of pantheism.

Maeterlinck, in his work *The Great Secret*,[2] seems to me to pierce to the heart of the Greek mystical position when he says that the most important parts of its ancient theosophy and philosophy, namely, those which treated of the Supreme Cause and the Unknowable, " were gradually neglected and forgotten by the classic theosophy and philosophy, and became, as in Egypt and India, the secret of the hierophants, forming, with more direct oral traditions, the foundations of the famous Greek Mysteries, and notably of the Eleusinian Mysteries, whose veil has never been pierced." But such unknowable elements as existed in the myths and otherwise were sufficient to destroy for the initiate the belief in the gods of the vulgar, " while at the same time he came to understand why a doctrine so perilous for those who were not in a position to realize its exalted nature had to remain occult. There was probably no more than this in the supreme revelation, because there is probably no other secret that man might conceive or possess ; that there never can have existed nor ever will exist, a formulæ that will give us the key of the universe."

It was likely, however, that the neophyte was

[1] Page 102   [2] Pages 137 ff.

initiated into an occult science of a more positive nature, such as that possessed by the Egyptian priests, and he must have been taught " the methods of attainment to union with the divine, or to immersion in the divine by means of ecstasy or trance," as M. Maeterlinck puts it, and, perhaps by hypnotic methods, more developed than our own. There was, in fact, developed within him all the mysterious forces of the subconscious self. But although I can find many assurances of this in connection with the Egyptian cult, I confess I cannot discover so many in the case of the parallel Hellenic societies.

M. Maeterlinck does not believe, however, that the occult fraternities of Greece knew much more of the great secrets of existence than what has been vouchsafed to us in the great revealed religions. It was not yet possible to know more, and had it actually been known, " we too should know it, for it is hardly conceivable that the gist of such a secret should not have transpired if so many thousands of men had known it for so many thousands of years." But from what has gone before, it must surely be plain enough that the earlier mystical knowledge in its perfection and grand simplicity had already been lost by the period of the floreat of the Eleusinian Mysteries, in the sixth century B.C. onward, which, in essence, were merely a lame attempt to relume and recapture the ancient knowledge of the Egyptians, and that, therefore, the possessors of such diluted arcane knowledge as they dispensed were scarcely in a position to reveal or bequeath the entire or pristine truth. The truth resided in the Mysteries of Egypt in their earlier form and recension, and in that alone.

But M. Maeterlinck will have it, nevertheless, that the conservators of the Greek Mysteries were in

possession of the secrets of the unknown forces of
nature in a much greater degree than are modern
scientists. By virtue of what knowledge, then, did
they attain to these heights if they were not in
possession of the grand and simple secret, the greatest
of all ? M. Maeterlinck seeks to justify his thesis by
indicating the architectural triumphs of the Egyptians
as so stupendous that they must have been erected
almost by occult means ! But this is mysticism run
wild, and well illustrates the danger of statements
made at random and without even a scintilla of
specialist knowledge so frequently made by mystics
who have not taken the trouble to acquaint themselves with the archæology of the past. There is
nothing occult about the manner in which the
Egyptian pyramids or obelisks were built, and the
methods employed are known absolutely to Egyptologists. This is not to say that these buildings may
not have *an occult or symbolical significance*, but
that is a world away from the belief or statement
that they were raised by " unknown means," thus
flagrantly assisting popular belief in the ponderous
rubbish which would make us believe that every
secret known to antiquity, and for that matter to
modernity, is " locked up " in the architecture and
plan of the Great Pyramid ! It is from this kind of
nightmare that true mysticism requires to be shielded
and protected, and which brings it into contempt, to
its immense loss and damage.[1]

To return to the spirit of the Greek Mysteries, it
may be said, in fine, that they were nothing else than
the poor shadows of the Egyptian, retaining more the

[1] Nor can I find good evidence that the Mysteries were celebrated
within the Pyramids. The funerary rites of the Pharaohs certainly
were, and in so far as these had a relationship with the Mysteries
this appears to be the only justification for such a theory.

letter and ritual than the spirit. But for this very reason alone they are valuable as preserving for us in part the ritual and ceremony which in all likelihood they received at first-hand from the priesthood of Egypt. I have always doubted, indeed, that the conservators of the Egyptian Mysteries would have vouchsafed much more than the bare forms and trappings of their tradition to foreigners, for whom they seem to have evinced a not unreasonable suspicion.

The place of the Egyptian Mysteries in the Secret Tradition is precise and distinct. In them was gathered up and made manifest all the wisdom and arcane knowledge of the ancient world, which was thus crystallized and systematized in such a manner that, had it been preserved in an unadulterated form, would most assuredly have saved later ages from many religious catastrophes and much false mysticism. But through the supineness and neglect of its conservators and perhaps through the cynical influences which impinged on them from abroad, its early divine beauty was gradually lost until at last only the skeletal forms of its ritual and ceremony remained. That the Christian religion was a practical attempt to restore its main ideas I do not doubt, and, indeed, facts are all on the side of such a hypothesis. Personal unity with the Divine through mystical rebirth was its main objective, as instanced in the patriarchal narratives, in the religion of Osiris, of the Indian sages, of practically all the great world-religions. And the precise manner in which it attained this great end it will be the endeavour of the ensuing pages to make clear, in order that the fresh and pristine marvel of the world's most simple yet profound system of correspondence with divinity may be made clear and serve to effect in some measure that restoration of ancient truth which mankind, wandering in the deserts of doctrinal folly and schismatic error, so grievously requires not only for its consolation, but for its ultimate salvation from the curse and evil spell of the material.

CHAPTER II

THE LITERARY SOURCES

THOSE writings which "describe" the Egyptian Mysteries (if such an expression can be employed where symbolic and arcane utterance is used rather than explicit statement) are numerous and fall into two classes : those which deal specifically and at length and "philosophically" or historically with them, such as the writings of Plutarch, Iamblichus, and Apuleius, or which fragmentarily preserve their intention, like the Book of the Dead ; and those which deal with them almost in passing as do many classical writers, such as Herodotus, Porphyry, Diodorus, Lactantius, and Arnobius. I have in the following chapters confined myself almost entirely to the former class, as practically every passage from the latter will be found in its appropriate place in this volume, and I have, with the exception of the Book of the Dead, arranged my précis of the authors cited in chronological order. At the end of the two chapters dealing with these sources I shall summarize the information they contain in order that the reader may carry that on in handy form so as to be able to apply it to the consideration of further arguments.

Herodotus (484–406 B.C.), whose knowledge of the Egyptian Mysteries had been gained through personal initiation, as he himself admits, invariably alludes to them with extreme caution and seems to have been especially fearful of revealing their secrets. I shall quote the little he tells us relating to the festivals and Mysteries *in extenso :*

" The Egyptians hold public festivals not only once in a year, but several times : that which is best and most rigidly observed, is in the city of Bubastis, in honour of Diana ; the second, in the city of Busiris, is in honour of Isis ; for in this city is the largest temple of Isis, and it is situated in the middle of the Egyptian Delta. Isis is in the Grecian language called Demeter. The third festival is held at Sais, in honour of Minerva ; the fourth, at Heliopolis, in honour of the sun ; the fifth, at the city of Buto, in honour of Latona ; the sixth, at the city of Papremis, in honour of Mars.[1]   Now, when they are being conveyed to the city Bubastis, they act as follows : for men and women embark together, and great numbers of both sexes in every barge ; some of the women have castanets on which they play, and the men play on the flute during the whole voyage ; the rest of the women and men sing and clap their hands together at the same time. When in the course of their passage they come to any town, they lay their barge near to land, and do as follows : some of the women do as I have described ; others shout and scoff at the women of the place ; some dance, and others stand up and pull up their clothes : this they do at every town by the riverside. When they arrive at Bubastis, they celebrate the feast, offering up great sacrifices ; and more wine is consumed at this festival than in all the rest of the year. What with men and

---

[1] These festivals were probably associated with the mysteries of gods other than Osiris or Isis. Of their nature we have at present little or no knowledge.

women, besides children, they congregate, as the inhabitants say, to the number of seven hundred thousand.

" I have already related how they celebrate the festival of Isis in the city of Busiris ; and besides, all the men and women, to the number of many myriads, beat themselves after the sacrifice ; but for whom they beat themselves it were impious for me to divulge. All the Carians that are settled in Egypt do still more than this, in that they cut their foreheads with knives, and thus show themselves to be foreigners and not Egyptians. When they are assembled at the sacrifice, in the city of Sais, they all on a certain night kindle a great number of lamps in the open air, around their houses ; the lamps are flat vessels filled with salt and oil, and the wick floats on the surface, and this burns all night ; and the festival is thence named ' the lighting of lamps.' The Egyptians who do not come to this public assembly observe the rite of sacrifice, and all kindle lamps, and this not only in Sais, but throughout all Egypt. A religious reason is given why this night is illuminated and so honoured.

" Those who assemble at Heliopolis and Buto perform sacrifices only. But in Papremis they offer sacrifices and perform ceremonies, as in other places ; but, when the sun is on the decline, a few priests are occupied about the image, but the greater number stand, with wooden clubs, at the entrance of the temple ; while others, accomplishing their vows, amounting to more than a thousand men, each armed in like manner, stand in a body on the opposite side. But the image, placed in a small wooden temple, gilded all over, they carry out to another sacred dwelling : then the few who were left about the image draw a four-wheeled carriage, containing the temple and the image that is in it. But the priests, who stand at the entrance, refuse to give them admittance; and the votaries, bringing succour to the god, oppose, and then strike, whereupon an obstinate combat with clubs ensues, and they break one another's heads, and, as I conjecture, many die of their wounds; though the Egyptians deny that any one dies. The inhabitants say they instituted this festival on the following occasion: they say, that the mother of Mars dwelt in this temple, and that Mars, who had been educated abroad, when he reached to man's estate, came, and wished to converse with his mother; and that his mother's attendants, as they had never seen him before, did not allow him to pass them, but repelled him; whereupon he, having collected men from another city, handled the servants roughly, and got access to his mother. In consequence of this, they say that they have instituted this combat on this festival in honour of Mars."[1]

Again: "At Sais also, in the sacred precinct of Minerva, behind the chapel and joining the whole of the wall, is the tomb of one whose name I consider it impious to divulge on such an occasion. And in the enclosure stand large stone obelisks, and there is a lake near, ornamented with a stone margin, formed in a circle, and in size, as appeared to me, much the same as that in Delos, which is called the Circular. In this lake they perform by night the representation of that person's adventures, which they call mysteries. On these matters, however, though accurately acquainted with the particulars of them, I must observe a discreet silence."[2]

Plutarch (A.D. 50–120) was a descendant of an

---

[1] Bk. II, 59–64.   [2] Bk. II, 170–171.

THE MYSTERIES OF OSIRIS
From a fresco at Herculaneum.

ancient family of Chæronea in Greece, and received his education at Athens under Ammonius, who grounded him well in Platonic studies and the treasures of Greek thought. He travelled in Egypt and Asia Minor, and became a lecturer at Rome, and a friend of Pliny and Tacitus. Later, he became a priest of Apollo at Delphi. His literary production was extensive, and he was obviously one of those people who find time for everything and for going everywhere. His *Lives* of the great figures of antiquity is the first, and certainly one of the greatest, biographical works ever written, and he was certainly the greatest Hellenist of his day.

Plutarch was a great life-champion, a man of lofty ideals, desperately anxious to reform the morality of his time. He saw what life might become if man could be moulded to the dictates of a temperate harmony. To him existence was a true initiation into the holy mysteries. He longed to bring order into the moral and social chaos of his time, and his method of doing so was an eclectic one, borrowing from any of those principles which might give support to character. Still, he was a Platonist and Aristotelian with a tincture of the Stoic in his composition. He had a profound belief in a threefold Providence exercised by a remote Supreme Deity.

In his treatise on Isis and Osiris he bases his opinions chiefly on Pythagorean mysticism, but, that notwithstanding, he certainly has many higher glimpses of the Divine. " While we are here below," he says, " encumbered by bodily affections, we can have no intercourse with God, save as in philosophic thought we may faintly touch Him, as in a dream. But when our souls are released, and have passed into the region of the pure, invisible, and changeless, this

God will be their guide and king who depend on Him and gaze with insatiable longing on the beauty which may not be spoken of by the lips of man."

He has " the vision of the one eternal, passionless Spirit, far removed from the world of chance and change." As a Platonist he reconciles himself to Greek and Egyptian mythology by a piously ingenious interpretation of ancient legend and by supposing a system of mediatory and administering spirits or genii, demiurges who moderate between God and man.

As Dill has said :[1] " It was assumed that the early myth-makers and lawgivers possessed a sacred lore of immense value and undoubted truth, which they dimly shadowed forth in symbolism of fanciful tale or allegory. The myth at once hides and reveals the mystery of the Divine. If a man comes to its interpretation with the proper discipline and acumen, the kernel of spiritual or physical meaning which is reverently veiled from the profane eye will disclose itself. And thus the later philosophic theologian is not reading his own higher thoughts of God into the grotesque fancies of a remote antiquity ; he is evolving and interpreting a wisdom more original than his own. In this process of rediscovering a lost tradition, he pushes aside the mass of erroneous interpretations which have perverted the original doctrine, by literal acceptance of what is really figurative, by abuse of names and neglect of realities, by stopping at the symbol instead of rising to the divine fact.

" The treatise of Plutarch on Isis and Osiris is the best illustration of this attitude to myth. Plutarch's theology, though primarily Hellenic, does not confine

[1] *Roman Society*, p. 423.

its gaze to the Greek Olympus : it is intended to be the science of human religion in general. It gives formal expression to the growing tendency to syncretism. The central truth of it is, that as the sun and moon, under many different names, shed their light on all, so the gods are variously invoked and honoured by various tribes of men. But there is one supreme Ruler and Providence common to all. And the lower deities of different countries may often be identified by the theologian under all varieties of title and attribute. So, to Plutarch as to Herodotus, the immemorial worships of Egypt were the proto- types or the counterparts of the cults of Greece. There was a temple of Osiris at Delphi, and Clea, to whom Plutarch's treatise is addressed, was not only a hereditary priestess of the Egyptian god, but held a leading place among the female ministers of Dionysus. It was fitting that a person so catholic in her sympa- thies should have dedicated to her the treatise in which Plutarch expounds his all-embracing theology.

" In this treatise we see the new theology wrestling in a hopeless struggle to unite the thought of Pytha- goras and Plato with the grossness of Egyptian myth. It is a striking but not a solitary example of the misapplication of dialectic skill and learning, to find the thoughts of the present in the fancies of the past, and from a mistaken piety, to ignore the onward march of humanity. Arbitrary interpretations of myth, alike unhistorical and unscientific, make us wonder how they could ever have occurred to men of intellect and learning. Yet the explanation is not far to seek. More elevated conceptions of God, the purged and clarified religious intuition, do not readily find a substitute for the old symbolism to express their visions. Religion, beyond any other institution,

depends for its power on antiquity, on the charm of
ancestral pieties. A religious symbol is doubly sacred
when it has ministered to the devotion of many
generations.

"In interpreting the powerful cult of Isis, which
was spreading rapidly over the Western world,
Plutarch had two objects in view. By reverent
explanation of its legends and ritual, he desired to
counteract its immoral and superstitious tendencies ;
he also wished, in discussing a worship so multiform
as that of Isis, to develop his attitude to myth in
general. We cannot follow him minutely in his survey
of the various attempts of philosophy to find the basis
of truth in Egyptian legend. Some of these explanations, such as the Euhemerist, he would dismiss at
once as atheistic. On others, which founded themselves on physical allegory, he would not be so
dogmatic, although he might reject as impious any
tendency to identify the gods with natural powers
and products. As a positive contribution to religious
philosophy, the treatise is chiefly valuable for its
theory of Evil and of dæmonic powers, and above all
for the doctrine of the unity of God, the central truth
of all religions."

In his treatise, *De Iside et Osiride*, Plutarch deals
principally with the allegories and symbolism by
which the ancients interpreted the nature of Osiris
and Isis. He disregards as impious the notions of
those who consider them to have been mortal
monarchs, but at the same time scoffs at the wholesale
credibility of all the tales and fables recounted of
them, an attitude with which, however, modern
criticism might not agree. The legend of Osiris, he
admits, is probably based on fact, but is so entangled
with allegory as to render it exceedingly obscure.

The name Isis, he tells us, signifies knowledge, according to the Greek interpretation thereof. She collects and compiles " a holy doctrine which she delivers to those who aspire after the most perfect participation of the divine nature, a doctrine which, by commanding a steady perseverance in one uniform and temperate course of life, and an abstinence from particular kinds of food, as well as from all indulgence of the carnal appetite, restrains the intemperate and voluptuous part within due bounds, and at the same time habituates her votaries to undergo those austere and rigid ceremonies which their religion obliges them to observe—the end of all which is by these means they may be the better prepared for the attainment of the knowledge of the first and supreme Mind, whom the Goddess exhorts them to search after, as dwelling near and constantly residing with her. For this reason is her temple, in the same language, called *Iseion*, alluding to that knowledge of the eternal and self-existent Being, which may be thus obtained, if it be properly approached, with due purity and sanctity of manners."[1]

The Greeks, he says, regarded Isis as the daughter of Hermes or of Prometheus, both deities of philosophic tendency, and for this reason they call one of the muses at Hermopolis Isis as well as Justice, or Wisdom, who points out the knowledge of divine truth to her votaries, the true Hierophori and Hierostoli, the former being those who carry " locked up in their souls as in a chest the sacred doctrine concerning the gods purified from all such superfluities as superstition may have annexed to it, whilst the holy habit with which the latter of these adorn the statues of these deities, partly of a dark and gloomy, and partly

[1] Samuel Squire's trans. Cambridge, 1744, pp. 2–3.

of a more bright and shining colour, seems aptly
enough to represent the notions which this doctrine
teaches us to entertain of the divine nature itself,
partly clear and partly obscure. And for as much as
the devotees of Isis after their decease are wrapped up
in these sacred vestments, is not this intended to
signify that this holy doctrine still abides with them,
and that this alone accompanies them in another life
. . . he alone is a true servant or follower of the
goddess who, after he has heard and been made
acquainted in a proper manner with the history of the
actions of these gods, searches into the hidden truths
which lie concealed under them, and examines the
whole by the dictates of reason and philosophy.''[1]

Many, Plutarch continues, are ignorant of the true
reason even of the most ordinary rites observed by
the Egyptian priesthood, and are satisfied with the
most superficial accounts of them, but the true reason
is the necessity for absolute purity in their quest for
the divine.   These purificatory observances were
founded not on fable or superstition, but with a view
to promote the morality and happiness of those who
were to observe them, to preserve the meaning of
some valuable passages in history, or to represent some
of the phenomena of nature.

But their philosophy is involved in fable and
allegory, exhibiting only dark hints and obscure
resemblances of the truth. This is insinuated, for
example, in the sphinx, a type of their enigmatical
theology, and in such inscriptions as that engraved
on the base of Minerva's statue at Sais, whom they
regard as identical with Isis : '' I am every thing that
has been, that is, and that shall be ; nor has any
mortal ever yet been able to discover what is under

[1] Samuel Squire's trans.   Cambridge, 1744, pp. 3–4.

my veil." "But to form true notions of the divine nature is more acceptable to them than any sacrifice or mere external act of worship can be," and one who realizes this is in no danger of falling into superstitions which their symbolism might seem to encourage.

Plutarch then details the mythological history of Isis and Osiris, " its most insignificant and superfluous parts omitted." Rhea (the Egyptian Nut, the sky-goddess), was the wife of Helios (Ra). She was, however, beloved by Kronos (Geb), whose affection she returned. When Ra discovered his wife's infidelity he was wrathful indeed, and pronounced a curse upon her, saying that her child should not be born in any month or in any year. Now the curse of Ra the mighty could not be turned aside, for Ra was the chief of all the gods. In her distress Nut called upon the god Thoth (the Greek Hermes), who also loved her. Thoth knew that the curse of Ra must be fulfilled, yet by a very cunning stratagem he found a way out of the difficulty. He went to Silene, the moon-goddess, whose light rivalled that of the sun himself, and challenged her to a game of tables. The stakes on both sides were high, but Silene staked some of her light, the seventieth part of each of her illuminations, and lost. Thus it came about that her light wanes and dwindles at certain periods, so that she is no longer the rival of the sun. From the light which he had won from the moon-goddess Thoth made five days which he added to the year (at that time consisting of three hundred and sixty days), in suchwise that they belonged neither to the preceding nor to the following year, nor to any month. On these five days Nut was delivered of her five children. Osiris was born on the first day, Horus on the second, Set on the third, Isis on the fourth, and

Nephthys on the fifth. On the birth of Osiris a loud voice was heard throughout all the world, saying: "The lord of all the earth is born!" A slightly different tradition relates that a certain man named Pamyles, carrying water from the temple of Ra at Thebes, heard a voice commanding him to proclaim the birth of "the good and great king Osiris," which he straightway did. For this reason the education of the young Osiris was entrusted to Pamyles. Thus, it is said, was the festival of the Pamilia instituted.

In course of time the prophecies concerning Osiris were fulfilled, and he became a great and wise king. The land of Egypt flourished under his rule as it had never done heretofore. Like many another "hero-god," he set himself the task of civilizing his people, who at his coming were in a very barbarous condition, indulging in cannibalistic and other savage practices. He gave them a code of laws, taught them the arts of husbandry, and showed them the proper rites where-with to worship the gods. And when he had succeeded in establishing law and order in Egypt he betook himself to distant lands to continue there his work of civilization. So gentle and good was he, and so pleasant were his methods of instilling knowledge into the minds of the barbarians, that they worshipped the very ground whereon he trod.

He had one bitter enemy, however, in his brother Set, the Greek Typhon. During the absence of Osiris his wife Isis ruled the country so well that the schemes of the wicked Set to take a share in its government were not allowed to mature. But on the king's return Set fixed on a plan whereby to rid himself altogether of the king, his brother. For the accomplishment of his ends he leagued himself with Aso, the Queen of Ethiopia, and seventy-two other conspirators. Then, after secretly measuring the king's body, he caused to be made a marvellous chest, richly fashioned and adorned, which would contain exactly the body of Osiris. This done, he invited his fellow-plotters and his brother the king to a great feast. Now Osiris had frequently been warned by the queen to beware of Set, but, having no evil in himself, the king feared it not in others, so he betook himself to the banquet.

When the feast was over Set had the beautiful chest brought into the banqueting-hall, and said, as though in jest, that it should belong to him whom it would fit. One after another the guests lay down in the chest, but it fitted none of them till the turn of Osiris came. Quite unsuspicious of treachery, the king laid himself down in the great receptacle. In a moment the conspirators had nailed down the lid, pouring boiling lead over it lest there should be any aperture. Then they set the coffin adrift on the Nile, at its Tanaitic mouth. These things befell, say some, in the twenty-eighth year of Osiris' life ; others say in the twenty-eighth year of his reign.

When the news reached Isis she was sore stricken, and cut off a lock of her hair and put on mourning apparel. Knowing well that the dead cannot rest till their bodies have been buried with funeral rites, she set out to find the corpse of her husband. For a long time her search went unrewarded, though she asked every man and woman she met whether they had seen the richly decorated chest. At length it occurred to her to inquire of some children who played by the Nile, and, as it chanced, they were able to tell her that the chest had been brought to the Tanaitic mouth of the Nile by Set and his accomplices. From that time children were regarded by the Egyptians as having some special faculty of divination.

By and by the queen gained information of a more exact kind through the agency of demons, by whom she was informed that the chest had been cast up on the shore of Byblos, and flung by the waves into a tamarisk-bush, which had shot up miraculously into a magnificent tree, enclosing the coffin of Osiris in its trunk. The king of that country, Melcarthus by name, was astonished by the height and beauty of the tree, and had it cut down and a pillar made from its trunk wherewith to support the roof of his palace. Within this pillar was hidden the chest containing the body of Osiris. Isis hastened with all speed to Byblos, where she seated herself by the side of a fountain. To none of those who approached her would she vouchsafe a word, saving only to the queen's maidens, and these she addressed very graciously, braiding their hair and perfuming them with her breath, more fragrant than the odour of flowers. When the maidens returned to the palace the queen inquired how it came that their hair and clothes were so delightfully perfumed, whereupon they related their encounter with the beautiful stranger. Queen Astarte, or Athenais, bade that she be conducted to the palace, welcomed her graciously, and appointed her nurse to one of the young princes.

Isis fed the boy by giving him her finger to suck. Every night, when all had retired to rest, she would pile great logs on the fire and thrust the child among them, and, changing herself into a swallow, would twitter mournful lamentations for her dead husband. Rumours of these strange practices were brought by the queen's maidens to the ears of their mistress, who determined to see for herself whether or not there was any truth in them. So she concealed herself in the great hall, and when night came Isis barred the doors and piled logs on the fire, thrusting the child among the glowing wood. The queen rushed forward with a loud cry and rescued her boy from the flames. The goddess reproved her sternly, declaring that by her action she had deprived the young prince of immortality. Then Isis revealed her identity to the awe-stricken Athenais and told her story, begging that the pillar which supported the roof might be given to her. When her request had been granted she cut open the tree, took out the coffin containing the body of Osiris, and mourned so loudly over it that one of the young princes died of terror. Then she took the chest by sea to Egypt, being accompanied on the journey by the elder son of King Melcarthus. The child's ultimate fate is variously recounted by several conflicting traditions. The tree which had held the body of the god was long preserved and worshipped at Byblos.

Arrived in Egypt, Isis opened the chest and wept long and sorely over the remains of her royal husband. But now she bethought herself of her son Harpocrates, or Horus the Child, whom she had left in Buto, and leaving the chest in a secret place, she set off to search for him. Meanwhile Set, while hunting by the light of the moon, discovered the richly adorned coffin and in his rage rent the body into fourteen pieces, which he scattered here and there throughout the country.

Upon learning of this fresh outrage on the body of the god, Isis took a boat of papyrus-reeds and journeyed forth once more in search of her husband's remains. After this crocodiles would not touch a papyrus boat, probably because they thought it contained the goddess, still pursuing her weary search. Wherever Isis found a portion of the corpse she buried it and built a shrine to mark the spot. It

is for this reason that there are so many tombs of
Osiris in Egypt.

Osiris, returning from the Otherworld, appeared to
his son Horus, and asked him to avenge his death.
Horus thereupon attacked Set with his followers, and
after a strife lasting many days gained a victory over
the usurper, Set himself being taken prisoner. But
he was freed by Isis, which so incensed Horus that he
tore off the insigna of her royalty, and instead of her
crown, placed on her head a helmet in the shape of
an ox's head.

Plutarch warns Clea, the pious priestess to whom
he dedicates his account, that a vast difference exists
between this version of the Osirian story and those
which poets and writers of fable have woven around
the personality of Osiris. It is "the reflexion of
something real," as can be proved by the attitude of
the Egyptian priesthood to the ceremonies associated
with the death of Osiris. "And this notion is still
farther suggested to us, as well from that solemn air
of grief and sadness, which appears in their sacrifices,
as from the very form and disposition of their temples,
in one place extended into long avenues and fair and
open aisles, and in another sinking into dark and
gloomy oratories, altogether resembling those subterraneous caverns which are allotted for the reception
of the dead."

The several theories current in his day regarding
the nature of the Osirian allegory are next set forth.
The first is that the divine beings alluded to in the
legend typified the constellations, secondly, that they
were genii or nature-spirits, again that Osiris personified the River Nile, which unites itself with Isis, the
land, and that Set is the sea, in which the river loses
itself ; or, alternatively, that Osiris signifies moisture

EXPULSION OF "DEMONS" FROM THE MYSTERIES OF ISIS

After Moreau le Jeune.

as the cause of generation and fructification, the male principle, so to speak. Set, on the other hand, represents whatever is adult and fiery, everything which is of a searching quality and destructive of moisture. Still another theory likens Osiris to the Sun, and Set to the drought or evil principle. A more elaborate explanation refers to Set as the sun and Osiris as the moon, the lunar orb, according to ancient philosophy, being productive of growth and the sun destructive, as might well be imagined in a climate like that of Egypt. Isis, according to this theory, is the generative influence resident in the moon, which is thus bisexual, " female, as it receives the influence of the Sun (Set) and male as it scatters the principles of fecundity." The last explanation refers the Osirian pantheon to the phenomena of eclipse, and states that the allegory of Osiris having been shut up in a chest signifies an eclipse of the moon.

Plutarch suggests very sensibly " that no one of these hypotheses taken separately contains the explication of the foregoing history, though all of them do together." By Set is meant the destructive principle at large. The world is made up of contrary powers, but good is predominant, yet the malignant principle cannot wholly be destroyed. By Osiris we are to understand the faculties of the Universal Soul, such as intelligence and reason, all that is regular and permanent in nature. The irrational and passionate part of nature is represented by Set.

The Egyptians, says Plutarch, mystically represented universal Nature by a right-angled triangle, the perpendicular side representing the masculine nature, the base the feminine, and the hypoteneuse the offspring of both, or respectively Osiris, Isis, and

Horus. In the same manner the sistrum or rattle of Isis was designed to represent that everything in nature must be kept in continual agitation, rousing it to action.

The sacred vestments of Osiris and Isis are of some importance. Those of Isis are dyed in a great variety of colours to signify her association with many-coloured nature. Those of Osiris, on the other hand, are of one uniform shining hue, as befits a first principle, pure intelligence unmixed and undefiled.

The essay of Iamblichus on the Mysteries is stated by the philosopher Proclus (A.D. 412–485) in his commentary on the Enneads of Plotinus to have been written in answer to an epistle of Porphyry (A.D. 233–306) which posed certain theological doubts. In replying to it, Iamblichus, a Syrian philosopher, who died in A.D. 339, assumed the name and style of a certain Egyptian priest, Ab-ammon, as being in character with the tone of the composition.

The epistle of Porphyry had been addressed to the Egyptian prophet Anebo, and inquired as to the nature and status of the gods. In replying to it, Iamblichus asks Porphyry to regard him as the person to whom his queries were addressed, " which after all, is a matter of no consequence." The only portions of the work which concern us are those which refer to the Egyptian Mysteries, and these may here be extracted and separated from the general body of the work.

In Section VII of his essay Iamblichus pays especial attention to the mystical symbolism of the Egyptians. " They exhibit," he says, " certain images through symbols of mystic, occult, and invisible intellections, just as nature . . . expresses invisible reasons through visible forms. . . . Hence the Egyptians, perceiving that all superior natures rejoice in the similitude to them of inferior beings, and thus wishing to fill the latter with good, through the greatest possible imitation of the former, very properly exhibit a mode of theologizing adapted to the mystic doctrine concealed in the symbols."

To comprehend the intellectual interpretation of symbols according to the conception of the Egyptians it is essential to forget their material nature and to elevate oneself to the status of intellectual truth. Neither do those veils by which arcana are concealed originate out of folly.

The Egyptians believed in one god, self-begotten and truly good, the fountain of all things, according to Hermes, called Kneph, the first and leader of the gods. The Demiurgic, or sub-creative nature is personalized by Ammon or Phtah. There are two natural " governments," o. e appertaining to the sun and the other to the moon, and, dividing the heavens into sections, they give to these a greater or less number of rulers. Thus unity rules multitude. " The Egyptians, likewise, do not say that all things are physical. For they separate the life of the soul and the intellectual life from nature, not only in the universe, but also in us. And admitting intellect and reason to subsist by themselves, they say that generated essences were thus fabricated. They likewise arrange the Demiurgus as the primary father of things in generation ; and they acknowledge the existence of a vital power, prior to the heavens, and subsisting in the heavens. They also establish a pure intellect above the world, and one impartible intellect in the whole world, and another which is distributed into all the spheres. And these things they do not survey by mere reason alone, but, through the sacerdotal theurgy, they announce that they are able to ascend to more elevated and universal essences, and to those that are established above Fate, viz. to God and the Demiurgus; neither employing matter, nor assuming any other thing besides, except the observation of a suitable time.

This deific and anagogic path Hermes, indeed, narrated, but Bitys, the prophet of King Ammon, explained it, having found it in the adyta of Sais in Egypt, written in hieroglyphics, and the same prophet also delivered the name of God, which pervades through the whole world. But there are, likewise, many other coarrangements of the same things; " so that you do not appear to me to act rightly in referring all things with the Egyptians to physical causes. For there are, according to them, many principles and many essences; and also super-mundane powers, which they worship through sacerdotal sanctimony."

Iamblichus touches, too, on the question of attaining unity with the gods, which was the main intention of the Mysteries. He says: " If the essence and perfection of all good are comprehended in the gods, and the first and ancient power of them is with us priests, and if by those who similarly adhere to more excellent natures, and genuinely obtain a union with them, the beginning and end of all good is earnestly pursued; if this be the case, here the contemplation of truth, and the possession of intellectual science are to be found. And a knowledge of the Gods is accompanied with a conversion to, and the knowledge of, ourselves. . . . It is better, therefore, in compliance with your request, to point out to you the way to felicity, and show you in what the essence of it is placed. For from this the truth will be discovered, and at the same time all the doubts may be easily dissolved. I say, therefore, that the more divine intelligible man, who was formerly united to the Gods by the vision of them, afterwards entered into another soul, which is coadapted to the human form, and through this became fettered with the bonds of necessity and fate.[1] Hence it is requisite to consider how he may be liberated from these bonds. There is, therefore, no other dissolution of them than the knowledge of the gods. For to know scientifically the good is the idea of felicity ; just as the oblivion of good, and deception about evil, happen to be the idea of evil. The former, therefore, is present with divinity ; but the latter, which is an inferior destiny, is inseparable from the mortal nature. And the former, indeed, measures the essences of intelligibles by sacred ways ; but the latter, abandoning principles, gives itself up to the measurement of the idea of body. The former is a knowledge of the father ; but the latter is a departure from him, and an oblivion of the god who is a superessential father, and sufficient to himself. The former, likewise, preserves the true life of the soul, and leads it back to its father ; but the latter draws down the generation-ruling man, as far as to that which is never permanent, but is always flowing. You must understand, therefore, that this is the first path to felicity, affording to souls an intellectual plentitude of divine union. But the sacerdotal and theurgic gift of felicity is called, indeed, the Gate to the Demiurgus of wholes, or the seat, or Palace, of *the Good*. In the first place, likewise, it possesses a power of purifying the soul, much more perfect than the power which purifies the body ; afterwards it causes a coaptation of the reasoning

[1] The Ka ?

power to the participation and vision of *the Good*, and a liberation from every thing of a contrary nature ; and, in the last place, produces a union with the Gods, who are the givers of every good.

" Moreover, after it has conjoined the soul to the several parts of the universe, and to the total divine powers which pass through it ; then it leads the soul to, and deposits it in, the whole Demiurgus, and causes it to be independent of all matter, and to be counited with the eternal reason alone. But my meaning is, that it peculiarly connects the soul with the self-begotten and self-moved God, and with the all-sustaining, intellectual, and all-adorning powers of the God, and likewise with that power of him which elevates to truth, and with his self-perfect, effective, and other demiurgic powers ; so that the theurgic soul becomes perfectly established in the energies and demiurgic intellections of these powers. Then, also, it inserts the soul in the whole demiurgic God. And this is the end with the Egyptians of the sacerdotal elevation of the soul to divinity."

It should be added, however, that Iamblichus makes it plain that in his belief the knowledge or intelligence of the Divine alone does not suffice to unite the faithful with God. It is the perfect execution and superiority of intelligence, of acts ineffable, the inexplicable power of symbols which convey the intelligence of divine things. This is a point of supreme importance.

CHAPTER III

THE LITERARY SOURCES (CONTINUED)

IT is from the *Metamorphoses*, better known as *The Golden Ass*, of Apuleius, a Latin Platonic philosopher of the second century A.D., that we obtain our fullest account of the Egyptian Mysteries in direct form. This is couched in the style of a novel, which recounts how one Lucius Patras is transformed into an ass by magic, and is only released from that form by the power of Isis. Later he becomes a neophyte of the goddess, and it is clear that the portion which deals with his initiation is really autobiographical, and refers to Apuleius himself, as is made plain enough by the fact that in the older original of the story, *Lucius or the Ass*, no mention is made of the Mysteries, and it would seem that a popular tale had thus been turned to the purposes of arcane teaching by an initiate.

That Apuleius was an initiate of the Mysteries of Isis seems on the whole probable, and it will best serve the purpose I have in view to quote at some length from his account of the manner in which he came to be sealed of the cultus of the goddess. We are informed that after he had been freed from ass's shape the priest of Isis exhorted him to " enrol his name in her sacred soldiery," and dedicate himself to the ministry of her faith. This he elected to do, and hired apartments within her temple : " For I had been admitted to the services of the goddess hitherto kept secret from me, and dwelt with her priests inseparably, and might not be parted from the worship of the mighty deity. Nor was there one night or one sleep of mine that was not gladdened by visions and admonitions of the goddess, but ever and again she commanded that I who had so long been destined for her mysteries should now at length be initiated therein. But I, though my desire for initiation burned strong, was held back by a certain religious awe and terror, for I had often been told that the service of the faith was hard, that the laws of chastity and abstinence were not easy to obey, and that my life must needs be hedged about by circumspection and caution against the manifold strokes of chance to which this flesh is exposed. And as I revolved these thoughts in my mind, not once only but continually, for all my eagerness I kept putting off the day. . . . I frequented the worship of the goddess, with all its exacting service, more zealously than ever, since my present good fortunes gave warrant for my expectations of the future. And daily my desire to be admitted to the mysteries increased ever more and more, and again and again I visited the high priest with the most urgent entreaty that he would at length initiate me into the secrets of the night that is holy to the goddess. But, he, being a man of steadfast character and famous for his observation of the strict laws of the faith, with kindly and gentle words, such as parents use to check the precocious desires of their children, put off my insistence and soothed the great trouble of my spirit by holding forth consolatory hope of greater bliss. For he said that the day of each man's initiation was fixed by the ordinance of the goddess, and that the

priest destined for her service was likewise chosen by
her providence, and that a like instruction appointed
the sum required for the expenses of the ceremony.
He bade me, like others, await all these ordinances
with reverent patience, warning me that it was my
duty to beware with all my soul of over-eagerness
and petulance, to avoid both these faults, and neither
to delay when summoned nor to hasten unbidden.
' There are none,' he said, ' of all the order of priests
of Isis so abandoned in spirit, or so given over to
death, as to venture rashly and sacrilegiously to under-
take the service of the goddess without her express
command and thus to contract mortal guilt. For the
gates of hell and the power of life are in the hands of
the goddess, and the very act of dedication is regarded
as a voluntary death and an imperilling of life, inasmuch as the goddess is wont to select those whose term
of life is near its close and who stand on the threshold
of the night, and are moreover men to whom the
mighty Mysteries of the goddess may safely be committed. These men the goddess by her providence
brings to new birth and places once more at the start
of a new race of life. Therefore thou too must await
the command of heaven although long since appointed
and ordained, by the clear and evident choice of the
great deity, to be highly favoured in thy service at
her shrine. And to that end, thou like other servants
of the goddess, shouldst henceforth refrain from
impious and unlawful foods, that so thou mayest
more righteously win thy way to the secret mysteries
of the purest of faiths.'

" So spake the priest, nor did I mar my service of
the goddess by any impatience, but with quiet and
gentleness, and edifying silence rendered zealous and
attentive service at the daily performance of the rites.

Nor did the saving grace of the great goddess play me false, or torture me by long deferment, but in the dark of night, in commands wherein was no darkness, she clearly warned me that the day of my long desire was come, whereon she would grant the fulfilment of my most earnest prayers. She decreed also what sums I must expend at the supplications, and ordained Mithras himself, her high priest, to reveal the Mysteries to me; for his destinies, she said, were closely bound with mine by the divine conjunction of certain constellations.

"By these and other gracious admonitions the supreme goddess gladdened my spirit, so that ere yet it was clear day I shook sleep from off me and hastened straightway to the priest's lodging. I met him even as he came forth from his bedchamber and saluted him. I had resolved to demand with yet greater persistence than my wont that I should be appointed to the service of the mysteries as being now my due. But he, as soon as he beheld me, anticipated me and said, 'Lucius, happy and blessed art thou, whom the august deity deigns to favour with such goodwill. Why,' he said, 'dost thou now stand idle and thyself delay thine own advancement ? The day so long besought by thine unwearied prayers is come, on which by the divine commands of the goddess of many names thou shalt be admitted by my hands to the most holy secrets of the mysteries.'

"Then, placing his right hand in mine, the kindly old man led me to the very doors of the great shrine, and after celebrating with solemn rite the service of the opening of the gates and performing the morning sacrifice, he brought forth from the hidden places of the shrine certain books with titles written in undecipherable letters. Some of these were in the shape of animals of all kinds, and seemed to be compendious symbols for the forms of speech ; others were defended from the curiosity of profane readers, inasmuch as their extremities were knotted or curved like wheels or closely interwoven like to the tendrils of the vine. At the same time he informed me of the various provisions which it was necessary for the aspirant to initiation to make. I lost no time, but with zealous liberality even greater than was required, either bought those things which were necessary myself or had them brought by my friends. And now the priest conducted me with an escort of the faithful to the nearest baths, for so, he said, the occasion demanded, and on my entering the bath, where it is the custom for the neophyte to bathe, after he had first prayed to the gods to be gracious to me, he besprinkled me with purest water and cleansed me. He then led me back to the temple and, the day being more than half spent, set me at the feet of the goddess herself, and after that he had confided certain secrets to me, things too holy for utterance, openly before all present bade me for ten consecutive days to abstain from all pleasures of the table, to eat no living thing, and to drink no wine.

" All these precepts I observed with reverent abstinence, and at last the day came for my dedication to the goddess. The sun was sloping westward and bringing on the evening, when lo ! on all sides crowds of the holy initiates flocked round me, each, after the ancient rite, honouring me with diverse gifts. Lastly, all the uninitiate were excluded, a linen robe that no man had yet worn was cast about me, the priest caught me by the hand and led me to the very heart of the holy place.

" Perchance, eager reader, thou burnest to know

what then was said, what done. I would tell thee,
were it lawful for me to tell, and thou shouldst know
all, were it lawful for thee to hear. But both tongue
and ear would be infected with like guilt did I gratify
such rash curiosity. Yet since, perchance, it is pious
craving that vexes thee, I will not torment thee by
prolongation of thine anguish. Hear, then, and
believe, for what I tell is true. I drew nigh to the
confines of death, I trod the threshold of Proserpine,
I was borne through all the elements and returned
to earth again. I saw the sun gleaming with bright
splendour at dead of night, I approached the gods
above, and the gods below, and worshipped them
face to face. Behold, I have told thee things of which,
though thou hast heard them, thou must yet know
naught.

"I will recount, therefore, only that which may
without sin be imparted to the understanding of the
uninitiate. So soon as it was morning and the rites
were accomplished, I came forth clothed in the
twelve cloaks that are worn by the initiate, a raiment
that is most holy but whereof no sacred bond forbids
me tell, since at the time whereof I speak many saw
me arrayed therein. For in the very midst of the
holy temple before the image of the goddess there
was a wooden dais whereto at the priest's bidding
I ascended, arrayed in a robe which, for all that it
was only made of linen, was so richly embroidered
that I was a sight for all men's eyes. The precious
cloak hung from my shoulders down my back, even
to my heels, and I was adorned, wheresoever thou
mightest cast thine eye, with the figures of beasts
broidered round about in diverse colours. Here were
dragons of Ind, there gryphons from the back of the
north wind, beasts after the semblance of a winged

bird, created by another world than ours. This cloak the initiates call the cloak of Olympus. In my right hand I bore a torch flaming with fire, and my head was garlanded with a fair crown of spotless palm, whose leaves stood out like rays. After I had been thus adorned as the sun and set up like to the image of a god, the curtains were suddenly withdrawn and the people thronged in to gaze upon me. Thereafter I celebrated this most joyous birthday of my initiation and there were feasts and merry banquetings. The third day was likewise celebrated with ceremonial rite, a solemn breaking of my fast was enjoined upon me and my initiation was duly consummated. Yet a few days longer I tarried there, and enjoyed the ineffable delight of dwelling with the image of the goddess, to whom I was now pledged by blessings such as I might never repay."

A year later " Lucius " was initiated into the Greater Mysteries, those of Osiris, and later into still higher Mysteries in which Osiris himself appeared to him, but mention of them is merely fragmentary and concludes the tale abruptly.

Does the Egyptian Book of the Dead, so-called, throw much actual light on the Mysteries ? The answer is both " yes " and " no," for whereas it cannot be expected that its pages should reveal to us very much explicit information regarding the procedure of the Mysteries, there can be little doubt that its doctrines and ideas were those of the very men whose duty it was to celebrate the Mysteries.

The Book of the Dead was a sort of *vade mecum* by means of which the spirit of the dead Egyptian might be enabled to make his way through the numerous dangers which beset it to the place of unity with and absorption in the being of the great

god Osiris. Now we have to bear in mind that the
Mysteries served a dual purpose—which, in effect, was
one—communion with the god during life, that is
direct and personal communication with the deity,
such as is described in the Scriptures by the phrase
" walking with God " and union eternal with Him
after death through mystical rebirth. The Book
of the Dead is a magico-religious treatise built up
during many centuries to ensure the safe arrival of
the souls of the just in the sphere of Osiris. It deals
scarcely at all with the subject of communion with
God during life, and only in passing with the final
absorption in Osiris, as might a guide-book or itinerary
deal with a destination.

The development or evolution of the Book of the
Dead was indeed a matter of centuries. The process
by which the dead were believed to find union with
the god differed at various periods in the long history
of Egypt, but the evolutionary tendency is plain
enough. In the texts of the Pyramid period (thirtieth
to twenty-fifth century B.C.), we find the prospect
of a glorious hereafter in the splendour of the sun-
god's presence. The state theology then centred in
the worship of Ra, the solar deity, with whom the
Pharaoh, and the Pharaoh alone, might gain final
communion. To the common people and even to the
nobles an undistinguished after-life in the netherworld
seems to have been the sole outlook. The king, in
fact, became Ra, the god himself, or was absorbed in
Ra. It was only later that ordinary mortals might
share such a destiny, and then under a rather different
dispensation.

The Pyramid texts, as they are called, that is, the
royal texts found in the Pyramids, are thus the
forerunners of the Book of the Dead, and afford us

a good general idea of the manner in which the king succeeded to union with the god. His soul must first of all bathe in the sacred lake in the Fields of the Blessed, the lesser gods officiating at the ceremony with towels and raiment ; or he must undergo lustration with the water of the Nile source at Elephantiné. In any case the object of the bath was one of ceremonial cleanliness, and was obviously the prototype of the initiates' bath in the later days when the ceremonial of the Mysteries had become fixed.

It was then necessary for the Pharaoh to cross the Lily Lake which separated him from the demesne of the sun-god, and in order to do so, he must gain the good graces of the Egyptian Charon, who bore the sinister name of " Face-behind," as it was necessary for him to face backward in order to pole the boat at the stern. Him the king must cajole, or else must take bird-shape and fly across the water. Once on the opposite shore, the great staircase of the sun must be ascended, reaching to the city of the sun. In each of these interludes we descry circumstances which at a very much later period came to be imported into the ceremonial of the Mysteries—the ferry-boat of the neophyte is, indeed, known to practically every mystical fraternity, and is the type of the solar barque, of the sun's daily progress through the heavens, while the golden staircase of the sun, composed of his beams reaching to earth from heaven, is likewise familiar in many rituals.

The king is now before the gates of the sun-city, and by means magical he must endeavour to open these. This is effected by means of a charm or spell, such as was later frequently employed in initiation. " The double doors of the sky are opened, the double doors of the firmament are opened to Horus of the gods." For, just as Horus had passed between these gates, so might the spirit of the dead king in his name.

In the Pyramid texts, too, we discover a circumstance which at once brings their whole method and aim into relationship with later practice in the Mysteries. That is the annunciation of the soul of the Pharaoh to the divine presence by heralds. The herald was one of the principal officials of the Greek Mysteries, and later of the Eleusinian and Druidic Mysteries as well, and it is as strange as interesting to find him alluded to in these most ancient texts, dating as they do more than twenty centuries before the Christian era. The herald in the Mysteries is, therefore, a figure of at least four thousand years' standing !

" Thy heralds make haste," says the text of King Pepi, " behold he comes," cries the herald Sehpu. The gods gather to greet the dead monarch. There is also mention of a gate-keeper, another very ancient office-bearer of the Mysteries, whose name is Methen. There is furthermore a divine scribe, whose place in some of the texts is actually taken by the dead king himself. Thus we see that practically every one among the officials of certain later Mysteries has his prototype in these primitive writings, so that little dubiety can exist regarding the origin of their offices.

Once accepted of Ra, the king enjoys the daily round of solar existence along with the god, sailing in the sun-barque, and tasting the delights of his effulgent glory. Now there is irrefragable evidence that the system set forth in the Pyramid texts was at first not only entirely separate from but theologically opposed to that of the Osirian faith, the religion of the god Osiris, who was regarded as the deity of the ordinary dead who dwelt in the dreary Underworld. But at some time a revulsion set in. The kings who in their death-records had most emphatically stated their freedom from the doom of Osiris were succeeded by others who as ardently prayed for communion with him. There were thus two groups of belief as regards the hereafter, one that concerning life with Ra the sun-god, which might be partaken of by the Pharaoh alone, and the other relating to a dreary future with Osiris, the god of the dead, in an underground hades. Osiris was not only the Nile personified, the god of growth and fertility, but he and the group of deities associated with him came to symbolize the ordinary everyday Egyptian himself. His history, and that of his sister-wife Isis, might indeed in some measure symbolize that of the Egyptian " John Citizen," so to speak. He was the archetype of Egyptian man, just as Horus, his son, typified in some ways the pious Egyptian son, and Isis the faithful wife. When dead every Egyptian became, or hoped to become, an Osiris, and as the centuries passed, a democratic desire seems greatly to have moved the people to place this popular deity on an equal status with Ra the sun-god, to give him like attributes with Ra, to make it possible for the Egyptian after death to become one with Osiris, just as formerly the kings alone had the privilege of union with Ra.

In the obscure period which followed the Pyramid Age these ideas appear to have fructified and to have been accompanied by others which considerably heightened the ethical and moral character of the Osirian cult. This in the event resulted in the almost complete fusion of the cults of Ra and Osiris, and of the figures of the two gods into that of the coalesced deity Ra-Osiris, who now partook of the attributes of both. But that the figure of Osiris triumphed in the end there can be small question.

Indeed we find the personages of the earlier mystical journey of the Pharaoh as described in the Pyramid texts becoming the property of the Osirian cult, the ferryman, the four celestial genii or Horuses, the golden staircase, and all the other associations of the more primitive cult.

Midway between the Pyramid texts and the Book of the Dead, however, stand those writings known as the " coffin texts," the directions of the priests to the dead Egyptian, placed in his coffin, and adjuring him as to the proper procedure to be taken during the journey to the Otherworld. These, dating from a period prior to the collection of the Book of the Dead into one corpus, still show the tendency which was especially to mark it out as a handbook to the deceased Egyptian as regards his manner of comporting himself during his journey to the locality where his union with Osiris would take place. The journey was, indeed, a dreadful one, and may be found reflected in the ritual of the Mysteries, therefore it is of especial interest to us. Most of the ordeals and risks to be encountered on the way were of a physical nature, and these were to be rendered nugatory by charms and other magical means.

These texts were already divided into chapters, such as " How to become a Magician," " How not to lose Magic in the Otherworld," " How a man may not decay in the Otherworld," and so forth. That these, for the most part, related to the grotesque notions of a superstitious people as to what might occur in the wastes and terrible deserts which lay between the hour of death and the Elysian Fields is,

of course, plain enough, and that they found their
way into the later Mysteries is also apparent. But we
must bear in mind that with simplicity of faith there
not infrequently goes hand-in-hand a residuum of
mythological or allegorical fiction, the legacy of that
religion of the lower cultus which precedes enlighten-
ment. And it is well to remember that such allegory
may quite possibly symbolize perils imminent enough
to the immortal spirit of an equally grievous if not
so gruesomely material character. Indeed, it seems
plain enough that at the later and more sophisticated
period of the Mysteries these horrors, once entirely
accepted in the materialistic sense, were regarded as
symbolical and to be taken in a psychological sense,
that is, as dangers to a soul which much less resembles
the actual body than it had done in the belief of the
more primitive folk of the Nileland. It will, however,
be more in keeping with the spirit of our quest if we
review these ideas as they are found in the Book of
the Dead itself, where they came to ultimate fruition.

The Book of the Dead is a magical book, inasmuch
as the sorcery of everyday life is placed at the disposal
of the dead in order that they may escape destruction
in the journey toward the Otherworld by means of
spells and magical invocations. Most of the texts
comprised in the work as we know it now are in one
form or another of much greater antiquity than the
dynastic period. Even at as early a date as 3300 B.C.
the writers who transcribed the ancient texts were so
puzzled by their contents as scarcely to comprehend
their meaning.

An inscription on the sarcophagus of Queen Khnem-
nefert, wife of Mentu-hotep, a monarch of the Eleventh
Dynasty (about 2500 B.C.), states that a certain
chapter of the Book of the Dead was " discovered in

the reign of Hesep-ti, a king who flourished about 4266 B.C." This in itself suffices to give a clue to the immense antiquity of this extraordinary body of ancient thought, which goes back at least fifty-four centuries beyond the present time. The Book of the Dead was known in its collected form in the Sixth Dynasty, or about 3233 B.C., although no actual manuscripts of that period have come to light, but the existence of many of its chapters in the pyramid inscriptions prove that it must have been in currency.

As we have previously noticed, the Book of the Dead was for their use from the moment when they found themselves inhabitants of the Otherworld. Magic was the very mainspring of existence in that sphere, and unless a spirit was acquainted with the formulæ which compelled the respect of the various gods and demons, and even of inanimate objects, it was helpless. The region to which the dead departed the primitive Egyptians called Duat. They believed it to be formed of the body of Osiris. It was regarded as dark and gloomy, containing pits of fire and dreadful monsters which circled the earth, and was in its turn bounded by a river and a lofty chain of mountains. The part of it that was nearest to Egypt was regarded as a description of mingled desert and forest, through which the soul of the deceased might not hope to struggle unless guided by some benevolent spirit who knew the paths through this country of despair. Thick darkness covered everything, and under veil of this the hideous inhabitants of the place practised all sorts of hostility to the new-comer, unless by the use of words of power he could prove his superiority over them.

But there was one delectable part in this horrid region—the Sekhet Hetepet, the Elysian Fields, which contained the Sekhet Aalu, or the Field of Reeds, where dwelt the god Osiris and his company. At first he had domain over this part of the Duat alone, but gradually he succeeded in extending it over the entire country of the dead, of which he was monarch. We find also a god of the Duat named Duati, but who appears to have been more a personification of the region that anything else. Now the wish of all good men was to win to the kingdom of Osiris, and to that end they made an exhaustive study of the prayers and ritual of the Book of the Dead, in order that they might the more easily penetrate to the region of bliss. This they might reach by two ways—by land and by water. The path by water was no whit less dreadful than that by land, the passage of the soul being barred by streams of fire and boiling water, and the banks of the rivers navigated were populous with evil spirits.

We learn from the Theban Recension or version of the Book of the Dead that there were seven halls or mansions in the Field of Reeds, all of which had to be passed through by the soul before it was received by the god in person. Three gods guarded the door of each hall—the doorkeeper, watchman, and questioner. It was necessary for the new-comer to address each god by his name. There were also names for the doors which must be borne in mind. The name of each god was in reality a spell consisting of a number of words. The Place of Reeds was divided into fifteen regions, each of which was presided over by a god. The first of these was called Amentet, where dwelt those souls who lived upon earth-offerings ; it was ruled over by Menuqet. The second was Sekhet Aalu, the Field of Reeds proper, the walls surrounding which were formed of the stuff of which the sky is made. Here dwelt the souls, who were nine cubits high, under the rule of Ra Heru-Khuti, and this place was the centre of the kingdom of Osiris. The third was the place of the spirit-souls, a region of fire. In the fourth dwelt the terrible serpent Sati-temui, which preyed on the dead who dwelt in the Duat. The fifth region was inhabited by spirits who fed upon the shadows of the weak and helpless souls. They appear to have been a description of vampire. The remaining regions were very similar to these.

We find other descriptions of the Duat in the Book of Gates and the Book of Him that is in the Duat, in which is outlined the journey that the sun-god makes through the Otherworld after he has set upon the earth-world. Immediately after sinking he takes the form of Osiris, which in this instance is that of a ram with a man's head. Coming to the antechamber of the Duat in the west, his entrance is heralded by songs of praise, raised by the Ape-gods, while serpents blow fire from their mouths, by the light of which his Pilot-gods steer his craft. All the doors are thrown open, and the dead, revived by the earthly air which Osiris carries with him, come to life again for a brief hour. All the creatures of this portion of the Duat are provided with meat and drink by command of the god. Such of the dead as dwell here are those who have failed to pass the various tests for entrance to his court, and all that they exist for is the material comfort provided for them by the brief diurnal passage of the deity.

When the sun, who in this form is known as Af-Ra, reaches the entrance to the second part of the Duat, which is called Urnes, the gods of the first section depart from him, and do not again behold his face until the following night. At this point the boat of

Af-Ra is met by the boats of Osiris and his attendant gods, and in this place also Osiris desires that the dead should receive food, light, and air. Here he grapples with the serpents Hau and Neha-her, as do most sun-gods during the time of darkness, and, having overcome them, is led into the Field of the Grain-gods, where he reposes for a while. When there he hearkens to the prayers of the living on behalf of the dead, and takes account of the offerings made by them.

Continuing his journey, he traverses the twelve sections of the Duat. In some of these we see what were probably quite separate realms of the dead, such as the Realm of Seker, a god who is perhaps of greater antiquity than Osiris. In this place his boat is useless, as there is no river in the gloomy kingdom of Seker, which appears completely alien to Osiris. He therefore repeats words of awful power, which compel the gods of the place to lead him by sub-terranean passages, from which he emerges into Amhet, where is situated a stream of boiling water. But he is not out of the kingdom of Seker until he reaches the sixth section, where dwell the dead kings of Egypt and the " ku " or Spirit-souls. It is at this point of his journey that Af-Ra turns his face toward the east and directs his course to the Mountain of the Sunrise ; previous to this he has been journeying from the south to the north. In the seventh section he is joined by Isis and other deities, and here his path is obstructed by the wicked serpent Apep, through whose body the attendant deities drive their daggers. A company of gods tow him through the eighth section, but his vessel sails itself through the ninth, and in the tenth and eleventh he seems to pass over a series of lakes, which may represent the lagoons of the eastern delta. In the latter section his progress is lighted by a disk of light encircled by a serpent, which rests upon the prow of the boat.

The twelfth section contains the great mass of celestial waters called Nu, and here dwells Nut, the personification of the morning. Before the boat looms the great serpent Ankh-neteru, and twelve of the gods, taking hold of the tow-line, enter this serpent at the tail and draw the god in his boat through the monstrous body, bringing Af-Ra out at its mouth ; but not as Af-Ra, for during this passage he has been transformed into Khepera, in which shape he is towed into the sky by twelve goddesses, who lead him before Shu, the god of the atmosphere of the terrestrial world. Shu places him in the opening in the semicircular wall which forms the end of the twelfth section, and he now appears to mortal eyes as a disk of light, having discarded his mummified form, in which he traversed the Duat. His progress is followed by the acclamations of his company of gods, who fall upon and destroy his enemies and sing hymns of praise to him.

In one of the chapters of the Book of the Dead we find Osiris seated in a large hall the roof of which is covered with fire and symbols of truth. Before him are the symbol of Anubis, the four sons of Horus, and the Devourer of the West, a monster who serves as his protector. In the rear sit the forty-two judges of the dead. The deceased makes his appearance before the god and his heart is placed in a great balance to be weighed by Anubis, Thoth, the scribe of the Gods, standing by to note the result upon his tablets. Having communicated this to Osiris, the dead man, if found worthy, is presented to the deity, to whom he repeats a long prayer, in which he states that he

THE JUDGMENT OF OSIRIS
From the Papyrus of Ani.

has not committed any evil. Those who could not pass the test were hurried away, and so far as is known were in danger of being devoured by a frightful monster called Beby, which awaited them outside. The justified deceased took part in the life of Osiris and the other gods, which appears to have been very much the same as that of the Egyptian aristocracy. As has been said, the deceased might also transform himself into any animal form he cared.

The life of the justified dead is well cutlined in an inscription on the tomb of Paheri, prince of El Kab, which is as follows : " Thou goest in and out with a glad heart, and with the rewards of the gods. . . . Thou becomest a living soul ; thou hast power over bread, water, and air. Thou changest thyself into a phœnix or a swallow, a sparrow-hawk or a heron, as thou desirest. Thou dost cross in the boat and art not hindered. Thou sailest upon the water when a flood ariseth. Thou livest anew and thy soul is not parted from thy body. Thy soul is a god together with the illuminated, and the excellent souls speak with thee. Thou art among them and (verily) receive what is given upon earth ; thou possessest water, possessest air, hast superabundance of that which thou desirest. Thine eyes are given to thee to see, and thine ears to hear speech, thy mouth speaketh, thy legs move, thy hands and arms bestir themselves for thee, thy flesh grows, thy veins are in health, and thou feelest thyself well in all thy limbs. Thou hast thine upright heart in thy possession, and thy earlier heart belongs to thee. Thou dost mount up to heaven, and art summoned each day to the libation table of Wennofre (Osiris), thou receivest the good which has been offered to him and the gifts of the Lords of the necropolis."

This part of the Book of the Dead is obviously an allegory of the passage of the sun through the Underworld. The sinking of the sun at nightfall would naturally arouse in primitive man thoughts as to where the luminary dwelt during the hours of gloom, for the sun was to early man a living thing. He could watch its motion across the sky, and the light and other benefits which he received from it came to make him regard it as the source of all good. It appeared plain to him that its diurnal career was cut short by the attacks of some enemy, and the logical sequel of the belief in the solar deity as a beneficent power was of course that the force hostile to him must be of evil disposition. It came to be figured as a serpent or dragon which nightly battled with the luminary and for a season prevailed. The gods of many religions have to descend into the Otherworld to do battle with the forces of death and hell.

Let us summarize the main points of the foregoing material, which constitutes practically all the literary sources we possess at first-hand concerning the Mysteries of Egypt, and see what it yields us.

Plutarch tells us that the cult of Isis prepares man for the attainment of the knowledge of the Supreme Mind. The goddess points out the knowledge of divine truth to her votaries, who carry the sacred doctrine regarding the gods locked up in their souls. He alone is a true servant of the goddess who, after he has become acquainted with her history (or myth), searches into the hidden truths which lie concealed under it. The " purificatory observances " associated with this quest for the divine were established with a view of promoting morality and happiness, to preserve the meaning of some valuable passages in history, or to represent some of the phenomena of nature. But this philosophy is involved in fable and allegory, showing only dark hints and obscure resemblances of the truth. The chief aim, however, is to form true notions of the divine nature.

The myth of Isis, as detailed by Plutarch, probably formed the mythic background of the Mysteries of that goddess. But Plutarch warns us that great differences exists between the version of the Osirian story as given by him and the popular version according to the poets and fabulists, as his recension is " the reflection of something real," as can be proved by the attitude of the Egyptian priesthood to the ceremonies associated with the death of Osiris.

Iamblichus tells us that to comprehend the Egyptian system of symbolism it is necessary to forget its material nature, and that those veils by which arcana are concealed do not originate out of folly. The Egyptians, through their sacerdotal theurgy, are able to ascend to more elevated and universal essences, to God and the Demiurgus, " neither employing matter, nor assuming any other thing besides, except the observation of a suitable time." This divine path is mentioned by Hermes, but Bitys, the prophet of King Ammon, explained it. (This obviously refers to a writing in hieroglyphics found by this sage in the adyta of Sais, and now lost to us.) The essence of all good is comprehended in the gods and the power of them is vested in the priests. The " more divine intelligible man," who was formerly united to the gods by the vision of them, afterwards entered into another soul, " which is coadapted to the human form, and through this, became fettered with the bonds of necessity and fate. Hence it is requisite to consider how he may be liberated from these bonds." Knowledge of the gods

is the only dissolution of these, for the scientific knowledge of the good is the idea of felicity. The deception
of evil and the oblivion of good constitute the idea
of evil. The first is divine the second mortal, the one
a knowledge of the Father, the other a departure from
Him. The one preserves the true life of the soul, the
other draws it down to that which is impermanent and
fluctuating.

The first is the first path to felicity and is known as
the Gate to the Demiurgus of Wholes, or the Palace
of the Good. The second stage is an adaptation of the
reasoning power to participation with, and the vision
of, the good, and in the last place a union with the
gods is produced. Moreover, after it has conjoined the
soul to the different parts of the universe, it deposits
the soul in the Demiurgus and unites it with the
eternal Reason.

Apuleius furnishes us with important matter
relating chiefly to the ritual of the Egyptian
Mysteries. Lucius, his hero, enrols his name in the
" sacred soldiery " of the goddess Isis, and hires
apartments within her temple, being admitted to
special services for the initiates, hitherto kept secret
from him. He was nightly visited by the vision and
admonitions of the goddess, but had perforce to wait
until the goddess gave her express command for his
initiation. The act of initiation is regarded as a
voluntary death and a new birth. Astrological
computation entered into the question of the time
of initiation of each individual, as the speech of Isis
makes clear.

The priest then instructed Lucius from certain
books written in Egyptian hieroglyphs, and what
seem to have been mnemonic symbols like the quipus
of the Peruvians or the Bobileth of the Druids.

Lucius then took the bath of the neophyte, and was asperged by the priest, who then confided to him certain secrets too holy for utterance, and enjoined fasting for ten days.

At evening on the day of dedication Lucius received gifts from the initiates, was clad in a linen robe, and introduced to the very heart of the holy place. He drew near to the confines of death, he trod the threshold of Proserpine, and was borne through all the elements and returned to earth again. He saw the sun gleaming at dead of night, approached the supernal and infernal gods, and worshipped them face to face.

In the morning, the rites being accomplished, he was clad in the twelve cloaks worn by the initiate, sewn with strange symbols. He stood on a wooden dais with a burning torch in his right hand, and on his head a crown of palm. The people then thronged in to gaze on him, and a banquet followed. His initiation was consummated on the following day, when he broke his fast.

The Book of the Dead was preceded by the Pyramid Texts, which recount the manner in which Egyptian royalty succeeded to union with the god. His soul bathed in the sacred lake, he underwent lustration with Nile water, and he then crossed the Lake of Lilies in the ferry-boat. He ascended the staircase of the sun and reached the city of the sun, after magically opening its gates by a spell, being announced by heavenly heralds.

The later coffin texts also afford directions as to procedure after death, and describe the perils to be encountered by the soul on its post-mortem journey.

In the Book of the Dead itself these earlier ideas are reduced to a strict canon or formulæ for the use of the spirit after death. It is unnecessary to recapitulate this here, as it will be dealt with, along with the matter furnished by Apuleius, in the chapters dealing with the Ritual of the Mysteries.

Let us then attempt with precision to fix and even to tabulate the information supplied by Plutarch and Iamblichus, who, as professional hierophants, deal with the spiritual essence or " theology " of the Mysteries. Plutarch lived at a period when it was still possible to glean much at first-hand regarding the Mysteries from living men in Egypt, where he had travelled, and Iamblichus, as a priest, who flourished at the beginning of the fourth century of our era, had a thorough knowledge of the Eleusinian and other Mysteries, and his inquiring mind must have gathered much of value concerning those of Egypt, of which he writes as though they were still maintained.

In Plutarch we find that :

(1) The cult of Isis was a preparation for the attainment of the knowledge of the Supreme Mind.

(2) Her votaries, who carry her sacred doctrine " locked up in their souls," study her history or myth and search into her hidden truths.

(3) Her " purificatory observances " or Mysteries are intended to preserve the meaning of valuable passages in history, and to represent the phenomena of nature.

(4) This philosophy is veiled by fable and allegory. Its aim is to form true notions of the divine nature.

Iamblichus tells us that :

(1) Egyptian symbolism has a spiritual basis.

(2) Through their sacerdotal theurgy the initiates of Egypt, observing a suitable time,[1] can aspire to union with the Divine.

---

[1] This, of course, refers to the astrological methods alluded to by Iamblichus.

(3) The essence of all good resides in the gods and the power of these is vested in the priesthood.

(4) The divine intelligible man, formerly united to the gods by vision, fell psychically, and his soul took on a more mortal form, becoming fettered by fate and necessity.

(5) Freedom from these bonds can only be accomplished by scientific knowledge of the gods.

(6) The first step to this freedom is known as the Gate to the Demiurgus of Wholes; the second is adaptation of the reasoning power to participation with the god, and the vision of the same; the third constitutes union with the Gods.

Now it is obvious that these statements of Plutarch and Iamblichus are complementary to each other. That of Plutarch is more methodical and descriptive of cult, that of Iamblichus more psychological and knowledgeable of the effect upon the soul.

More at this juncture it is unnecessary to say. The results of our inquiry will be found contained in the chapter on the Philosophy of the Mysteries.

CHAPTER IV

ORIGIN OF THE MYSTERIES

THE origin of the Egyptian Mysteries may, with more aptness than is usually associated with the use of the term, be said to be lost in the mists of antiquity. Arising out of patriarchal practice in communion with the Deity, they came, at some later period, to be systematized into a regular associational ritual and allegory under the guidance and care of the priesthood. This, not unnaturally, derogated from their primal simplicity and effectiveness, nevertheless they remained for centuries as the highest possible human expression of that straining toward the sublime which the spirit of man has ever found essential to its growth and well-being.

That similar confraternities of arcane tendency have been discovered among the most primitive peoples in Asia, America, Africa, and Australia is perhaps the surest proof not only of the very early origin of a mystery-religion of world-wide scope, but it also affords good evidence that the cult in question had its rise and inception in the Nile Country, although there are not wanting certain peculiarities which give rise to the assumption that the first seat of this faith and system may have been located farther west, in Spain or North-west Africa. Be that as it may, it was certainly in Egypt that it rose to its greatest height and celebrity.

The relationship between the Mysteries and the religions of the lower cultus, totemism, animism, and the like, raises a question fraught with considerable difficulty. As has already been said, the researches of Lang have made it clear that even the most primitive races known to modern anthropology have a knowledge of a deity or Allfather, transcending the " powers " or mere godlings associated with the totemic or other pristine gropings. But whether this conception preceded or followed totemism or animism is still obscure. Some authorities of standing are of opinion that totemism, the religious part of which credits the blood-relationship with animals, is a relatively late religious stage, or even a deteriorate one, while others think that it may well have proceeded concurrently with the Allfather belief. But everything seems to point to the conclusion that it is a system of exceedingly early provenance, as, indeed, its type seems to indicate and its relatively long existence and wide dissemination would seem to show. There can be little question that in its religious and even its social implications totemism not only preceded but also accompanied the course of the practice of the Mysteries in earliest Egypt and elsewhere for countless generations.

But it must not be too rashly assumed that the animal-like gods of Egypt retained their totemic significance at the period of the dynasties of greater enlightenment. That they were originally totemic in character no reasonable student of early religion can doubt, but the probabilities are that in later and more civilized times they came to have rather an allegorical character than a totemic one. There exists, moreover, another and perhaps more striking reason for the acceptance of such a theory. Totemism, or at least its " religious " side, though not its social, was associated with the idea of sacrifice, of the union of the worshipper or client of the animal-god with his patron by the ceremonial eating of its flesh at fixed seasonal intervals. That this notion prevailed and survived in the practice of the Mysteries and in that of the higher religions for centuries, and, that it is indeed to be found in a higher sense in the Christian faith itself, we know ; still, in its cruder form it soon ceased to exist in the practice of the higher cultus, where it gave way to the idea of a spiritual rather than a material communion, or oneness, with God.

In all likelihood the ritual and practices as well as the ideas of the higher and lower cults reacted upon one another, were mingled, accepted, rejected, as time proceeded. But all were deeply tinged with Magic. It is by no means more derogatory to Magic than to Religion, indeed it is not at all derogatory, that it had its beginnings in what appears to us to be the grossest superstition. Like all early thought and science it was empirical, as it was bound to be. Even to-day man's thoughts are founded on the shifting sands of early supposition and imagination, and for that they are none the worse, in that the foundation can be all the more readily changed when necessary.

But Magic, groping its way upward, found a humble if effective culture-bed in superstition, and one must not deride its growth there any more than he must deride the similar growth of Religion or science, its sister organisms. Its entire tendency, even where that appears to be in an opposite direction, was assuredly toward the light. The stumblings of blindness are not criminal, and even ignorance contains the germs of intelligence. Every magical act, however seemingly profane in our modern eyes, was a step taken in darkness toward knowledge, toward the higher Magia.

That traces of Mysteries in the Old Stone Age have been discovered in the Dordogne and elsewhere in France as well as in Spain, is clear from the researches of Osborn, Macalister, Obermeier, and other archæ-ologists. The Aurignacian caves in the Dordogne especially exhibit this influence. Their walls are covered with drawings of animals—deer, elephants, and horses, which undoubtedly had some religious significance, and statuettes or "idols" of goddesses, believed to have been those of the Great Mother, a figure resembling Isis or Demeter, have been found at or near these sites. There exists, indeed, considerable proof that the idea of initiation into a mystic cult may actually have originated in France or Spain among the Aurignacians, or perhaps in North Africa, whence they may have come to Europe. There are obvious religious as well as cultural associations between the Aurignacians and the ancient races of the Balearic Isles and Crete, all of whom appeared to have fostered similar mystical societies like that the vestiges of which have been found in France. It is, indeed, typical of early man that he should found such societies or fraternities.

Initiatory mysteries are inevitable in early human society. But before we discuss this question further, let us glance for a moment at that of the origin of magic. Considerable diversity of opinion exists regarding this subject among present-day anthro-pologists, and the works of Frazer, Marett, Hubert and Mauss, etc., although differing widely as regards its foundations, have thrown much light upon a hitherto obscure problem. All writers on the subject, how-ever, appear to have ignored one notable circumstance in connexion with it—that is, the element of wonder, which is the true fount and source of veritable magic. According to one of the warring schools of anthropology, nearly all magic is sympathetic or mimetic in its nature, as, for example, when the barbarian medicine-man desires rain he climbs a tree and sprinkles water upon the parched earth beneath, in the hope that the deity responsible for the weather will do likewise; when the ignorant sailor desires wind, he imitates the whistling of the gale. This system is universal, but, if our conclusions are well founded, the magical element does not reside in such practices as these. It must be obvious, as Frazer has pointed out, that when the savage performs an act of sympathetic magic he does not regard it as magical— that is, to his way of thinking it does not contain any element of wonder at all; he regards his action as a cause which is certain to bring about the desired effect, exactly as the scientific man of to-day believes that if he follows certain formulæ certain results will be achieved. Now the true magic of wonder argues from effect to cause; so it would appear as if sympathetic magic were merely a description of proto-science, due to mental processes entirely similar to those by which scientific laws are produced and scientific acts are performed—that there is a spirit of certainty about it which is not found, for example, in the magic of evocation.

It would, however, be rash to attempt to differentiate sympathetic magic entirely from what I would call the " magic of wonder " at this juncture; indeed, our knowledge of the basic laws of magic is too slight as yet to permit of such a process. We find considerable overlapping between the systems. In passing, I may say, for the sake of completeness, that

I believe the magic of wonder to be almost entirely spiritistic in its nature, and that it consists of evocation and similar processes. Here, of course, it may be quoted against me that certain incenses, planetary signs, and other media known to possess affinities for certain supernatural beings were brought into use at the moment of their evocation. Once more I admit that the two systems overlap; but that will not convince me that they are in essence the same.

Like all magic, Egyptian magic was of prehistoric origin. As the savage of to-day employs the sympathetic process, so did the savage of the Egyptian Stone Age make use of it. That he also was fully aware of the spiritistic side of magic is certain. Animism is the mother of spiritism. The concept of the soul was arrived at at a comparatively early period in the history of man. The phenomenon of sleep puzzled him. Whither did the real man betake himself during the hours of slumber? Palæolithic man watched his sleeping brother, who appeared to him as practically dead—dead, at least, to perception and the realities of life. Something seemed to have escaped from the sleeper; the real, vital, and vivifying element had temporarily departed from him. From his own experience the puzzled savage knew that life did not cease with sleep, for in a more shadowy and unsubstantial sphere he re-enacted the scenes of his everyday existence. If the man during sleep had experiences in dreamland or in distant parts, it was only reasonable to suppose that his ego, his very self, had temporarily quitted the body. Grant so much, and you have two separate entities, body and soul, similar in appearance, because the latter on the dream plane exercised functions identical with those of the former on the corporeal plane.

The significance of this digression is to indicate that both types of magic entered into the Mysteries of Egypt, the sympathetic was abundantly employed, as was the spiritistic, as we shall have opportunity to observe.

The Greeks believed that colonies of Egyptians settled in Argolis and Attica, and several Greek authors assert that Dionysus and Demeter were one and the same with Osiris and Isis. Moreover, the Egyptians of the Greek or Ptolemaic period accepted the identification. In the fourth century B.C. a temple of Isis was founded at Piræus, near Athens, and under the successors of Alexander the Isiac fraternities multiplied exceedingly.

In certain tombs at Eleusis of the Mysteries an Egyptian scarab has been found along with other Egyptian articles similar to those employed in the cult of Isis, along with a statuette of the goddess.[1] It is also remarkable that although direct Egyptian influence is not visible in the architecture of the temples raised to the native Greek deities, it is most noticeable in the plan of the temple of Demeter at Eleusis, and that of the goddesses Mneia and Azesia at Aphasia in the Ægean, the patrons of which were merely variants of Demeter and Persephone, the deities of Eleusis. The daughters of Danaus were fabled to have brought the secret rites of Demeter at Eleusis from Egypt,[2] and these, as practised in the fifth century B.C., reveal an aspect of the Egyptian Isis as protector of marriage and the family. The Greeks settled at Naucrates in Egypt and an image of Isis nursing Horus, housed in the Cairo Museum, was assuredly consecrated by a Greek of Naucrates at some time in the fifth century B.C.

[1] *Report of the Archæological Society*, Athens, pp. 30 ff., 1898.
[2] Herodotus II.

In the middle of the second century, says Foucart, a colony of fugitives from Egypt arrived at Argolis in Greece, and founded a powerful dynasty which lasted for sixty years. They inculcated the worship of Isis under the name of Demeter, and adored her as the goddess of agriculture and fecund nature.[1]

Not only is it possible to equate Demeter with Isis, but it is equally permissible to say that the Eleusinian cult of the former goddess constituted an entirely new religion in Greece.

To return to the question of primitive Mysteries, it may be well in this place to touch briefly on them as indicating the natural development of initiatory rites. As has already been said, all primitive societies possess mysteries of one kind or another, indeed, the " Men's House," where these are performed, is usually a feature of the village or hut-cluster of most savage or barbarous folk. Within its walls the young men of the clan or tribe undergo at the age of puberty tests of manhood of the severest kind, and secrets are there unveiled which are never revealed to women or children.

But above and beyond these were the secret fraternities of the priesthood, composed of grades of illumination, only to be entered by those willing to undergo trying ordeals. The Algonquin Indians of North America had formerly three such grades, the *wabeno*, the *mide*, and the *jossakeed*, the last being the highest. To this no white man was ever admitted. All the tribes of the Red Man, indeed, possessed such societies. The Indians of the Orinoco, for example, maintained one called the Botuto or " Holy Trumpet," whose members must vow celibacy and submit to severe scourgings and fasts. In Peru the Collahuayas

[1] *Les Mystères d'Eleusis*, p. 39.

and in Mexico and Central America the Naguals composed castes of mystical secrecy with elaborate initiatory rites, and these were quite apart from the popular religious organizations. In Australia, secret societies of a mystical tendency have been known from time immemorial, and the same applies to Africa and many parts of Asia and Europe.

It is here essential that we should examine the Anthropological position with regard to the Mysteries. This seems to me to be dependent almost entirely on the idea that man formerly resided with the gods " in the sky " and that he was cast thence to earth for misdemeanour or rebellion. The Mysteries, I believe, constitute an attempt to enable him to return to the place of his divine origin.

Frobenius tells us that the Kich people of the Nile relate how in the beginning men lived in heaven. Some of them irritated the Deity, who sent them down to earth by a long golden cord, whence those who improved their ways climbed back again. But a blue bird pecked at the cord until it was torn, whereby the connection with heaven was broken off.[1] This myth of modern Nileland I believe to be the surviving " representative " of an ancient Egyptian myth, now lost, of similar character.

It explains the whole *raison d'être* of the Mysteries in one word. It describes an instinct fixed and inalienable to the mind of man. As Mr. A. E. Waite has admirably phrased it : " If we take in succession the chief initiating orders which have, within the historical period, existed in the various countries of the world, and if we attempt to summarize shortly the legitimate inferences concerning them, we shall find that, in spite of their variations, they have all in

[1] Frobenius, *Childhood of Man*, p. 335.

reality taught but one doctrine, and, in the midst of enormous diversities in matters of rite and ceremony, there has still prevailed among all one governing instruction, even as there is one end. The parables differ, but the morality is invariably the same. From grade to grade the candidate is led symbolically from an old into a new life. The archaic mysteries of Greece have been described as an introduction to a new existence ruled by reason and virtue, and to both these terms something much deeper and fuller than the conventional significance is attached. With this notion of a new life there is also unfailingly connected the corresponding idea of a return ; in other words, the new life is really an old life restored to the initiate, who recovers, symbolically at least, that state of perfection and purity which he is supposed to have enjoyed originally as a spiritual being prior to what Greek mysticism regarded as the descent into genera-tion. From this it is clear that the doctrine of all the mysteries is the doctrine of pre-existence, sometimes operating in the form of reincarnation, but more usually apart from specific teaching as to any mode of the metempsychosis.''

If then we admit so much—and how simple and natural does the admission seem to any but those miserably blind to the divine scheme by reason of existence in a comparatively low stage of psychic mentality ?—we have still not to explain, but to describe the development of this belief in the human mind and the steps taken by primitive man to ensure reunion with divinity. We can leave to one side the totemic phase as having little significance in our quest, for although its intimations and ritual practices assuredly continued into the age of greater enlighten-ment, they did so just as certain admittedly barbarous customs still cling to modern dispensations and cannot readily be jettisoned for conventional or sentimental reasons. There is nothing to hinder us in the belief that the " Fall of Man " may have been credited in totemistic times and that reunion with an animal deity may have been hoped for. That alters not at all the instinctive character of the belief in divine reunion ; it is merely the barbarous version of it.

The belief that the sun was the divine country lost to man is strong in the primitive mind. In any case it symbolized the lost paradise, and the belief in that former state centred easily and naturally in it. The one supreme aim of early religion, then, was the return of the soul to this golden and glorious land, the country of its ancestors. But how is this to be accomplished ? By magical or semi-magical means. Primitive man conceives a ladder of magical arrows shot into the sky, remaining supernaturally fixed in space, by which he can climb upward. As in Mexico and elsewhere he rears a pole or mast, by which the soul can clamber past the clouds, on sacrificial occasions. Like the Haida Indian, he may conceal himself in the belly of a whale to reach the sky-country, or, on the death of a man, he may slay a bird in the hope that it will bear the soul of the deceased to the regions of the blest, as the South Sea Islanders formerly believed, along with the American Indians of the North-West.

But the solar barque provides the most typical example of the process in many lands. Among the Dyaks of Borneo the soul-ship of Tempon-telon is merely a variant of that of Ra or Osiris in Egypt, yet even the idea of this ship is evolved from that of the bird, the rhinoceros-hornbill, as paintings of it in the Berlin Museum well illustrate. Every twenty-four

hours Tempon-telon sets sail with his freight of the
dead. It meets with terrific weather on the voyage,
and dangers of fire and tempest assail it, yet at length
it reaches port in the City of Souls.

In the Egyptian Texts we observe a similar set of
ideas. Osiris has his barque of the dead. But this,
possibly, was a comparatively late introduction into
Egyptian mystical thought. The early Pyramid
Texts, and coffin texts, make no mention of such a
soul-ship. They favour the impression that the soul
was regarded as taking bird-shape to reach the Otherworld, although certainly a ferry-boat is included in
the myth as an alternative. In any case the Egyptian
solar barque is, like that of Tempon-telon, probably
developed from the idea of the bird. Nor do the
Greek myths of Eleusis and the other Hellenic
Mysteries allude to a passage by soul-ship, but rather,
like certain Egyptian rituals, to a progress through
the Underworld, or through a region of gloom to one
of light.

How came it then to be presumed that the soul
must necessarily traverse the infernal before it could
win to the supernal plane? I can see no other
explanation save that the primitive myth of direct
progress from earthly banishment to the ancestral sky
became confused with the allegory of the birth and
death of the grain-god Osiris or the goddess Persephone or Proserpine who dwelt half the year below
ground, and that it was inferred by his or her
worshippers to be essential to their salvation to
experience the selfsame journey. Personally I
cannot perceive any particular weakness in this
theory, and we know that the Osirian cult became
fused with that of Ra, the sun-god. I would add
that I believe the Egyptian and Eleusinian Mystery

myths to have been thought out by people acquainted with existence in sandy, marshy, and rocky regions—a statement of the rather obvious, perhaps, as the dreary journey in search of Osiris and Persephone, which seems to have composed part of the Mysteries, reveals.

It is important for us to understand the full significance of the Greek Mysteries, the offspring of those of Egypt. It is equally important that we should understand at this stage of our inquiry not so much the ritual and ceremony of the several cults, which will be described later, but those religious and psychological laws which underlay them.

In Greece the rise of the Mysteries was associated with a novelty of thought which in some ways took almost the character of a religious revolution. For the first time in the history of Hellas, religion, hitherto strictly tribal or even domestic, that is, patriarchal, took a universal tendency. In the sixth century B.C. new rites and cults arose, membership in which was not confined to the people of a certain town or district, but to all, citizens, strangers, and slaves alike, could they satisfy the hierophants of these cults as to their fitness for initiation.

The Greek mystical cults were not necessarily new religions, indeed in them the old deities of the tribe or gens might be, and were, worshipped, although with new rites. Indeed there was no compulsion for any of their members to leave the state or local religion to which they already belonged when joining the cults of Eleusis, or Bacchus. In the Semitic countries of Asia Minor a tendency had arisen to cast aside the notion of sacrifice to the gods as a gift tendered in order that these divine beings might in turn send man greater gifts, and to put in its place the idea of closer communion with God. This theory, Egyptian in origin, seems also to have been introduced into Greece under Semitic and Western Asiatic auspices. It brought with it a more hopeful view of the life after death. The gift-sacrifice had merely embraced the hope of betterment in the immediate and material future, but the new cults held out the likelihood of a much more delectable existence after death than that previously credited by the Greeks, whose Hades was merely a subterranean dungeon, and whose Paradise, the Blessed Isles or Hesperides, seems to have been reserved for certain castes or classes alone.

The effort to achieve closer companionship with the Divinity was thus marked by greater confidence as regarded the future of the soul. The religious part of totemism at best had been a hope to participate in the divine life of the sacred animal, and this had usually a more or less alimentary tendency. But now a religious basis was provided by the Mysteries, however imperfectly they were conceived in Greece, for that belief in immortality which in its first form had been an accompaniment of primitive thought. The hope of a future world was associated with and in a measure dependent upon spiritual communion in this life.

From Egypt, and by way of the Greek cities of Asia Minor, came the new influence, spreading itself over Greece itself and finally over Italy. At first the ritual associated with the movement seems to have taken the form of purificatory rites. These were administered by a caste known as *Agyrtæ*, or " collectors," from the circumstance that they were in the habit of making a collection of goods or money after the performance of their ritual, The *Agyrtes* travelled from city to city with his apparatus, a pile of sacred books, a tame serpent, a drum, and a magic mirror laden on a donkey's back, much as might an itinerant magician of a later age. Arrived in a town or village, he pitched his tent in which the mysteries were to be celebrated, and then, beating his drum, and preceded by a man carrying a portable shrine, or miniature temple, he went through the town, dancing wildly, and occasionally gashing his legs or cutting his tongue till the blood flowed, until at last he attracted a crowd. This he drew gradually toward the tent, where he was consulted by those desirous of companionship in his especial mystery, or of testing his knowledge on things mystical.

This, of course, was merely the primitive priest of the tribal mystery alluded to above as a travelling hierophant. It was impermanent, but it was a beginning. Certain *Agyrtæ* settled in one place and founded a permanent religious association, and this it was which gave the new movement a less haphazard aspect and rendered it more truly institutional. There were already among the Greeks societies known by the various names of *thiasi, erani,* and *orgeones,* voluntary associations for religious purposes, which differed from the cult of the national gods in that whilst these latter were open only to members of the state, the societies alluded to were open to all without respect of class or sex, if found suitable.

These societies had special codes or laws of their own, dealing with the conditions of admission, times of assembly, amount of subscription, and so forth. They had both lay officials and officiating priests and priestesses who conducted the rites, presided over the initiation of members and celebrated the mysteries. The sacred premises consisted usually of a temple, a banqueting hall and accommodation for initiates

THE PINAX OF NANNION
Depicting the Lesser and Greater Mysteries of Eleusis.

during the period of their preliminary exercises. In
the ritual books of these private or semi-private
societies the precise acts to be performed by the
novice, his attitude and gesture at each stage in
the proceedings were prescribed and contained.

The general procedure in vogue (and we are always
dealing with early Greece) seems to have been very
much as follows : The candidate for initiation was
placed under the protection of the presiding deity
by having the skin of a fawn cast over his shoulders.
A rite of purification followed. The neophyte was
stripped naked and made to kneel, when bowls of
water were poured over him to fit him symbolically
for the coming rites. Sometimes the candidate was
smeared or cleansed with clay, mud, or a mixture of
clay and bran.

The neophyte, during this purification, was en-
couraged by loud and ecstatic cries from the surrounding initiates, and after the ceremony was
ordered to rise and to exclaim : " I have escaped
the bad and I have found the better." This signified
that he was now purified in heart and prepared
spiritually for the actual mystery. This rite, in the
case of certain of the early Greek mysteries, was of the
nature of a sacramental meal, a reversion to the early
practice of attempting to achieve communion with
the god by the consumption of his animal representatives.

A procession was then formed which paraded the
streets, the new initiate wearing a garland of fennel
or poplar, or bearing the mystic cist, or the sacred
winnowing-fan, or even a serpent above his head in
both hands. Thus accommodated he danced along,
crying : " Evœ Sabœ ! Hyês Attês, Attês Hyês ! "

It is obvious that the ceremony of initiation would

have been imperfect without some oral instruction or interpretation of the nature of the Mysteries from the lips of the hierophant. What was the nature of this sermon or harangue? From several ancient texts we can gauge its character with considerable accuracy.

The Legomena, as it was called, was a communication to the Greek mystic promising him safety in his progress through the unknown, and giving him the necessary courage to face the ordeal. We cannot doubt that it was modelled on similar Egyptian practice. But the hierophant had no choice in the expressions he was to make use of. These were ritually fixed.

We know from Saint Hippolytus that one of the formulæ employed on this occasion was: " The divine Brimo, the infant Brimos, the divine child." This was the ritual revelation of the secret name of the god Dionysus. The Legomena, we may be sure, consisted of a number of short ritual phrases of the kind which completed the revelation of what the mystics had seen and explained the nature of their visions.

The Egyptians believed the space betwixt Heaven and Earth to be a place in which incessant reactions and changes took place. They represented Heaven as their proper earth, watered by a celestial Nile, where dwelt the great gods, the various orders of spirits, the genies and demons of their abounding mythology. The life of these beings resembled that of man on the earth. But they were subjected to the invasions of the forces of evil, and identified as they were by the stars, the motions and changes of these luminaries were thought of as indicating the progress of the heavenly war with the evil powers.

On these planetary changes the priests based their

astrological and magical computations. Dramas were staged in the temples, in which the wars of the gods were enacted in consonance with the alterations of stellar cosmography. Such a drama was that held at Abydos. Such a drama, too, was that celebrated in Eleusis, in which the priests took the part of divinities. There Zeus came to be united to Demeter, and the union assured to men the advantages of full crops and such prosperity as they had enjoyed aforetime.

We know that at Abydos in Egypt a description of " passion-play " enacting the myth of Osiris was annually presented, but how far it was actually associated with the Mysteries themselves is not apparent. That it probably afforded a popular version of them is, however, not unlikely. The play itself is completely lost, but the memorial stone of Ikhernofret, an officer of Sesostris III, now preserved in Berlin, furnishes an outline of it. The drama evidently lasted for several days, and the people themselves seem to have participated in it.

It seems to have consisted of eight acts. The first was a procession in which the ancient god of death, Upwawet, made straight the way for Osiris. In the second the great deity himself appeared in the sacred barque, which was also placed at the disposal of a limited number of the more illustrious of the visiting pilgrims. The voyage of the vessel was retarded by actors dressed as the enemies of Osiris, Set and his company. A combat ensued in which actual wounds seem to have been given and received, but, like Herodotus, Ikhernofret is silent as to the death of the god, the sacred character of the event defying description. This event seems to have taken place during the third act, which was an allegory of the triumphs of Osiris. The fourth depicted the going out of Thoth, probably in search of the divine victim's body. Then followed the ceremonies in preparation for the burial of Osiris, and the march of the populace to the desert shrine beyond Abydos to lay the god in his tomb. A great battle between the avenging Horus and Set was next staged, and in the final act Osiris appeared, restored to life, and entered the temple of Abydos in triumphal procession amid the plaudits of the multitude.

The actual text or rather programme of these proceedings, which took place nearly fifteen hundred years before a similar representation was witnessed by Herodotus, is as follows :

(1) " I celebrated the ' Procession of Upwawet ' when he proceeded to champion his father (Osiris).

(2) " I repulsed those who were hostile to the Neshmet barque, and I overthrew the enemies of Osiris.

(3) " I celebrated the ' Great Procession,' following the god in his footsteps.

(4) " I sailed the divine barque, while Thoth . . . the voyage.

(5) " I equipped the barque (called) ' Shining in Truth,' of the Lord of Abydos, with a chapel ; I put on his beautiful regalia when he went forth to the district of Peker.

(6) " I led the way of the god to his tomb in Peker.

(7) " I championed Wennofer (Osiris) on ' That Day of the Great Battle ' ; I overthrew all the enemies upon the shore of Nedyt.

(8) " I caused him to proceed into the barque (called) ' The Great ' ; it bore his beauty ; I gladdened the heart of the eastern highlands ; I (put) jubilation in the western highlands, when they saw the beauty

of the Neshmet barque. It landed at Abydos and they brought (Osiris, First of the Westerners, Lord) of Abydos to his palace."[1]

The ceremony, as enacted by Ikhernofret is described by M. Moret[2] much as follows : The Mystery in question was known as the Peut âat, in " grand funeral procession," and was enacted by persons representing the gods and goddesses, Isis, Nephthys, Thoth, Anubis, and Horus. Ikhernofret himself assumed the part of Horus, the son of Osiris. He procured a barque built of sycamore and acacia encrusted with gold, silver, and lapis lazuli. Inside, he instilled a statue of Osiris in wood and supplied the necessary amulets of lapis lazuli, malachite, and electron.

A procession was formed, and the " body " of Osiris passed down the banks of the Nile at Abydos. The barque was carried across the place of the Nedyt (unknown). Anubis, in his character of the day, searched for the corpse and found it. But when the friends of Osiris attempted to place the body in the barque a battle took place between them and the partisans of Set, the enemy, in which the Osirians triumphed.

The cortège then proceeded, and bore the body to the Repeqer, the tomb of Osiris. During this time Horus continued his strife with the assailants. Triumphant, he came at last to the Repeqer, where a statue was dressed in the garments of the god and took the place of his cadaveric image. The sacred barque then returned to Abydos and the god entered his temple and took his seat on the throne in the holy of holies.

---

[1] Breasted, *Religion and Thought in Ancient Egypt*, p. 289.
[2] *Mystères Égyptiens*, pp. 9 ff.

The occasional representation of such a " mystery " as the above naturally gave Osiris an extraordinary popularity among the people of Egypt, and many of the tablets found at Abydos contain prayers sent up by the pilgrims that after death they may be permitted to participate in such pageants. The passion-play spread from one town to another, and its frequent presentation spread the hope in a future existence and the belief that the magical agencies employed by Isis to raise the dead Osiris would be efficacious in the case of all men.

Herodotus, writing of this sacred drama, says : " At Sais also, in the sacred precinct of Minerva, behind the chapel and joining the whole of the wall, is the tomb of one whose name I consider it impious to divulge on such an occasion. And in the enclosure stand large stone obelisks, and there is a lake near, ornamented with a stone margin, formed in a circle, and in size, as appeared to me, much the same as that in Delos, which is called the Circular. In this lake they perform by night the representation of that person's adventures, which they call mysteries. On these matters, however, though accurately acquainted with the particulars of them, I must observe a discreet silence."

This appears as though the Father of History had considered the play at Sais to have been of the nature of a guarded mystery. Indeed it is just possible that what he witnessed at Sais in the Delta may have had a much more arcane significance than the popular " passion-play " enacted at Abydos, which seems to have been the Oberammergau of Egypt. Allowance must be made, however, for the extraordinary length of time which had elapsed between the representations as described by Ikhernofret and Herodotus, a period as long as that between the landing of Julius Cæsar in this island and the Wars of the Roses !

M. Alexandre Moret, in his *Kings and Gods of Egypt*, provides quite an elaborate explanation of the sacred drama as enacted in public. It was, he says, celebrated at the beginning of winter in sixteen of the large towns of Egypt, and his reconstruction of it is based upon the texts discovered in the tombs and temples.

The opening scene, he tells us, represented the death of Osiris. The dismemberment of the god's body was actually shown, and its fragments were scattered about. From the " Hymn to Osiris " on a stela in the Bibliothèque Nationale, Paris, M. Moret concludes that the next scene consisted in the search for the fragments of the dead Osiris by Isis, aided by Horus, Thoth and Anubis.

" When Osiris had been found, the play proceeded to bring together his dismembered body. Diodorus relates how Isis restored to life each member of the mutilated god, as it was recovered. ' She enclosed each fragment in a life-size effigy of Osiris, made of wax and perfumes.' This suggests a magic process, the first step of which is to fashion an image of Osiris. The fictitious body, on contact with the piece of flesh placed within it, was supposed to become alive according to magic creed. After these brief and partial obsequies, the family of Osiris effected in detail an entire reconstruction of the divine body. The Rituals state that Horus made for Osiris a large statue (we would term it a ' mummy ') by joining together all the parts that Set had severed. ' Thou hast taken back thy head,' say Isis and Nephthys to their brother ; ' thou hast bound up thy flesh ; thy vessels have been given back to thee ; thou hast regained thy members.' The gods take part in this difficult operation. Geb, the father of Osiris, presides over the ceremony; Ra sends from heaven the goddesses Hawk and Uræus, those who encircle like a crown the forehead of the gods, ' in order to put the head of Osiris in its place and to join it to his neck.'

" The description we read of in the Rituals was carried out faithfully in practice. At the solemn festivals of Osiris, two complete statues of the god were fashioned from earth mingled with wheat, incense, perfumes, and precious stones; but the fragment of the body assigned by Isis to each sanctuary was fashioned apart, and when the priest brought the clay to pour it into the mould, he recited these words : ' I bring to Isis these fragments of the mummy of Osiris.'

" Near to the statue, now clad in the clinging shroud which would henceforth be the characteristic garb of Osiris, Isis and Nephthys, in mourning robes, their hair unbound, their head and breast bruised with repeated blows, intone a kind of *vocero*, a funeral dirge. They implore Osiris ' to return to inhabit his reconstructed body.' "[1]

The second act, M. Moret believes, consisted of scenes depicting the return of the soul of Osiris and the resurrection of the god. The rebirth of Osiris was enacted in an allegorical form, the statue being placed for seven days on branches of sycamores, the number seven being symbolical of the seven months passed by the god in the womb of his mother, Nut, the goddess of the sycamore tree. This assured to the statue a veritable rebirth, and this image, made of earth,

---

[1] These details, says M. Moret, are taken from " The Lamentations of Isis and Nephthys," which may be found in English in A. Wiedemann's *Religion of the Ancient Egyptians*, p. 211.

barley, wheat, and perfumes was buried beneath the holy sycamore trees on the day of the Feast of the Fields, that is, at seedtime, so that the statue, full of seeds, might " return to life " through the agency of vegetation.

At Dendereh and Philæ are bas-reliefs which illustrate the resurrection of Osiris. The body of the god is stretched on a funeral bed, while Isis and Nephthys urge on the recreation of the skeleton, its reclothing with flesh, by magnetic or magical passes, as is shown by the action of the hands. Little by little the legs, body, and head appear in response to the magical passes. At length the god moves, turns on his side and raises his head. This rite, in all likelihood, was enacted in the course of the dramatic representation.

The preservation of the life restored was the subject of the third act of the drama. The statue was elaborately dressed and painted in the hues of life, perfumed and anointed, each specific act having a magical significance of its own. Then the god was placed before a table laden with " all things good and pure that heaven gives, that earth creates, that the Nile yields from her stores," bread, meats, fruits, and beverages. Finally the image was laid in a shrine, the doors of which were locked and sealed. Henceforth Osiris lived a new life. He was the prototype of the soul reborn. If any god or man desired to be so reborn at a second existence he must undergo a similar process of ritual.

The fact that drama entered into the Egyptian Mysteries is eloquent of their origin. As Marrett says, early religion was rather a thing to be " danced out " than thought out, that is, it was inspirational rather than philosophical. But this, notwithstanding, we do not require to believe that the whole sum and essence of the Mysteries was contained in dramatic ritual. That it was not is proved by the existence of several stages of the Mysteries, Lesser and Greater.

But we must not omit to mention, while still dealing with the public Mysteries, the ceremony of dad or tetu. This " fetish," so-called, was a pillar with four capitals, representing four pillars in perspective, and is considered by some authorities to symbolize the backbone of Osiris, though others believe it to be the sycamore or tamarisk in which Osiris was enclosed, according to the myth of Plutarch. When lying on the ground it symbolized Osiris dead, but when raised, Osiris resurrected. At the festival in question, the dad pillar was raised by cables, the Pharaoh himself bearing a hand.

That agricultural and alimentary implications lie at the very root of the Mysteries is obvious, and these mingle strangely with their more lofty aspects. If man were to know full communion with God in the Afterworld, it was essential that he should reside there in a sufficiently comfortable state. This the Egyptian texts prove conclusively. The dead man is made constantly to demand of the gods a sufficiency of bread, geese, beer, and other nourishment.

That this comparatively low outlook is to be found side by side with the nobler idea of unity with God does not seem strange to the student of Comparative Religion. It emanates from a period when the soul was still regarded as partaking more of the material form and habit than future generations conceived it. The hungry ghost then constituted a very real social and religious problem, and those responsible for the dead man, his sons and male relatives, felt their responsibility keenly and made such offerings at his tomb as would keep him in good humour. The alternative was haunting and vampirism.

This belief, in its beginnings, could scarcely have coincided with that of unity with divinity in the Otherworld. But it remained and persisted, even when the idea of spirit took on a less material form, although in the case of food offerings a species of magical composition was effected by painting provisions on the walls of the tomb. The alimentary character of the bargain, however, is clear, and, along with the rite of " eating the god," invaded and seized upon the sacred ideal of communion, of which it even became the symbol. In a word the idea of spiritual absorption in the god became not unnaturally confounded with the material absorption of the god. The only method early man could conceive of effecting actual unity with the god was by devouring him, absorbing him into himself, thus partaking of his godhead, at first as an animal, and at the later agricultural stage as bread or corn. Corn, we know, was the last great symbol unveiled in the Mysteries of Eleusis, the goddess in excelsis, the symbol of the patroness of bread by which man lives.

Associated with the agricultural character of the Mysteries was the rite of dismemberment reflected in the myths of Osiris in Egypt and Zagreus-Dionysus in Greece. The scattering of the mangled remains of the god may be an allegorical way of expressing either the sowing or winnowing of the grain, and this theory is assisted by the tale that Isis placed the severed limbs of Osiris on a corn-sieve. Again, it is not improbable that it may be a reminiscence of a custom of sacrificing a human victim as a representative of the corn-spirit and distributing his flesh over the fields in order to fertilize them. We have it on the authority of Manetho that the Egyptians were in the habit of burning red-haired men, whose ashes were scattered with winnowing fans, and it is significant that this sacrifice was offered by the kings at the grave of Osiris, so that the likelihood is that the victims represented Osiris himself, or were his surrogates.

Says Frazer on this point : " According to one story Romulus the first king of Rome, was cut in pieces by the senators, who buried the fragments of him in the ground ; and the traditional day of his death, the seventh of July, was celebrated with certain curious rites, which were apparently connected with the artificial fertilization of the fig.   Again, Greek legend told how Pentheus, king of Thebes, and Lycurgus, king of the Thracian Edonians, opposed the vine-god Dionysus, and how the impious monarchs were rent in pieces, the one by the frenzied Bac-chanals, the other by horses.   These Greek traditions may well be distorted reminiscences of a custom of sacrificing human beings, and especially divine kings, in the character of Dionysus, a god who resembled Osiris in many points, and was said, like him, to have been torn limb from limb. We are told that in Chios men were rent in pieces as a sacrifice to Dionysus : and since they died the same death as their god, it is reasonable to suppose that they personated him. The story that the Thracian Orpheus was similarly torn limb from limb by the Bacchanals seems to indicate that he too perished in the character of the god whose death he died."[1]

Myth was, of course, an essential accompaniment of the Mysteries. This must not be taken as meaning that the several gods of the Egyptian pantheon who were associated with the cultus of the Mysteries were

[1] *Golden Bough*, Vol. II., pp. 98–99.

in anywise mythical or merely the sport of man's inventive faculty. Primitive man did not " create " the gods as so many students of Comparative Religion, destitute of imagination, sympathy, and all religious genius, appear to think. What he actually did, often quite subconsciously, was to apply names and quasi-human faculties to these " powers " or phenomena which he rightly enough believed to be the manifestations of the divine. That, at a later stage at least, he considered these as demiurges or phases of the one God is sufficiently obvious.

Myth, in its relationship to the Mysteries, is more of the nature of that species of allegory or narrative symbolism which arose as a concomitant of primitive religious thought. As I have said before, Mr. R. R. Marett remarks in one of his suggestive essays, early religion was more a thing to be " danced out " than to be found associated with those higher developments of thought which modern minds connect with the expression " religion," that is, it was an allegory or drama of the life of a god, lord of the crops or master of the animal food-supply, was theatrically represented in its seasonal changes and so forth as a species of terpsichorean drama. This dance-myth represented the birth of the corn-god (let us say, for example), his growth, his arrival at full age, and, at a later season, his death. In time it came to be accepted not only as an allegory of the deific existence but of the life of man himself, of his passage from the cradle to the grave, and the period passed by the god of grain beneath the soil in the dark months of his terrestrial imprisonment or " burial " came to be regarded as symbolical of the sojourn of man in Hades, and his subsequent resurrection.

That such a myth formed part of the Egyptian

Mysteries we cannot doubt. Not only does the ritual of the Elusinian Mysteries point most directly to such a conclusion, but the very nature of those Egyptian deities most closely associated with the Nilotic form of the Mysteries renders it positive. Osiris was most assuredly a god of the crops, of wheat or barley. Not only do certain mural and other paintings depict him actually as the soil sprouting and flourishing with crops, but it was customary to cover the coffins of the dead with lids on which a thin stratum of soil had been sewn with corn-seed. This in time germinated and grew, and was considered not only to be symbolic of the resurrection of the human spirit, but actually to supply that sympathetic magic which rendered such a process possible.

Primitive man not only feels himself more closely allied to nature and the cosmic forces than his civilized brother, but he implicitly believes that these forces manifest in him precisely as they do in the case of the soil, the crops, the trees, in vegetation generally. " We Indians shall not for ever die," said an Indian chief to a Moravian missionary, " for, like the corn, our spirits shall reproduce themselves elsewhere." This simple and striking testimony, indeed, puts the whole philosophy of primitive man regarding resurrection in a nutshell.

We have, then, the best possible reasons for believing that, as in the Eleusinian and other Mysteries, the Egyptian Mysteries contained in their revelations passages which depicted the life, death, and resurrection of Osiris in his character of the corn-plant. Indeed this is made clear in the passage which deals with the dramatic passion-play of Osiris. At one part of the Eleusinian Mysteries, the moment of complete revelation, we are told an ear of corn was held up by the hierophant before the neophytes, and they were solemnly assured that it represented the heart and depths of their mystery, that it symbolized in itself all they had undergone so much to understand.

For, just as the highest possible literary distinction lies in noble simplicity, so in things spiritual the height of celestial significance is reached through the plain, the natural, the seemingly undistinguished. Just as the humble flower brought Wordsworth thoughts " too deep for tears," just as Paracelsus assures us that the Grand Mystery may often better be apprehended by a woman sitting at her spinning-wheel than by scholarship the most profound, so the most sublime secrets of God and nature are most truly understood when they are placed before us not in the symbols of priestcraft, which are too often merely the patronizingly " paternal " foppery of a conceited hierarchy which believes that its people are too ignorant to apprehend deep truths except in pictorial forms, but in these more soul-inspiring natural symbols which signify birth and death, life and decay. and the " mightier movements," as Stevenson so aptly called them. Simple and even common objects have indeed been employed by the Christian Church from the beginning to convey its deepest truths and mysteries—the Lamb, the Mother and Child, bread, wine, the burning bush, the Grail—these are far more effective and inspiring than any of those more involved and hieratic emblems which stultify rather than ennoble spiritual existence.[1]

Summarizing the material at our disposal concerning the origin of the Egyptian Mysteries, we find that :

[1] I do not intend here to derogate from the veridical and appropriate employment of symbols, which are essential to the setting forth of the Mysteries, but to their irrational, profuse, and occasionally quite illogical use.

Similar confraternities of arcane tendency have been discovered among the most primitive peoples in Asia, Africa, America, and Australia.

That these were associated with totemic belief, but did not necessarily originate in it.

That Magic entered into the philosophy and ritual of the Mysteries, both in its "Sympathetic" and Spiritistic forms.

The Greeks believed their especial Mysteries to have been of Egyptian origin, and for this belief archæological proofs are not wanting.

The Mysteries are associated with the venerable belief in the Fall of Man. Man, it was thought, formerly resided in the sun or the sky, and had been cast down to earth for misdemeanours. The Mysteries revealed the path by which he might return to the place of his divine origin.

A myth of the Kich people of the Nile country reveals the present existence of such a belief. It is probably of ancient Egyptian origin, but beyond and above that it represents an instinctive idea in the mind of man.

Man concerted more than one magical attempt to enable him to return to his place of divine origin. These culminated in the idea of the solar barque of souls, a soul-ship, evolved from bird-like form.

The idea, as expressed in the Egyptian and Greek Mysteries, that the soul must first traverse the infernal regions ere it could emerge on the supernal plane, arose out of confusion with the myth of an agricultural deity, Osiris, whose allegory described his history as the grain-plant buried or planted in the earth for several months in the year.

In Greece the rise of the Mysteries was accompanied by a novelty of thought which partook of the character of a religious revolution. It gave rise to universal rather than tribal tendencies in faith. Also the idea of communion with God took the place of justification by sacrifice, and brought a more hopeful view of life after death. In the first instance the new dispensation took the form of purificatory rites.

The Egyptians believed the sky to be a region in which constant astrological action and reaction took place, the wars between the divine and evil powers. These were staged in the temples as mystery dramas. Such a drama was associated with Osiris at Abydos, but how far it was connected with the actual Mysteries is not apparent, although a similar drama at Sais seems to have constituted part of the Mysteries.

The origin of the Mysteries of Egypt, then, seems to reside in the idea of the Fall of Man, and the possibility of his return to the divine sphere he formerly inhabited. With this came to be associated the " agricultural " allegory of the annual burial of the grain-god, necessitating the passage of the soul through the infernal regions he inhabited during a portion of the year.

As regards the place of origin of the Egyptian Mysteries, and, therefore of all mysteries, I must confess that I lean to the theory that they originated in prehistoric France or Spain among the Aurignacian people at some time about the sixteenth millennium before our era. I think I see in the bull-cult of the Aurignacians the prototype of those of Crete and Egypt, and the legends of the Mysteries of the Cabiri having been brought from North-west Africa to Egypt " by Osiris," strengthens the belief that the mystic cult of Osiris and the bull was imported into Egypt from Spain by way of North-west Africa. But, frankly, our data on the subject are still too scanty to permit us to dogmatize, and perhaps it is better that we should presently regard the Mysteries of Egypt as having for all practical purposes originated in the Nile country, where, after all, they took on not only a character distinctly their own, but became the parent form of many later mysteries.

CHAPTER V

THE PHILOSOPHY OF THE MYSTERIES

REGARDING the philosophy of the Egyptian Mysteries science altogether fails us. We must not here be entrapped into the consideration of theories advanced by anthropologists or mythologists. These are useful in so far as they supply analogies from ritual and folk-custom, but when we approach the spiritual, the ineffably sacred and divine, the appropriation of such aids becomes a blasphemy, a practice to be abhorred and discouraged by the earnest mystic. It is because of fundamental differences in psychological and mental origin and attitude that the mystic can never altogether accept the shallow conclusions and materialistic arguments of the scientist. These he may employ in respect of the mere facts of material occurrences and historic happenings, but in the more exalted atmosphere of spiritual affairs the intrusion of the scientist becomes an impertinence not only to be discouraged but to be sternly resisted.

The realm of spirit is properly closed to the profane. Not only is it fenced round by the walls and turrets of divine height and screened by the impenetrable fogs and forests of mystic terror, but it is denied to them by reason of their own invincible ignorance and by their inhibitions of pride and folly. The jewel of veneration is given to the few out of the divine wisdom, just as

the allied gift of imagination or inspiration is the
possession of those stamped with the angelic seal of a
superior humanity.

Nevertheless, it is possible to employ spiritual
analogies in spiritual circumstances. Where we find
the divine philosophy made plain in one instance we
may reasonably apply it in another. It has already
been said that the whole purpose of the Mysteries
was to attain fellowship or unity with the Divine here
and hereafter. This was not to be achieved by mere
doctrine, but by the exercise of the Higher Magic.
The outward form of this Magic was expressed in
ritual, in actual allegory. It was emblematic,
symbolical, for the good reason that in emblem and
symbolism and dramatic rite reside the only available
human means for outwardly expressing the inward
desire for at-one-ment with deity. But, let it be
remembered, that these are after all merely the
enacted impulses of the inward thought and belief.
The ancient men who established these rites were well
aware that a striking and dramatic rehearsal of the
process of achieving unity, a material and symbolic
representation of what is actually a psychical process,
could not but assist it by bringing the mental and
bodily parts of man into magical and rhythmic
response with his psychic part and thus with the
upward movement as a whole. The circumstance
that a prolonged preparation on the part of the
neophyte was essential to the great undertaking of
the Mysteries clearly establishes a recognition of the
fundamentally moral and spiritual intention underlying their outward expression.

It is not alone that the powers of death and darkness must be overcome. That is naturally implied by
and embraced in the idea of union with the Divine.

It is a becoming of the Divine, a complete absorption in and identification with Him which is intended and hoped for. This does not signify a loss of individuality, but rather an expansion of it from the mortal to the immortal scope, the blossoming of the human seed, sprouting through the soil of this life's death and mortality up to the free air of eternity.

The frequent enactment of the Egyptian Mysteries demanded the presence of several of their initiates on every occasion when a neophyte entered their circle, and thus it is clear that the drama and process of initiation must have been most familiar to them. Indeed the frequent enactment of the Mysteries must have been an essential to the proper understanding and development of the life mystical. Just as our Lord makes it clear that the frequent celebration of the sacrament of communion is necessary to the efficacy of the Christian life as bringing home to those who partake of it the whole circumstances of the divine allegory of atonement, so the statutory celebration of the Egyptian Mysteries was indubitably of similar moral efficacy and mnemonic virtue.

It is essential that we should understand what the Egyptians implied in speaking of what we call " soul." They believed that the Ba, as they called the indestructible spirit, would survive eternally, provided that the body it inhabited were preserved. Originally, no doubt, the idea prevailed that the essential and eternal part of man resided in the bones, as prehistoric belief and burial would certainly seem to indicate. This the Egyptians denominated the *Ka*, or double, a species of corporeal soul, a shadowy ghost or reflection of the fleshly body, invisible to men. It could materialize in a statue, portrait, or mummy, which, indeed, attracted it.

This belief it was which inspired the Egyptians to build tombs in the manner of dwellings in which the ghost of the dead man might reside. Such a life was purely material, and the deceased was thought of as enjoying all the comforts of a well-appointed residence.

Although the notion lasted throughout the whole course of Egyptian history, it came later on to be accompanied by another of higher conception. The idea of unity with the god brought about a more sublime comprehension of the destiny of the human spirit, and this by degrees took the place of, if it did not destroy, the primitive notion of the Ka. This was the knowledge that a more spiritual soul and destiny are the inalienable possessions of mankind. Along with the corporeal soul or Ka the Egyptians came to believe in a spiritual soul, the Ba, which they represented by a bird with a man's head, the symbolism having undoubted reference to the soaring nature of man's immortal part. In all likelihood the idea of a more ethereal future life was at first regarded as the possession of the Pharaoh alone, but, by degrees, came to be recognized as possible for all. But the Ba, as has been strangely overlooked, came into existence for the first time at the death of the individual,[1] that is, he must become a Ba, and many ceremonies were resorted to to secure this result.

But apart from and along with this belief the doctrine of transmigration of souls was unquestionably held by the ancient Egyptians. This belief, introduced into Greece during the sixth century B.C. by Pythagoras, is said to have been discovered by him in the Nile country. The cause of transmigration, he tells us, is sin, and its term no less than 30,000

[1] This would seem to associate the Ba with the idea of the bird-ship.

THE EGYPTIAN BA, OR SOUL
From a statuette.

years, the final goal of the human spirit, after serving that term and perfecting itself, being godhead or unity with the Divine Spirit. That is, the nature of transmigration is a cycle and the soul which escapes from that cycle becomes as a god, or is dissolved in the One, the All.

Pythagoreanism, which is merely a Greek form of the Egyptian doctrine of transmigration of souls, differs from the Buddhist or the Hindu conception of soul-transference in several important particulars, especially those which refer to its cause, sin, its nature as a cycle, the fact of escape from it and the method of escape. Says Jevons : " This, combined with the tradition of antiquity that Pythagoras derived his doctrine from Egypt, would suffice to prove its Egyptian origin. But there are further resemblances. The Egyptian philosophy which taught that the soul returns to the divine essence from which it sprang, is reproduced in the Pythagorean teaching that the soul emanated from and finally returns to the ether, the starry sky. And just as the Egyptian philosophers adopted religious terminology to convey their speculations, and taught that to become God or a god, Osiris or an Osiris, was the same thing as being merged in the divine essence, so Pythagoreanism taught that for the soul to become *theos* or *daimon* was the same thing as for it to dissolve into ether or into the starry sky, of which it was the offspring. But even granting that Pythagoras could and did invent out of his own head a theory exactly resembling in its cardinal points a doctrine which in Egypt was the result of slow centuries of evolution, still we must think it strange that the minor details and non-essential accessories should be the same. Let us illustrate this point. In the Pythagorean inscription already quoted, the

departed soul is represented as anxiously eager to
drink of cool, flowing water. No such anxiety is ever
expressed in literature, as far as I am aware, by any
Greek ghost not holding Pythagorean doctrines.
But in the inscriptions on tombs in ancient Egypt
the deceased commonly prays for this lustral water.
This may, however, be a fortuitous agreement, for
libations of water are offered in ancestor-worship by
the Hindus. But the Hindus did not conceive some
supernatural being as giving the water to the deceased,
whereas, as we have seen, the Pythagoreans did.
And, oddly enough, so did the Egyptians. And again,
though such an idea as the Pythagorean notion of
supernatural 'guards' giving the ghost water to
drink is unknown elsewhere in Greece, it is an ordinary
feature of the pictures on Egyptian tombs: the
most usual representation of this is the picture in
which the goddess Nut pours out the water of life to
the deceased from the interior of a sycamore-tree.
In a picture published by M. Chabas, the deceased
kneels before Osiris, and receives from him the water
of life from a vessel under which is written *anch ba*,
'that the soul may live.' Again, in the Egyptian
Book of the Dead the deceased is directed to protect
himself, in his long and perilous journey through the
underworld with its monsters of all kinds, not only
by the use of amulets and talismans, but by pro-
claiming 'I am Osiris.' So the Pythagorean ghost
is to proclaim that he is divine. Again, it is not likely
that the idea of issuing a guide to the underworld
occurred straight off to Pythagoras, whereas the
Egyptian Book of the Dead took centuries to form.
If it be said that a small gold tablet is not to be
compared with the Book of the Dead, which has
hundreds of chapters, the answer is that the verses

on the Pythagorean tablets are but extracts from a greater work ; and that in Egypt the most important of the talismans which were buried (like the Pythagorean tablets) with the deceased was one which had an extract from the Book of the Dead (namely, Chapter XXX) engraved upon it : ' the rubric directs it to be placed upon the heart of the deceased person.' "[1]

Jevons proceeds to say that " there is nothing in Pythagoreanism which is not to be found in the religion of ancient Egypt." Transmigration, then, was an evil which the soul had to avoid at all costs. If it had sinned then it must suffer an age-long round of development from the lowliest to the highest forms. Were it sinless and justified, it proceeded at once to the apotheosis of union with the divine.

It is here that the importance of the Mysteries becomes apparent. Were the wise to escape the fate of transmigration, were they to avoid the frightful fate of enforced evolution from larval forms to divine apotheosis, could virtue and wisdom combined save them from this immense disaster, it must be effected by means of some sanction not only extraordinarily sacred, but equally compelling through the force of the great art of Magic. We cannot say how the mystæ were aware or become aware either of having passed through the dread cycle or being in danger of so doing, but the fact that Pythagoras declares he actually had experienced it proves that they believed themselves to have the means of assessing the truth in this respect.

That initiation into the Mysteries secured protection for the soul from the ordeal of transmigration must be not only assumed but unhesitatingly accepted. The

[1] *Introduction to the History of Religion*, pp. 322–23.

terrible anxiety of the ancient Egyptian that he would not win through the dangers of the Otherworld and achieve communion with his god is so apparent in the Book of the Dead that it is highly improbable that some much more consistent means of achieving this end than is visible in that work would not have been considered and perfected.

But it is equally obvious that only to the few would such an avenue be held open. In the first place, immortality was anciently comprehended as the privilege of royalty alone, and the idea that it was the preserve of the wise and learned few would certainly die hard. The simple peasant and the evil rich man, his costly preparations against psychic destruction or submergence notwithstanding, would scarcely appeal to the erudite or the instructed adept as persons qualified for apotheosis. Only the man of wise heart and pure and stainless life could hope to achieve unity with the Divine, and indeed it would be regarded as profane and dangerous to select any other for the experience of such an ordeal.

Therefore it appears much more than probable that the Mysteries, besides dramatizing the life-story of the god and affording the novice an opportunity of passing through the same phases as divinity itself in the hope of achieving a like end, also magically portrayed and enacted that other process of under-going the cycle of transmigration of 30,000 years in order that the initiate might be spared the risk of such a prolonged separation from deity. Indeed my personal belief is that whereas the Mysteries enacted the divine drama of communion, they were also associated with those magical processes by which the neophyte was believed to free himself from the chance of undergoing transmigration by having already magically and by imitative processes passed through the entire cycle of metempsychosis. Now this presupposes a drama in which the neophyte had to enact the passages through various animal forms, and of the existence of such a drama we have a certain amount of evidence in the Book of the Dead. The guardians, demons, or genii of the several doors, those spirits who keep the path to paradise, and who must be exorcised by a knowledge of their names on the part of the deceased, are these not typical and representative of the various animal and other forms which the spirit must inhabit in the cycle of metempsychosis ? Many of them are animal-headed and bear names of animal provenance, such as " Eater-of-entrails " (hyena ?), " Two-eyes-of-Flame " (wolf ?), and so forth, and cats, hawks, and dogs are represented. If these do not signify the phases of transmigration, what, then, do they signify ?

We know that in the Greek Mysteries the neophyte had perforce to grovel on the ground and later to go on all fours in the earlier part of the ceremony. Did this not symbolize first the reptilian stage which the soul doomed to metempsychosis must undergo and later the animal or mammalian phase ? And did not the ritual of the Egyptian Mysteries include some such pantomime ? I believe it did, and I find a certain amount of corroboration for the theory in the late Miss Jane Harrison's *Prolegomena*, where, writing of the wheel or cycle of existence as depicted in the Greek Mysteries of Orpheus,[1] which were certainly of Egyptian origin, she gives it as her opinion that at some part in the ritual proceedings the mystic enacted the escape from the Wheel of Purgation, " he passes with eager foot over the Ring or circle . . . he enters

[1] Pages 588 ff.

and perhaps passes out of some sort of sacred enclosure. As to the actual rite performed we are wholly in the dark."

The Greek neophytes who endure passage through the Mysteries took animal form—kids, fawns, dogs. They were reborn as young animals, in a word they passed through bestial forms in pantomime to that of man, and I believe the incident where they were covered with mud symbolized the passage of larval forms from the mire upward. What is all this but the drama of transmigration ?

The chief difference between the Egyptian and Hindu ideas of transmigration was that whereas Karma is transmitted in a direct line which may be continued to infinity, the Egyptian doctrine supposed only a cycle of changes to be suffered. Escape in this case is dependent on the completion of the cycle, and the favourable judgment of Osiris, with whom union, complete and everlasting, ensues, whereas in the Buddhistic and Hindu notion of transmigration escape depends neither on the judgment of the god nor consists in the absorption of the soul into the godhead. Jevons indicates that both in India and in Egypt " the dominant religion and the lower forms (totemism, etc.) acted and reacted on one another " so that the theory of retribution had to be reconciled with the belief in totemism, or the idea of religious association with the animal souls. " But," he continues, " though in India as in Egypt, the totemist faith has been generalised and dissociated from the totem animal, and though in both countries the migrating soul may return to human form, here all resemblance ceases. In Egypt, metempsychosis was first made a means of rewarding the righteous exclusively, and then exclusively an instrument for punishing the wicked.[1] But in India it was applied to both good and bad alike : the retribution theory was infused into metempsychosis—all men were born again, but the good got a good birth, the bad a bad one according to their deeds and deserts. In the next place, there was a cycle of transformations in Egypt, with the possibility of escape on the completion of the cycle. But in India there was no cycle and no escape : the good got a good birth, and then bad behaviour might cause him to be born lower in the scale—but whether the soul behaved well or ill, it always had to be born again."

But that the *ascent* of the soul was also portrayed in a part of the Mysteries is clear enough from the analogy of Greek and Latin practice, as Virgil, Plato, Apuleius, and Proclus assert. " The sources of the soul's existence," says Taylor, " are also the principles from which it fell." These sources are the Demiurgus or mundane intellect, or Bacchus, according to the Orpheans, as Plato states in his *Phædo*. " The soul," he says, " descends Corically, or after the manner of Proserpine, into generation, but is distributed into generation Dionysiacally, and she is bound in body Prometheiacally and Titanically : she frees herself, therefore, from its bonds by exercising the strength of Hercules, but she is collected into one through the assistance of Apollo and the saviour Minerva, by philosophizing in a manner truly cathartic."

But this belief was associated with a vision or comprehension of the causes of the soul's descent, as is obvious from a passage in Apuleius. " I approached,"

[1] That is, it was, under a totemistic regime, " good " to be united with the totemic or animal god ; but, under a more enlightened dispensation, union with the animal form came to be abhorred and escape from it an essential to felicity and ultimate union with the (now preferable) divine god.

he says, " the confines of death, and treading on the threshold of Proserpine, and being carried through all the elements, I came back again to my pristine situation. In the depths of midnight I saw the sun glittering with a splendid light, together with the infernal and supernal gods : and to these divinities approaching near, I paid the tribute of devout adoration."

Plato, in his *Phædrus*, also remarks : " But it was then lawful to survey the most splendid beauty, when we obtained together with that blessed choir, this happy vision and contemplation. And we indeed enjoyed this blessed spectacle together with Jupiter ; but others in conjunction with some other god ; at the same time being initiated in those mysteries, which it is lawful to call the most blessed of all mysteries. And these divine Orgies were celebrated by us, while we possessed the proper integrity of our nature, and were freed from the molestations of evil which awaited us in a succeeding period of time. Likewise, in consequence of this divine initiation, we became spectators of entire, simple, immovable, and blessed visions, resident in a pure light ; and were ourselves pure and immaculate, and liberated from this sur- rounding vestment, which we denominate body, and to which we are now bound like an oyster to its shell."

It is thus clear that the most sublime part of that portion of initiation which was known as " inspec- tion " consisted in beholding the gods themselves invested in a resplendent light (the sun), and that this symbolized these visions which the justified soul would eternally enjoy in a future state, and thus the ascent of the soul to the highest, to apotheosis. Proclus in his essay on the *Republic* of Plato says :

" In all initiations and mysteries, the gods exhibit many forms of themselves, and appear in a variety of shapes : and sometimes, indeed, an unfigured light of themselves is held forth to the view ; sometimes this light is figured according to a human form, and sometimes it proceeds into a different shape."

One of the magic oracular utterances of Zoroaster says : " Invoke not the self-conspicuous image of Nature, for you must not behold these things before your body has received the purification necessary to initiation." Now what is this " self-conspicuous image of Nature " ? Proclus, writing on the *Timæus* of Plato, tells us that " the moon is the cause of nature to mortals, and the self-conspicuous image of fontal nature," and Taylor, the Platonist, writing on this passage, remarks that : " If the reader is desirous of knowing what we are to understand by the fontal nature of which the moon is the image, let him attend to the following information, derived from a long and deep study of the ancient theology : for from hence I have learned, that there are many divine fountains contained in the essence of the demiurgus of the world ; and that among these there are three of a very distinguished rank, viz. the fountain of souls, or Juno, the fountain of virtues, or Minerva, and the fountain of nature, or Diana. This last fountain, too, immediately depends on the vivific goddess Rhea, and was assumed by the Demiurgus among the rest, as necessary to the prolific production of himself. And this information will enable us besides to explain the meaning of the following passages in Apuleius, which, from not being understood, have induced the moderns to believe that Apuleius acknowledged but one deity alone. The first of these passages is in the beginning of the eleventh book of his Metamorphosis, in which the divinity of the moon is represented as addressing him in this sublime manner : ' Behold Lucius, moved with thy supplications, I am present ; I, who am Nature, the parent of things, queen of all the elements, initial progenitor of ages, the greatest of divinities, queen of departed spirits, the first of the celestials, and the uniform appearance of gods and goddesses : who rule by my nod the luminous heights of the heavens, the salubrious breezes of the sea, and the deplorable silences of the infernal regions ; and whose divinity, in itself but one, is venerated by all the earth, according to a multiform shape, various rites, and different appellations—hence the primitive Phrygians call me Pessinuntica, the mother of the gods ; the native Athenians, Cecropian Minerva, the floating Cyprians, Paphian Venus ; the arrow-bearing Cretans, Dictynnian Diana ; the three-tongued Sicilians, Stygian Proserpine ; and the inhabitants of Eleusis, the ancient goddess Ceres. Some again have invoked me as Juno, others as Bellona, others as Hecate, and others as Rhamnusia : and those who are enlightened by the emerging rays of the rising sun, the Æthiopians, Ariians, and Ægyptians, powerful in ancient learning, who reverence my divinity with ceremonies perfectly proper, call me by a true appellation, queen Isis.' "

Now this has an even deeper natural and primitive meaning than Taylor guessed. This significance is enshrined in the folklore belief, current in many lands, that the moon is a reservoir of life and soul-force. The Melanesian peoples believe in a reservoir of supernatural or magical force which they call *mana*. This, like the *orenda* of the North American Indians, is thought to be stored in the moon, which forms a huge tank of this power, which seems to be considered by these primitive peoples as the source of all life and energy. Most goddesses of the moon preside over the child at birth, and the orb of night is thought of among such races as possessing greater power to quicken the growth of plants than even the sun himself. The fairies, we know, are connected with the moon. They are also notorious midwives, ever ready to assist mortals in this respect. They are thus spirits of life, bringing the soul which animates the body of the newly-born child. Hence all the tales of changelings with which they were connected. And this leads, through supplementary proof, to the assumption that a confusion of beliefs occurred, and that at some time or another the notion of the transmigration of souls was imported into fairy mythology and that the fairy became confounded with the soul which returns again and again to earth.

CHAPTER VI

THE PHILOSOPHY OF THE MYSTERIES
(CONTINUED)

PLATO, indeed, asserts that the ultimate design of the Mysteries was to lead humanity back to the principles from which it originally fell. With antiquity, as with barbarism to-day, the fall of man was a persistent belief. Some peoples, indeed, as for example the ancient Welsh, and a tribe of Indians in Arizona, believed man to have struggled upward from lower forms, thus anticipating the Darwinian theory of evolution. But an almost universal tradition credited his moral and ethical downfall from a state of innocence.

The tradition was, of course, associated with the idea of carnal knowledge and the breaking of taboos, and the story of the fall from heaven and the broken cord or mast which descended to earth.

The prayer which, in Apuleius, Psyche addresses to Ceres certainly alludes to the descent of the soul : " I beseech thee, by thy fruit-bearing right hand, by the joyful ceremonies of thy harvests, by the occult sacred concerns of thy cistæ, and by the winged car of thy attending dragons, and the furrows of the Sicilian soil, and the rapacious chariot, and the dark descending ceremonies attending the marriage of Proserpine, and the ascending rites which accompanied the luminous invention of thy daughter, and by other arcana which Eleusis the Attic sanctuary conceals in profound silence, relieve the sorrows of thy wretched supplicant Psyche."[1]

The rape of Proserpine, says Taylor, signifies the descent of the soul, as is evident from the passage in Olympiodorus in which he says the soul descends Corically, and this statement is, indeed, confirmed by Sallust in his *De Dies et Mundo:* " And as the rape of Proserpine was exhibited in the shows of the mysteries, as is clear from Apuleius, it indisputably follows, that this represented the descent of the soul and its union with the dark tenement of body. Indeed if the ascent and descent of the soul, and its condition while connected with a material nature, were represented in the shows of the mysteries, it is evident that this was implied by the rape of Proserpine. And the former part of this assertion is manifest from Apuleius, when, describing his initiation, he says, in the passage already adduced, ' I approached the confines of death, and treading on the threshold of Proserpine, and being carried through all the elements, I came back again to my pristine situation.' "

How far is this psychic descent associated with the idea of transmigration ? It has, I believe, a very substantial connection with it, and one which has been rather neglected or lost sight of. Symbolically, the descent of Proserpine alludes to seed corn being placed in the ground. Proserpine, was, indeed, the goddess of the corn-seed, just as her mother Kore was the corn-plant itself. Now corn is associated with the idea of transmigration, as more than one

---

[1] We observe well here how even the incidentals of myth become " sacred " and capable of use in adjuration, that to mention the mere adjuncts or scenery of a legend enforces a certain mysterious power in supplication.

remarkable legend makes clear. The British goddess Keridwen, who is unquestionably a grain-goddess, and perhaps merely a variant of Kore, pursued Gwion, whom she had set to watch her magic cauldron. Each takes various animal shapes in the course of the pursuit, and at last Gwion adopts the disguise of a grain of wheat. Keridwen swallows him, and he is reborn as the mystic poet Taliesin. This is not only a legend of transmigration in which the corn-plant figures, but an allegory of the rebirth of the mystic through the ritual mysteries of Keridwen. Moreover Keridwen was addressed by at least one of her adepts as the moon, and she is called Ogyrven Amhad, " the goddess of various seeds," a statement which equates her with Ceres.[1]

When Gwion unwittingly tasted the virtue of her Cauldron of Inspiration he pursued him; he transformed himself into a hare, when she became a greyhound, turned him, and chased him toward a river. He leapt into the stream and became a fish, but as she pursued him as an otter, he took the form of a bird. Transforming herself into the guise of a sparrowhawk, she was gaining upon him, when he perceived a heap of wheat upon a floor, dropped into the midst of it, and assumed the form of a single grain. Keridwen then changed herself into the shape of a black, high-crested hen, descended into the wheat, scratched him out, and swallowed him, and, as the history relates, he was born of her in due time as the beautiful babe Taliesin, who was found in the fishing weir of Elphin.

Now the whole myth certainly bears allusions to the rite of initiation. Keridwen first transforms herself into a female dog. Virgil, in the sixth book of

[1] See my *Mysteries of Britain*, pp. 196 ff.

his *Æneid*, describing all that it was lawful to reveal of the Eluesinian mysteries, says that one of the first things observed by his hero as the priestess conducted him toward the mystic river was a number of female dogs, and Pletho in his notes upon the Magical Oracles of Zoroaster, remarks that it is the custom in the celebration of the mysteries to exhibit to the initiated certain phantoms in the figures of dogs. The dog was, indeed, the guardian of the Underworld, and it seems probable that, as the initiate was supposed to enter this gloomy region when undergoing his ordeal, the presence of dogs may have entered symbolically into the ceremony. Indeed, Diodorus, dealing with the mysteries of Isis, mentions that the whole solemnity was preceded by the presence of dogs, and he even terms the priests of the mysteries " dogs," although he believes that the Greeks mistook the Hebrew word *cohen*, a priest, for their own word *kune*, dog.[1] However, the dog of Gwyn ap Nudd, the British Pluto, is named Dormarth, " the gate of sorrow," so it would seem that the animals represented in the British mysteries somewhat resembled the classical Cerberus or the Egyptian Anubis, and that they had a similar significance—that they were, indeed, of the same character as the Proserpine Limen which Apuleius approached in the course of his initiation.

Then we find that the aspirant was converted into a hare, a sacred animal among the Britons, as we learn from Cæsar, but perhaps here symbolizing the great timidity of the novice. This hare is turned and driven toward a river. The first ceremony in the Greek mysteries was that of purification, which was

[1] The " dog " of the Egyptian Mysteries was, of course, Anubis, and one of the officiating priests wore his canine mask.

celebrated upon the banks of rivers. The Athenians, for example, performed his ceremony at Agra on the Ilissus, a river of Attica, whose banks were called " the mystical," and whose stream itself was named " the divine."

According to the myth, the aspirant now plunges into the stream, and the otter here seems to symbolize the priest who attended to his lustrations. His form then changes into that of a bird, probably the *dryw*, which means both a wren and a Druid, and, indeed, elsewhere Taliesin informs us that he had once taken that form. His adversary becomes a hawk, reminiscent of Egyptian mythology. At last he takes the shape of a grain of pure wheat, mixing with an assemblage of the same species, and thus assumes a form eminently sacred to Ceres or Keridwen, who receives him into her bosom, whence he is reborn.

There can thus be little question that the Egyptian and Greek Mysteries in that part of them which dealt with the descent of the soul were associated with the idea of transmigration or metempsychosis.

Fable or allegory, remarks Sallust, the Platonic philosopher, is theological, so far as it pertains to pure philosophy ; when it is physical it appertains to the realm of poetry. But when it is mingled in character it applies to initiatory rites, " since the intention of all mystic ceremonies is to conjoin us with the world of the gods." This I regard as a most important light to our comprehension of the Mysteries, as it shows us that they must have been understood as affording a bridge or nexus, so to speak, between the mortal and the divine. Such a bridge is, indeed, alluded to in the Jewish mystic writings and in those of certain Islamic mysteries, a species of psychic arc, of which divinity is the head and man the first ascending steps, as Zoharistic and Cabbalistic pronouncements infer.

Both the descent and the ascent of the soul were thus envisaged and enacted in the course and practice of the Egyptian Mysteries. We must think of the drama of descent as showing and revealing the course of a soul from anthropomorphic or human likeness through the cycle of being to the human again, from man to the lowest forms of life, the worm, the serpent, the mammal. Did an appropriate thought-process accompany the process ? We cannot say, but doubtless it did. Self-abasement there must have been, and pantomimic representation there certainly was. The neophyte grovelled as reptile, went on all fours as dog or fawn, was disguised in the skins of animals, until, his allegorical evolution completed, he rose again to mortal deportment and stature. Such, then, was probably the basic nature of the outward ceremonies of a part of the Mysteries.

But still more important was the quality of thought, the consideration which accompanied this, and the magical means by which freedom from bestial forms was supposed to be won. As I have said, self-abasement must have been a concomitant of the bestial status. Was it accompanied by any form of words, of ritual ? Says Miss Jane Harrison of the Greeks : " Diogenes Laertius, who is concerned to glorify Pythagoras, said that he was the first to assert that ' the soul went round in a changing Wheel of necessity, being bound down now in this, now in that, animal.' A people who saw in a chance snake the soul of a hero would have no difficulty in formulating a doctrine of metempsychosis. They need not have borrowed it from Egypt, and yet it is probable that the influence of Egypt, the home of animal worship, helped out the doctrine by emphasizing the sanctity of animal life. The almost ceremonial tenderness shown to animals by the Pythagorean Orphics is an Egyptian rather than a Greek characteristic. The notion of kinship with the brute creation harmonized well with the somewhat elaborate and self-conscious humility of the Orphic."

" A kid, I have fallen into milk," recited the Orphic neophyte. The Greek initiate believed himself reborn as a kid, a certain reminiscence of a change in animal progression derived from the still older Egyptian ritual. We know, too, that the Bacchic initiate " became " a fawn. That these changes were accompanied by alterations in thought-process who can doubt ? Each ascent must have been accompanied by appropriate spells and prayers.

But greatly more important was the thought-process which must have accompanied the ritual of the soul's ascent, the drama of the Osirian death and rebirth. This has frequently been decried, and it has been opined on no reasonable grounds, that the ritual of the Mysteries included their entire celebration, that by the magical potency of ritual alone the initiates hoped for union with the Divine. Such an opinion would mean that the Mysteries remained always as a part of the religion of the lower cultus, a mere " dancing out " of myth, and that they never took on the significance accruing to a wisdom-religion. The evidence of Iamblichus, Plutarch, and many others easily disposes of a theory so absurd.

That the wanderings of the soul, that is, of Isis, were symbolized as a part of the ritual, a part which came prior to the actual drama of rebirth, we can scarcely doubt. According to the Eleusinian Mysteries, the soul descended from the planetary galaxy, from the tropic of Cancer, into the planet Saturn, which Capella compares to a sluggish and voluminous river, and which is symbolized by the sea, in which the mystics bathed. Later it was supposed to fall into the lunar orb, and still later into the terrestrial sphere, that is, the body.

At this point we have to consider the myth of the matron Baubo, as given by the Christian father Arnobius, as illustrating the bodily association of the soul. Arnobius, of course, narrates it for the purpose of decrying the Mysteries, but it is none the less useful for our means.

The goddess Ceres, when searching through the earth for her daughter, in the course of her wanderings arrived at the boundaries of Eleusis, in the Attic region, a place which was then inhabited by a people called Autochthones, or descended from the earth, whose names were as follow: Baubo and Tripto-lemus; Dysaules, a goatherd; Eubulus, a keeper of swine; and Eumolpus, a shepherd, from whom the race of the Eumolpidi descended, and the illustrious name of Cecropidæ was derived; and who afterwards flourished as bearers of the caduceus, hierophants, and cryers belonging to the sacred rites. Baubo, there-fore, who was of the female sex, received Ceres, wearied with complicated evils, as her guest, and endeavoured to sooth her sorrows by obsequious and flattering attendance. For this purpose she entreated her to pay attention to the refreshment of her body, and placed before her a miscellaneous potion to assuage the vehemence of her thirst, But the sorrow-ful goddess was averse from her solicitations, and rejected the friendly officiousness of the hospitable dame. The matron, however, who was not easily repulsed, still continued her entreaties, which were as obstinately resisted by Ceres, who persevered in her refusal with unshaken constancy and invincible rigour. But when Baubo had thus often exerted her endeavours to appease the sorrows of Ceres, but without any effect, she, at length, changed her arts and determined to try if she could not exhilarate by prodigies, a mind which she was not able to allure by serious attempts. For this purpose she freed from concealment that part of her body through which the female sex produces children, and derives the appellation of woman. This she caused to assume a purer appearance, and a smoothness such as is found in the private parts of a stripling child. She then returns to the afflicted goddess, and, in the midst of those attempts which are usually employed to alleviate distress, she uncovers herself, and exhibits her secret parts ; upon which the goddess fixed her eyes, and was delighted with the novel method of mitigating the anguish of sorrow ; and afterwards becoming cheerful through laughter, she assuages the ardour of her thirst with the miscellaneous potion which she had before despised.

This myth unquestionably belongs to that body of arcane discourse, fulfilled with mystical meaning which is one of the undoubted legacies of the Mysteries. As Iamblichus observes : " Exhibitions of this kind in the mysteries were designed to free us from licentious passions, by gratifying the sight, and at the same time vanquishing desire, through the awful sanctity with which these rites were accompanied, for the proper way of freeing ourselves from the passions is, first, to indulge them with moderation, by which means they become satisfied ; listen, as it were, to persuasion, and may be thus entirely removed."

Baubo, the matron, may be conceived as the

symbol of the passions or female quality of corporeal life by means of which spirit or soul is united with the terrestrial body. The soul caught in the nets of the terrene, descends and is born into the corporeal sphere, thus passing from the divine splendour into darkness, and psychical as well as bodily infancy. Ceres or Kore, the intellectual part of the soul, in the course of her wanderings or evolutions through the realms of matter, is captivated by the arts of Baubo, the corporeal life, which amuse or divert her, and cause her to forget her sorrows. In like manner is man obfuscated and drawn from the consideration of things divine by the interesting or diverting phantasmagoria of this terrestrial existence, which make him forget the immediate cause of his being and the intense need for psychical progression. In his folly he seizes at the shadow of the material or sensual, and neglects the substance of the divine. The potion of Baubo typifies the mixed and impure draught of earthly existence, leading to corruption and death.[1]

But the " wanderings of the soul " must have been experienced by the Egyptian neophyte in a very much more intense and even afflicting manner during these days in which he concentrated upon them than it is possible for any but an adept to comprehend. The mental and psychic passage through the several elemental or " planetary " spheres, that is the several planes of being, must indeed have been an experience of sublime anguish which left its mark for ever on the initiate. This voyage among the deeps of the great ocean of the spiritual could not but be fraught with terrors and agonies almost impossible of estimation

[1] This part of the myth might scientifically be explained as an effort to make Demeter become prolific by sympathetic magic. The women who, according to Herodotus, exposed themselves at the festival of Osiris probably did so for similar reasons.

by those ignorant of or inexperienced in such a quest.
That the neophyte actually journeyed in spirit
through the gulfs and glooms of the eternal it would
be impious to question. Accompanied by the divine
Isis, he must have penetrated, while his corporeal
part lay in the cell of meditation, through many a
region of awful majesty and ancient fear.

The approach of the goddess, his guide and
guardian, heralded by the frenzied rattle of her divine
sistrum, must in itself have appalled the stoutest
heart. The initial steps of the voyage, terrific in the
novelty of spiritual freedom, untrammelled by bodily
incumbency, cannot but have filled the soul, now
whirled into the valleys of the extra-terrestrial sphere,
now transported to the peaks of the sublime, with
such amazement that each phase of the journey would
inevitably be deeply imprinted on its consciousness.
As coast upon coast of the mystic continents of the
eternal were approached and passed what turmoil of
sensations must have afflicted even the wisest and
most resolved ? That the awful quest was not
infrequently attended with mortal results is surely
a matter of little surprise. Many who essayed the
journey never returned. Whence they fared, on what
shoals of horror those unprepared spirits were wrecked
and lost, we cannot say. But to us, profiting from
these disasters, there remains the great and abiding
lesson of wisdom that only to the highest and noblest,
the most courageous and stainless, is the way of
complete initiation open.

Fools in their folly, without preparation or even
adequate consideration, still frequently attempt the
dread path. Madness, or at best derangement, is too
often the result. Lured by the agencies of evil, these
ignorant ones essay what even to the greatest is an

undertaking of frightful significance and jeopardy. Let none who read these lines and is neither fitted nor who has not undergone the prescribed preparation under adept guidance dare to risk the perils of the uncharted deeps of the mysterious and the sublime. In itself the blasphemy is unspeakable and of a description peculiarly revolting, and that condign and terrible punishment awaits it let no man question. I say no more on a subject where silence is best, and all sane and knowledgeable men will bear witness to the need for silence in this place.

But, after all, the result of the Mysteries was but a vision or foreshadowing of the desired union with deity, and not that union itself. The mystic now knew, was assured, of the sublime destiny which awaited him did he faithfully carry out his sacred responsibilities during the remainder of his earthly pilgrimage. He was indeed reborn in the spiritual sense. He counted the day of his initiation as the first of his new life. That some rite allegorical of this rebirth was actually celebrated we have good proof. Says M. Moret on this point :[1] " In Egypt, in order to represent gestation and rebirth, either a statue or the mummy of the deceased was placed inside the hide of a sacrificed animal or inside a wooden cow ; or, a priest would lay himself down within the hide on the night of the funeral, as a substitute for the dead man. Next morning, the priest was considered to issue from the skin as from a womb. Mythology coming to the aid of magic, the deceased became identified with the Sun Ra, born under the form of a calf from the cow Nut, who was goddess of Heaven. Both Plutarch and Apuleius mention the wooden image of a cow, which was borne upon the priest's shoulders in the procession

[1] *Kings and Gods of Egypt*, pp. 186 ff.

of Isis. Did the wooden cow mean for the Isiacs what it meant for the Egyptians, the ' womb ' from which the dead are born anew ? Judging from the episode of Aristæus in the Georgics, the Romans were acquainted with the rite of the hide. Virgil gives to the bee-breeders a recipe which will bring about spontaneous generation of bees. By the action of magic rites, a swarm can be brought into existence within the hides of sacrificed bulls. This miraculous process, as the Latin writers knew, was derived from Egyptian and Orphic traditions. On the other hand, the Egyptians were familiar also with the idea that the soul issued from the skin of victims under the form of a bee. Was this tradition, which Virgil presents in a popular form, propounded to the neophyte with its mystic significance ? At any rate, the presence on the walls of the megarum of a bee and a fœtus surrounded with ears of corn suggests that those symbols were in some way or other employed to illustrate the mysteries of new birth."

It has been said of initiation into the Eleusinian Mysteries that " The soul at the moment of death experiences the same sensation as those experience who are initiated into great mysteries. Word and thing are alike : we say teleirtan (to die) and teleisthai (to be initiated). There are, at first, steps to be taken at random, painful wanderings astray from the right path, anxious and unavailing journeys through the darkness. Then, before the end, the crisis of fear, the shudder, the shiver, the cold sweat, the terror. But afterwards, a marvellous light breaks upon the eyes ; the soul enters into pure regions, and meadows echoing with the sound of voices and of dances ; sacred utterances, divine apparitions inspire the soul with awe."

But that the goddess who had led the initiate through the terror of spatial experience would guard him during the rest of his earthly days is plain from a passage in Apuleius. Isis, speaking to Lucius, says : " Thou shalt lived blessed, thou shalt live crowned with glory beneath my protection, and when thy life is run and thou goest down to the Nether World, there also, in that nether atmosphere, thou shalt see me shining in the inmost halls of Styx ; and thou shalt dwell in the Elysian Fields, and continually make offering of worship to me, and I will smile upon thee. Nay, if by sedulous observance and religious service and persistent chastity thou bear thee worthy of my godhead, thou shalt know that I alone have power to prolong thy life beyond the space ordained by fate." At the same time righteous living is essential to long life and future bliss.

The experience won in the Mysteries changed and altered the entire future earthly life of the initiate. He knew, and with the torch of his illumination burning before him, worked peacefully, yet triumphantly through the remainder of his earthly pilgrimage, prepared for death whenever it might come to him. Equipped with the epoptic vision, nothing was hidden from him, and he might tread the avenues of the past or the future with ease and certainty. Nor were the inner thoughts of men in any way hidden from him.

But to have penetrated to the Absolute must have awakened in the illuminated mind a large impatience to be translated from the material sphere to that which he had upheld in psychic vision. Once having experienced the marvels of the divine plane, it could scarcely have tolerated earthly proximity for long. As the poet strains after Faerie, the country of his imagination, as the composer conjures up spheres where the larger planetary music rolls in thunder, joy, and passion, so must the initiate have yearned for the divine splendours in which he had once breathed, the ineffable glories of the unearthly approach, the summits of divine communion.

Summarizing the results of this chapter in the order of the theories and opinions quoted, we find that :

(1) It is hopeless to expect much, if any, assistance from scientific theory alone. Sublime understanding, what might vulgarly be termed " uncommon sense " alone will help us in this quest, yet spiritual analogies may be employed.

(2) The Mysteries were in part the enacted symbolism or magic of an inward impulse toward unity with or absorption in the Divine.

(3) The Egyptian idea of spirit was first expressed by the semi-material Ka ; later by the purely spiritual Ba.

(4) Besides this the Egyptians believed in the doctrine of the transmigration of souls, which differed from the Hindu or Buddhist conception in that it was confined to a period of 30,000 years. With the Egyptians transmigration was an evil to be avoided, and escape from this peril was probably effected through initiation into the Mysteries. In all likelihood this was accomplished by a dramatic representation of transmigration which magically rendered metempsychosis unnecessary, and passages in the Book of the Dead and in the Greek Mysteries seem to assist this theory.

(5) That the descent and ascent of the soul were also portrayed in the Mysteries is clear from Greek and Latin practice. The latter included the vision of the gods.

(6) The sun and moon were symbolically and psychically observed by the neophyte.

(7) The " Fall of Man " was portrayed in the Mysteries.

(8) The descent of the soul is probably associated with the idea of transmigration.

(9) " The intention of all mystic ceremonies," says Sallust, " is to conjoin us with the world of the gods." That is, they afforded a bridge or nexus between the mortal and the divine.

(10) The thought-processes which accompanied the ritual of the Mysteries were greatly more important than the ritual itself.

(11) Rebirth, symbolical and psychical, was a concomitant of the process of unity with the Divine.

And lastly : how, precisely, do those writings on the Egyptian Mysteries which we reviewed, in the second and third chapters bear on the theories and opinions we have advanced or quoted in this ? They agree with the opinions of Plutarch and Iamblichus as follows :

(1) That a knowledge of the Supreme Mind was the purpose of the Egyptian Mysteries. That their philosophy was veiled in allegory, but that their aim was to form true notions of the divine nature.

(2) That their symbolism, as Iamblichus says, had a spiritual basis.

(3) That their initiates aspired to union with the Divine.

(4) That man fell psychically, and that the " more mortal form " of his soul, as Iamblichus expresses it, was expressed by the semi-material Ka.

(5) That freedom from the bonds of materialism was only to be accomplished in the Egyptian belief, by " scientific knowledge of the gods."

We have certainly here no proof that, as Plutarch says, the Mysteries were intended " to preserve the meaning of valuable passages in history," but that can be posited from the analogy of the primitive rites of other peoples which recite and describe divine histories.   The myths of Osiris and Isis take the place of these primitive " histories " in other mystery systems and probably sprang from like origins.   That they represented the phenomena of nature is equally probably, as Plutarch says, personal history and nature-myth frequently becoming amalgamated.

CHAPTER VII

MYSTERIES IN OTHER LANDS

THE subject of the existence of Mysteries in other lands than Egypt is important to the student of the occult and the mysterious, not only as illustrating the possible Egyptian origin of these rites and ceremonies, but as recording those analogical circumstances which may be capable of throwing light on Egyptian mysticism and arcane practices. In practically every portion of the globe we discover the existence of mystico-religious societies of a character so similar that their pristine common origin cannot logically be disputed. In Greece, Africa, Australia, America these arcane bodies flourished with such amazing vigour and similitude that not to posit for them some extremely ancient common source seems not only unscientific but merely foolish.

This association I have already outlined in the chapter dealing with the origin of the Mysteries. It remains to give some account of those non-Egyptian systems which appear most likely to assist comprehension of the Egyptian school. That Greece actually borrowed the idea of the Eleusinian and Dionysian Mysteries from Egypt the work of Foucart and Moret has made abundantly clear, though Jevons and Farnell appear to be of opinion that the process may have taken place through the medium of western Asiatic faiths. But M. Foucart, in his *Recherches sur l'origine et la nature des mystères d'Eleusis*, has proved to admiration that the Demeter of Eleusis is merely a hellenized Isis.[1]

Egyptian association with ancient Hellas is proved by the inscriptions on the mounments of the Theban Dynasty, which records that in the sixteenth century B.C. the officials of King Thoutmosis III and his successors frequently visited the islands of the Ægean Sea in Phœnician vessels.[2] The worship of Demeter, the corn-mother, although it may originally have been Hellenic, certainly took on the colouring of that of Isis, and at some time in the sixth century B.C. had undoubtedly absorbed the whole Osirian and Isiac ideals. " It is not necessary," says Maspero, " to be a learned Egyptologist to recognize the Isis of the Delta under the Greek name and robe, the fertile earth, lady of the harvests and of bread, who awards her faithful ones the same fate which she assured to her husband Osiris, and who guides them to a shining paradise through the horrors of the darkness beyond the tomb."[3]

The revelations vouchsafed to the initiate of the Eleusinian Mysteries were free to all who were found worthy, and consisted in a traditional ritual revelation of the life beyond. They comprised the elements of drama, the unveiling of certain sacred objects, and instruction in formula. The drama enacted the rape of Kore or Persephone by Hades, god of the Underworld, the consequent grief of her mother Demeter, her journeys in search of her daughter, her union with Celeus, and the birth of Euboleus, and the manner in

---

[1] With this theory the late Mr. Andrew Lang did not agree, believing that savage analogies could be found for practically every instance in Hellenic mystery cults. See his *Custom and Myth*, p. 81.

[2] Deveria, *Mémoires et Fragments*, Vol. I, pp. 35–53.

[3] Maspero, *New Light on Ancient Egypt*, p. 56.

which Triptolemus delivered his half-sister Kore. In another series of scenes the hierophant and the priestess of Demeter enacted the marriage of Zeus and Demeter, and presented to the spectators the ultimate result, the blade of ripe corn, product of heaven and earth. The representation took place in the sacred enclosure, and in the halls of the temple. There were few scenic decorations, and, says, Foucart, no mechanical or complicated devices.

"The silence of the night," says this profound student of the mysteries, " the alterations of light and shade, the majestic voice of the sacred herald, the imposing robes of the hierophants and ministers engaged in the solemnities, the singing of the choir, now plaintive, now triumphant, exercised a strong influence on the senses and imagination. The heart thus excited by the preparation that preceded the initiation, mystery easily held sway in the sacred precincts ; the promises and semi-revelations of the mystagogue to whom the instruction of the novice was entrusted, the retreat into the Eleusinium of Athens, the fasting, the repeated purifications and sacrifices, the songs and dances of the procession from Athens to Eleusis, the continual shouts of ' Iacchos,' the arrival by torchlight in the holy city, and, above all, the impatient and anxious anticipation of what was to be revealed, combined to incline a man to strong emotion. And when at last the hierophant disclosed the sacred effigies to his view, in a form and with attributes unknown to the profane, must he not have felt nearer to the gods, as if admitted to contemplate them face to face ? "

Theo of Smyrna states expressly that there were five parts of initiation into the Eleusinian Mysteries, " the first of which is previous purgation, for neither

are the mysteries communicated to all who are willing
to receive them ; but there are certain characters
who are prevented by the voice of the cryer, such as
those who possess impure hands and an inarticulate
voice ; since it is necessary that such as are not
expelled from the mysteries should first be refined by
certain purgations, but after purgation the tradition
of the sacred rites succeeds. The third part is
denominated inspection. And the fourth, which is
the end and design of inspection, is the binding of the
head and fixing the crowns ; so that the initiated may,
by this means, be enabled to communicate to others
the sacred rites in which he had been instructed ;
after this he became a torch-bearer, or an interpreter
of the mysteries, or sustains some other part of the
sacerdotal office. But the fifth, which is produced
from all these, is friendship with divinity, and the
enjoyment of that felicity which arises from intimate
converse with the gods. Similar to this is the tradition
of political reasons for, in the first place, a certain
purgation precedes, or an exercise in convenient
mathematical disciplines from early youth. For thus
Empedocles asserts, that it is necessary to be purified
from sordid concerns, by drawing from five fountains,
with a vessel of indissoluble brass : but Plato, that
purification is to be derived from the five mathematical disciplines, viz. from arithmetic, geometry,
stereometry, music, and astronomy ; but the philosophical tradition of theorems, logical, political and
physical, is similar to initiation. But he (that is,
Plato) denominates inspection, an occupation about
intelligibles, true beings, and ideas. But he considers the binding of the head, and coronation, as
analogous to the power which any one receives from
his instructors, of leading others to the same con-

templation. And the fifth gradation is the most perfect felicity arising from hence, and, according to Plato, " an assimilation to divinity, as far as is possible to mankind."[1]

The reason for the popular adoption of the Mysteries of Eleusis in Greece has been explained by Jevons[2] who makes it clear that the discontent arising out of a native faith which held out little or no expectation of a future existence beyond that of a dreary sojourn in an underground Hades literally drove man to seek for a " larger hope," as the theologians of the late nineteenth century would have expressed it. The sixth-century Greeks, craving for a happy Other-world, hearkening to the alien doctrine of a fairer future, eagerly sought out sanctuaries in which the mysterious archaic ritual still prevailed, and which had almost certainly received that ritual from a foreign source. The sanctuary where the ritual was most peculiarly striking chanced to be Eleusis, near Athens, which offered the Athenians precisely the kind of worship of which they were in search, and in the Hymn to Demeter they discovered the necessary mythic or traditional background which gave it sanction.

The Eleusinian goddess had a cereal character, and the corn-plant had originally been the totem of the district, which later developed into a goddess. The rites connected with her worship were gloomy, mysterious, and impressive. The myth of the goddess " explained " how her daughter Kore, the corn, came to reside for six months of the year with her mother, and for the remainder with Hades, King of the Under-world, not only by the history of the corn-plant itself,

---

[1] *Mathematica*, p. 18.
[2] *Introduction to the History of Religion*, pp. 358–362.

watered from above and fructified below the earth, but in virtue of her marriage with Hades, which gave her power over the future of men after death. The whole represented not only an allegory of the life-history of the corn-plant, but that of the resurrection of man. The life, death, and return of the wheat seemed, indeed, to primitive man the best and most apt allegory of his own existence here and hereafter.

Thomas Taylor, the Platonist, provides us with a deeply mystical theory of the higher objects involved in the Eleusinian Mysteries. " The lesser mysteries," he writes, " were designed by the ancient theologists, their founders, to signify occultly the condition of the impure soul invested with a terrene body, and merged in a material nature : or, in other words, to signify that such a soul in the present life might be said to die, as far as it is possible for soul to die ; and that on dissolution of the present body, while in a state of impurity, it would experience a death still more durable and profound. That the soul, indeed, till purified by philosophy, suffers death through its union with body, was obvious to the philologist Macrobius, who, not penetrating the secret depth of the ancients concluded from hence that they signified nothing more than the present body, by their descriptions of the infernal abodes. But this is manifestly absurd, since it is universally agreed that all the ancient theological poets and philosophers inculcated the doctrine of a future state of rewards and punishments in the most full and decisive terms, at the same time occultly intimating that the death of the soul was nothing more than a profound union with the ruinous bonds of the body. Indeed if these wise men believed in a future state of retribution and at the same time considered a connection with body as the death of the soul, it necessarily follows that the soul's punishment and subsistence hereafter are nothing more than a continuation of its state at present, and a transmigration, as it were, from sleep to sleep, and from dream to dream."

The one objection to this view is that it is scarcely in accordance with Egyptian doctrine, which most assuredly believed in the resurrection of the material body itself. Indeed one of the chief objects of the Egyptian Mysteries, and of Egyptian Religion in general, was the survival of the material body in a glorified form, and one cannot doubt from the general character of the Eleusinian rites that the same idea pervades them—the survival of the material body through the provision of an adequate food-supply hereafter. That this came to have a much deeper and more occult allegorical significance, however, we cannot doubt.

The Orphic or Bacchic Mysteries represent the gradual infiltration of religious ceremonies from Asia Minor and Egypt distinct from the public ceremonies of Greece. These were not only merely of a ritual character, but held also ascetic implications. Thus the Orphic life, as it came to be known, forbade animal food and on certain occasions the use of woollen clothing, both restrictions practised by the Egyptian priests.

In Homeric and other early Greek poetry Bacchus and Demeter are seldom encountered. But during the interval between Hesiod and Onomacritus the rise in public favour of the Mysteries brought these deities into the front rank of the Greek pantheon. That their cults were intertwined or in some way associated is clear from the genealogical connection of the principal deities, for according to the Orphic

doctrine, Zagreus, the first " avatar " of Bacchus or
Dionysus, was the son of Persephone, daughter of
Demeter, and later rose from the confusion of his
destruction as Dionysus.

The change in Hellenic ideas seems to have taken
place about the end of the seventh and the beginning
of the sixth century B.C., when Egypt was first fully
open to the Greeks, and was certainly due to communication with the Nile land as well as to commercial
and political association with Thrace, Phrygia, and
Lydia.   Dionysus and Demeter became identified
with Osiris and Isis, so that what was borrowed from
the Egyptian worship of these gods naturally fell to
their equivalents in the Greek system.   It was the
Phrygian element in these cults which gave them the
orgiastic and frenzied character seldom found in the
Egyptian Mysteries.

Among the rites and orgies now introduced into
Greece were those of the Idæan Zeus in Crete, the
cult of Demeter at Eleusis, of the Cabiri in Samothrace,
and of Dionysus or Bacchus at Delphi and Thebes.
That they bore much the same character is proved
by the way in which they became confused in the
minds of those who wrote about them, and that they
were actually confounded in practice is shown, for
example, by the case of an aged priestess who passed
from the service of Demeter to that of the Cabiri and
again to that of Cybele.[1]

That agencies other than Egyptian went to compose
these cults is clear enough, although we must not
forget the pseudo-orgiastic character of the festival
of Isis at Busiris, described by Herodotus, when the
Egyptians are spoken of as beating themselves

---

[1] Kallimachus, Epigram 42.

unmercifully. Says Grote : " The rites grew to be more furious and ecstatic, exhibiting the utmost excitement, bodily as well as mental : the legends became at once more coarse, more tragical, and less pathetic. The manifestations of this frenzy were strongest among the women, whose religious suscepti- bilities were often found extremely unmanageable, and who had everywhere congregative occasional ceremonies of their own, apart from the men—indeed, in the case of the colonists, especially of the Asiatic colonists, the women had been originally women of the country, and as such retained to a great degree their non-Hellenic manners and feelings. The god Dionysos, whom the legends described as clothed in feminine attire, and leading a troop of frenzied women, inspired a temporary ecstasy. Those who resisted the inspiration, being disposed to disobey his will, were punished either by particular judgments or by mental terrors ; while those who gave full loose to the feeling, in the appropriate season and with the received solemnities, satisfied his exigencies, and believed themselves to have procured immunity from such disquietudes for the future. Crowds of women, clothed with fawn-skins and bearing the sanctified thyrsus, flocked to the solitudes of Par- nassus, or Kithæron, or Taygetus, during the conse- crated triennial period, passed the night there with torches, and abandoned themselves to demonstra- tions of frantic excitement, with dancing and clamorous invocation of the god. They were said to tear animals limb from limb, to devour the raw flesh, and to cut themselves without feeling the wound. The men yielded to a similar impulse by noisy revels in the streets, sounding the cymbals and tambourine, and carrying the image of the god in procession."

Herodotus seems to have been convinced that the cult of Dionysus was derived from Egypt, brought over by Cadmus, inventor of the Greek alphabet, and taught by him to Melampus, who introduced the Bacchic dance with its fanatical excitement. Moreover the myth of the dismemberment of Zagreus, the first form of Dionysus, is one and the same with that of Osiris, and the wailing and mourning of the Bacchantes, which found expression in the myth of Penthus, torn in pieces by his own mother, is strikingly reminiscent of the awful grief of Isis on discovering the death of Osiris, the dismemberment and the subsequent mourning of Isis and Nephthys at the bier of the god. The Thracian Orpheus later became the Moses, so to speak, of a sect which performed the Mysteries of Dionysus with peculiar care, minuteness, and fervour, besides observing certain rules in respect to food and clothing, and it was the opinion of Herodotus that these rules, as well as the Pythagorean, were borrowed from Egypt.

To come to the description of specific mystic systems in Greece, the Eleusinian Mysteries were locally thought of as having been instituted by the goddess Demeter herself. Demeter, in the Eleusinian legend, is said to have come from Crete and to have been plunged into deep sorrow by the seizure of her daughter Persephone by Hades who had carried her off to the Underworld. After searching for her by day and by night with torches, the nature of her loss was revealed to her by Helios. Dolefully she came to Eleusis, and became nurse to Demophoon, son of King Keleos, as Isis had to the son of the king of Egypt. Like Isis, too, she plunged the child Demophoon into a sacred fire nightly, but was at length restrained from so doing by the terrors of Queen

Metaneira, to whom Demeter revealed her godhead, giving express injunctions to the queen to erect a temple and altar for her worship, in which she took up her abode.

But she would not permit the barley to sprout in the soil, and mankind might have perished had not Zeus, in alarm, sent Hermes to Hades to bring Persephone back. Hades, however, prevailed upon her to swallow a grain of pomegranate (the food of the dead), which rendered it impossible for her to remain the whole year away from him.

Before returning to Olympus Demeter revealed to Keleos, Triptolemus, Diocles, and Eumolpus the nature of the rites and ceremonies which she required to be observed in her honour, and thus were the venerable Mysteries of Eleusis established, the lesser mysteries celebrated in February, in honour of Persephone, the greater in August in honour of Demeter herself.[1]

As Miss Jane Harrison has shown in her *Prolegomena to the Study of Greek Religion*, the " primitive harvest festival " of the Eleusinian Mysteries borrowed nearly all of its *spiritual* significance from the cult of Dionysus.

Considerable doubt exists as to the character of the Greater and Lesser Mysteries at Eleusis. The Lesser seem to have been sacred to Persephone and not to her mother Demeter, and to have been of later origin. The scholiast in the *Plutus* of Aristophanes says : " In the course of the year two sets of mysteries are performed, the Lesser and the Greater. . . . The Greater were of Demeter, the Lesser of Persephone, her daughter." The Lesser were a sort of purification for the Greater, he tells us. Stephen of Byzantium

---

[1] See the Homeric Hymn to Demeter

adds that " the Lesser Mysteries, performed at Agra, were an imitation of what happened about Dionysus." Thus Dionysus shared the Lesser Mysteries with Kore, or Persephone.

M. Georges Foucart is a student of the Eleusinian Mysteries so admirably equipped that what he has to say regarding their significance is of the utmost value to a full consideration of the subject of the mysteries in general.   Unlike the late Miss Jane Harrison, whose theories are reviewed in a later part of this chapter, he does not agree that the Orphic cult had other than a symbolical influence in Eleusinian practice.

The Lesser Mysteries, he tells us, were celebrated in the springtime at Athens in the Temple of Agra in the month Anthesterion, a few months prior to the celebration of the Greater Mysteries.   They were preceded by a trial or preparation of not less than fifty-five days.   The festival, as has been said, did not take place at Eleusis, but at Agra on the left bank of the River Ilissus, where stood the temple of Demeter and Kore, or Proserpine, and the rites were celebrated by the priestly classes of the Eumolpidæ and Keryces.   The former were a hierophantic sect of Thracian origin, while the latter were originally a caste of women whose business it was to collect polluted things and carry them off to the sea for purification or destruction.

At these Lesser Mysteries the mystæ performed purificatory ablutions in the river Ilissus.   Stephen of Byzantium tells us that the Lesser Mysteries con- sisted of " an imitation of the history of Dionysus," a part of his myth unknown to the profane, and which would permit them to understand better the revelation of the Greater Mysteries.   The birth of the god was exposed to their eyes, or rather his death and rebirth, or perhaps his union with Kore. Concerning the Lesser Mysteries of Eleusis this is all the certain information we possess.

The Greater Mysteries were celebrated partly at Athens, partly at Eleusis. On the 14th of the month Boedromion the sacred objects were carried from Eleusis to Athens. They were deposited in the sacred chapel of the shrine at Agra, in cists or boxes, and were accompanied by the three Eumolpidæ. During the journey the procession arrived at the extremity of the plain of Thria, where the lakes called Rhetoi were situated, marking the boundary between Eleusis and Athens. These were consecrated to Demeter and Kore, and their fishes were reserved for the priests of Eleusis alone. At a later date the cortège took its way by the seashore, and was received by the council and citizens of Athens in concourse.

The sanctuary of Agra was surrounded by high walls, like that at Eleusis, intended to keep out the profane.

The festival commenced at the 15th Boedromion, with the new moon. The first day, called Agyrmos, was marked by the assembly of the mystæ in the shrine Poecile, which was situated hard by the Eleusinion. At that time those interdicted from taking part in the Mysteries were enumerated, such as criminals, the sacrilegious, murderers, and barbarians. The costume and nourishment of the mystæ were furthermore prescribed.

On entering the Eleusinion the mystæ were asperged with water from a sacred vase placed in the gateway. On the second day, the mystæ went down to the sea to undergo a rite of purification at the cry of the heralds : " Alade mystai," " Mystæ to the sea ! "

The next day was known as " Iacchos " and was called after a spirit or deity of the cycle or myth of Demeter. On this day the image of the god in question was placed in a chariot and drawn in procession, accompanied by the priests and priestesses of the temple, to Eleusis, where the chief rites were to be performed. The procession entered the village with torches and rejoicings.

The image of Iacchos was accompanied by mystical objects which were used in ceremonies of initiation. Strangely enough, Strabo describes Iacchos as "the dæmon of Demeter, the founder of the Mysteries," and it was his name that was called out by the initiates in the procession. His statue holding a torch stood in the Temple of Demeter, and he seems to have had his especial priests, although he had no particular shrine of his own. Indeed, as Professor Farnell says : " He comes as a stranger and a visitor and departs at the end of the sacred rite." He appears, indeed, to have been a deity of late acceptance, although he was sufficiently popular. Is his name merely a corruption of that of Bacchus ? The answer is almost certainly " yes," as the ode in Sophocles' *Antigone* reveals. He was regarded as the son of Zeus and Persephone, and was probably adopted into the Eleusinian rites because of his great Athenian popularity.

As I have said before, the Eleusinian Mysteries enshrined secrets and were indeed established on a basis of secrecy, not, as Jevons seems to think, because of " religious infection," but for very much deeper reasons. Their secrecy was established by law, and its profanation by Alcibiades raised a veritable tempest at Athens. Æschylus also suffered for revealing them in his tragedies.

On the morning of the twentieth Boedromion a

solemn sacrifice was offered to Demeter and Kore with the object of obtaining favourable results. The movements of the sacrificed animal and the condition of its entrails showed whether the omens were favourable or otherwise. The victim was usually a pig, and a portion of it seems to have been eaten as a sacred repast. The actual business of initiation now commenced. Strabo says that the secret of the Mysteries gave a majestic idea of divinity, and brought home to the initiate its nature which was unveiled to their understanding. The mystical play of Demeter and Kore was now enacted, and it seems probable that the high priest and priestess took a part in it. Tertullian says : " Why is the priestess of Ceres (or Proserpine) carried off unless Ceres herself had suffered the same experience," and Apuleius in his story of Psyche makes her mention " the unspoken secrets of the mystic chest, the winged chariots of thy dragon-ministers, the bridal descent of Proserpine, the torch-lit wanderings to find thy daughter, and all the other mysteries that the shrine of Attic Eleusis shrouds in secret." From such references we may feel certain that the great myth of Demeter and her daughter was enacted before the eyes of the mystæ in the Telesterion. The symbolic wanderings in search of Peresphone seem to have been made at night over the adjoining countryside. It was also pretty certain that an allegorical marriage took place, a representative act whereby the whole company of the initiates entered into mystic communion with the deities, for marriage in the primitive mind is closely identified with communion ; but that there was anything of a gross or indecent nature in the allegory we have not the slightest evidence, the statements of certain ill-informed classical writers notwithstanding.

Subsequently to this it is also fairly clear that the symbolical birth of a holy child was enacted. This was a very ancient episode in Greek ritual. Indeed some of the oldest Greek sacred dances illustrated such an allegory. I believe it is to this incident that Origen alludes when he tells us that the priest called aloud : " The goddess Brimo has given birth to Brimos, the holy child."

There appears to be some doubt regarding this particular incident in the minds of certain authorities. The amazing thing is that what is practically an identical rite is to be discovered in ancient Mexico where the birth of the maize-god was symbolized at a public festival, and this was preceded by the rite of a sacred marriage.[1]

I do not mean to infer that there is any cultural connection between the two, but it seems to me that the identical character of the rites is too striking altogether to ignore, and this identity may strengthen the assumption as regards Eleusis.

Maximus Tyrius maintains that all such festivals as that at Eleusis had an agricultural significance, and Varro tells us that " there was nothing in the Eleusinian Mysteries that did not refer to corn." He thus took the selfsame view as the anthropologists, ignoring altogether the latter-day intention of these ceremonies, which undoubtedly was directed towards the secrets of the after-life. I stress this because there is an ever-present danger in perusing works on Folklore to lose sight of this paramount characteristic of the Mysteries.

To come to more minute considerations concerning the actual ritual. The privation from food seems to have symbolized the fast of Demeter. This was broken

---

[1] See my *Gods of Mexico*, pp. 162–3.

by the ceremonial eating of food out of the sacred chests, meal, honey, wine, cheese, and herbs. The chest seems to have been made of osiers in a cylindrical form, and the kalathos appears to have been a similar basket of a rather longer shape in which the vestments of Demeter were held. The Cyceon was the cup from which the mystic wine was drunk. After partaking of these the mystæ appear to have been crowned with myrtle.

Certain revelations were then made to the mystæ. Themistius mentions that in approaching the sanctuary of the goddess at this stage the neophyte felt himself seized with vertigo and experienced much trouble and doubt, finding difficulty in entering the shrine, but when the hierophant opened its gates and raised the vestments of the statue displaying its beauty, when they beheld the resplendent marble inundated with a divine light, then their fears were dissipated and their intelligence seemed to rise out of the abyss. In the place of the shadows which had enveloped them they emerged into the light. This seems to apply to something more than clarity of mortal vision, and almost certainly admits of the assumption at least that the neophytes at this stage received their first glimpse of immortal splendour.

The mystæ had now to traverse either symbolically or spiritually the world of shadows into which Kore had descended, and as I have dealt at some length on this phase in another chapter there is no necessity to reconsider the nature of the journey in this place. From this region of terror they passed into the Elysian Fields suffused with light, and contemplated the sacred objects which have already been enumerated. The sermon or address which has also been described, was then given, and this appears to have concluded the initiation of the Lesser Mysteries.

The final or Epoptic stage or phase of the Mysteries is less known to us in its details, but authorities are agreed that it dealt almost entirely with the rite of the ear of corn. Indeed it is the only rite mentioned in connection with the Greater Mysteries at Eleusis which were associated with Dionysus rather than with Demeter. We find that large numbers of initiates seem to have been content with entrance to the first degree, and that the second was conferred after an interval of at least a year. We get a certain amount of footing from references in the writings of St. Hippolytus, enigmatical as these are. He tells us that an ear of wheat was exhibited in silence, and he says so with such brevity and precision that we can scarcely doubt the accuracy of his statements which assist us to link up the Eleusinian second degree with Egyptian practice. Dionysus or Iacchos, then, was the patron god of the Greater Mysteries of Eleusis, and there can be little question that the myth of his life furnished the material for the higher mysteries. We have already perused this myth and have indicated its significance according to Taylor and others. That it was for all purposes practically identical with that of Osiris I cannot bring myself to doubt.

CHAPTER VIII

MYSTERIES IN OTHER LANDS (CONTINUED)

IT is essential here to summarize what the late Miss Jane Harrison wrote on the subject of the Eleusinian Mysteries in her *Prolegomena to the Study of Greek Religion*. She believed them to be originally but a local Eleusinian version of the Haloa, or feast of Demeter, Kore, and Dionysus, on the occasion of the cutting of the vines, and the tasting of the wine made from them. Their ultimate splendour and spiritual prestige are due to the fact that Athens adopted them for political purposes, and that at some unknown date they became associated with the Mysteries of Dionysus and the cult of Orpheus.

" In general by a mystery is meant a rite in which certain sacra are exhibited, which cannot be safely seen by the worshipper till he has undergone certain purifications."[1]

Subsequently to the bringing of the sacred objects from Eleusis to Athens, the assembling of the candidates for initiation took place on the 15th Boedromion. On the 16th was held the rite known as " to the Sea, ye mystics," from the cry that heralded the act of purification. This was a banishing of evil,

---

[1] This may hold true of some rites encountered under the head of " mysteries," or mysteries at a comparatively low stage of development, but such a statement has no regard for the secondary stage of mystery cults, for the explanatory myths which crystallize round their ritual, or for the moral sanctions they possess.

and on the six-mile journey each of the mystics took with him a young pig, with which he bathed in the sea. " Mysteries," says Miss Harrison, quoting Lydus, are derived " from the separating away of a pollution (musos) as equivalent to sanctification "— a very much better derivation or rather definition than that she herself proposed.

On the night of the 19th–20th the procession of purified mystics left Athens for Eleusis, carrying with them the image of Iacchos, " and after that we have no evidence of the exact order of the various rites of initiation."

First fruits were offered, and the ritual followed, including the drinking of the kykeon (or sacred brew) and the handling of certain sacred objects. The confession or formulary of the mystic regarding these " is not a confession or dogma or even faith, but an avowal of ritual acts performed. Of the sacred objects taken from the chest, placed in the basket and returned to the chest " we know nothing." Like the sacra of the Thesmophoria, another festival, a ball, a mirror, a cone, they may have been of an equally trivial character.

" Late authors in describing the Eleusinian rites use constantly the vocabulary of the stage." Miss Harrison then quotes the valuable account of Psellus (the significance of which she obviously discovered from Taylor, who also quotes it in his work), as follows : " Yes and the mysteries of these (demons), as for example those of Eleusis, enact the double story of Deo or Demeter and her daughter Pherephatta or Kore. As in the rite of initiation love affairs are to take place, Aphrodite of the Sea is represented as uprising. Next there is the wedding rite for Kore. And the initiated sing as an accompaniment ' I have eaten from the timbrel, I have drunk from the cymbals, I have carried the kernos, I have gone down into the bridal chamber.' Then also they enact the birth-pains of Deo. At least there are cries of entreaty of Deo, and there is the draught of gall and the throes of pain. After these there is a goat-legged mime' because of what Zeus did to Demeter. After all this there are the rites of Dionysos and the cista and the cakes with many bosses and the initiated to Sabazios and the Klodones and the Mimallones who do the rites of the Mother and the sounding cauldron of Thesprotia and the gong of Dodona and a Korybas and a Koures, separate figures, mimic forms of demons. After this is the action of Baubo."

This, according to Miss Harrison, is " the sacred pantomime according to Psellus . . . Dionysus and the other Orphic divinities are daimons rather than gods. The religion of Orpheus is religious in the sense that it is the worship of the real mysteries of life, of potencies rather than personal gods ; it is the worship of life itself, in its supreme mysteries of ecstasy and love." As Murray, in his *Ancient Greek Literature,* phrased it : " Reason is great, but it is not everything. There are in the world things, not of reason, but both below and above it, causes of emotion which we cannot express, which we tend to worship, which we feel perhaps to be the precious things in life. These things are God or forms of God, not fabulous immortal men, but ' Things which Are,' things utterly non-human and non-moral which bring man bliss or tear his life to shreds without a break in their own serenity." So far Miss Harrison.

This sentiment it was, then, which inspired the Mysteries in their later cultus—not only the binding of man to God, the man becoming the god, but the recognition that Love and Ecstasy are and actually constitute God, and that all human barriers and taboos are incapable for ever of standing between man and God in these forms. This truth the poet and the musician know through rhythm, which is ecstasy, this truth the artist knows through colour, which is the material solidification of rhythm—and the charitable, the generous, and the affectionate know it through what is greatly nobler—the love of man for his fellow, the sacrifice which love ever inspires whether it be for humanity in the mass or for the individual. For love, wanting sacrifice, is not only as unwise as art lacking restraint, but as incomprehensible as body without soul. This splendid gift, then, it was the province of the Orphic cult to bring to the half-formed rite of Eleusis, as we shall see.

Regarding the Bacchic or Dionysiac Mysteries, said to have been instituted by Orpheus, those depended upon the following arcane narration: Dionysus or Bacchus, while he was yet a boy, was engaged by the Titans, through the stratagems of Juno, in a variety of sports, with which that period of life is so vehemently allured, and among the rest, he was particularly captivated with beholding his image in a mirror, during his admiration of which he was miserably torn to pieces by the Titans, who, not content with this cruelty, first boiled his members in water and afterwards roasted them by the fire. But while they were tasting his flesh thus dressed, Jupiter, excited by the steam, and perceiving the cruelty of the deed, hurled his thunder at the Titans, but committed his members to Apollo, the brother of Bacchus, that they might be properly interred. And this being performed, Dionysus, (whose heart during his laceration was snatched away by Pallas

THE VEILED NEOPHYTE

The neophyte is veiled.   The priestess holds the mystic fan (?) over his head.

and preserved), by a new regeneration again emerged, and being restored to his pristine life and integrity, he afterwards filled up the number of the gods. But in the meantime from the exhalations formed from the ashes of the burning bodies of the Titans, mankind was produced.

" In order to understand properly the secret meaning of this narration," says Taylor,[1] " it is necessary to repeat the observation that all fables belonging to mystic ceremonies are of the mixed kind. . . . In the first place, then, by Dionysus, or Bacchus, according to the highest establishment of this deity, we must understand the intellect of the mundane soul; for there are various processions of this god, or Bacchuses derived from his essence. But by the Titans we must understand the mundane gods of whom Bacchus is the summit : by Jupiter, the Demiurgus, or artificer of the universe : by Apollo, the deity of the Sun, who has both a mundane and supermundane establishment, and by whom the universe is bound in symmetry and consent, through splendid reasons and harmonizing power : and lastly, by Minerva we must understand that fontal, intellectual, imperatorial, and providential deity, who guards and preserves all middle lives in an immutable condition, through intelligence and a self-energizing life, and by this means sustains them from the depredations of matter. Again, by the puerile state of Bacchus as the period of his laceration, the flourishing condition of an intellectual nature is implied ; since, according to the Orphic theology, souls, while under the government of Saturn, who is pure intellect, instead of proceeding as now, from youth to age, advance in a retrograde progression from age to

[1] *Eleusinian and Bacchic Mysteries*, p. 137.

youth. The arts employed by the Titans, in order to ensure us, are symbolical of those apparent and divisible energies of the mundane gods, through which the participated intellect of Bacchus becomes, as it were, torn in pieces : and by the mirror we must understand, in the language of Proclus, the inaptitude of the universe to receive the plenitude of intellectual perfection."

The symbols of the rites of Bacchus, says Taylor, were, according to Clemens Alexandrinus, a wheel, a pine-nut, physical games, the fruit of the Hesperides, a mirror, a fleece of wool and the ankle-bone. These represent intellectual energy, the matrix of the soul, the energy of the mundane intellect, the incorruptible nature of the intellect, truth, the locomotion of intellect and the progression of Bacchus with nature.

Jevons naturally supplies a more modern reading of the myth. He says : " Zeus in his anger smote the evil Titans with his thunderbolts, and reduced them to ashes. From those ashes sprang the human race. Hence the two elements in man, the Titanic and the Dionysiac, the evil and the divine, the material and the spiritual. Thus the folk-tale of early Orphic literature was made to afford a basis for the Pythagorean teaching of the opposition of the body to the soul, and the efforts of the latter to escape from imprisonment in the former and to rejoin the world-soul, the divine essence, which was sometimes by accommodation termed Ouranos, sometimes Zeus. In the same vein the Orphic myth of the dismemberment of Zagreus by the Titans was made to bear witness to Pythagorean pantheism : the body of Zagreus was the one reality, the divine essence of all things, which is robbed of its divine unity by the action of the Titanic or evil element and split up into the manifold of the phenomenal world. But the longing of the soul to escape from its fleshly prison, to merge itself in the divine essence and so shuffle off its individual existence, is a testimony at once to the original unity which existed before its harmony was broken by the intrusion of evil, and to the ultimate destiny of the soul when purified."

M. Maeterlinck, with his customary shrewdness, has at once pierced to the heart of the comparative character of the Bacchic legend. He says, " Dionysus, the child-god, slain by the Titans, whose heart Athene saved by hiding it in a basket, and who was brought to life again by Jupiter, is Osiris, Krishna, Buddha ; he is all the divine incarnations ; he is the god who descends into or rather manifests himself, in man ; he is death, temporary and illusory, and rebirth, actual and immortal ; he is the temporary union with the divine that is but the prelude to the final union, the endless cycle of the eternal Becoming."

Heraclitus, who was regarded as the philosopher of the mysteries, explains the nature of this cycle. " On the periphery of the circle the beginning and the end are one." " Divinity is itself," says Auguste Dies, " the origin and the end of the individual life. Unity is divided into plurality, and plurality is resolved into unity, but unity and plurality are contemporaneous, and the emanation from the bosom of the divine is accompanied by an incessant return to divinity. All comes from God, all returns to God ; all becomes one, one becomes all. God, or the world, is one : the divine idea is diffused through every quarter of the universe. In a word, the system of Heraclitus, like that of the *Vedas* and the Egyptians, is a unitarian pantheism."

But by far the most illuminating contribution as

to the precise nature of the Orphic Mysteries is that of the late Miss Jane Harrison, who, in her *Prolegomena to the Study of Greek Religion*, made it abundantly clear that Orpheus was "a real man, a mighty enigma, a prophet, and a teacher," who was martyred, and whose tomb became a mantic shrine. For this theory Conan, Strabo, and Pausanius are her chief authorities. Orpheus, she thinks, "took an ancient superstition, deep-rooted in the savage ritual of Dionysus, and lent to it a new spiritual significance." Orpheus probably came from the South, and his cult in its most primitive form is best studied in Crete. "In Crete, and perhaps there alone, is found that strange blend of Egyptian and primitive Pelasgian which found its expression in Orphic rites. Diodorus says Orpheus went to Egypt to learn his ritual and theology."

Just as the worshippers of Dionysus believed that they were possessed by the god, it was but a step further to the conviction that they became the god, as the worshippers of Osiris after death became Osiris, were made one with him.

A more spiritual implication was imported into the ancient Bacchic rites by Orpheus. The intoxication and madness which characterized it gave place to a quieter and much more dignified pose and ritual. "The great step that Osiris took was that, while he kept the old Bacchic faith that man might become a god, he altered the conception of what a god was, and he sought to obtain that godhead by wholly different means. The grace he sought was not physical intoxication, but spiritual ecstasy." The cardinal doctrine of Orphic religion was the possibility of attaining divine life.

A fragment of the *Cretans* by Euripides gives us

the clue to Orphic doctrine and practice, in which the leader of the mystics confesses his faith and the nature of the ritual acts associated with it. He says that he has fulfilled the god's "red and bleeding feasts." The allusion is to the sacrifice of the bull, probably connected with the Cretan legend of the Minotaur, and (I believe) a legacy from the very much older bull-worship of the prehistoric Aurignacians of Southern France. The principal part of this ritual was the tearing asunder of the victim and the devouring of its raw flesh.

"I will not," cries Clement, "dance out your mysteries, as they say Alcibiades did, but I will strip them naked, and bring them out to the open stage of life, in view of those who are the spectators at the drama of truth. The Bacchoi hold orgies in honour of a mad Dionysos, they celebrate a divine madness by the Eating of Raw Flesh, the final accomplishment of their rite is the distribution of the flesh of butchered victims, they are crowned with snakes, and shriek out the name of Eva, that Eve through whom sin came into the world, and the symbol of their Bacchic orgies is a consecrated serpent." This is the horrified protest of a Christian Father who abhorred the "pagan mysteries" and wished to prove them savage orgies, picking out for the purpose the most ancient and barbarous of these rites. But, as Miss Harrison justly observes : "Because a goat was torn to pieces by Bacchants in Thrace, because a bull was at some unknown date, eaten raw in Crete, we need not conclude that either of these practices regularly obtained in civilized Athens."

In the *Dionysiaca* of Nonnus we learn that it was the custom of the mystæ to bedaub themselves with white clay, as an act of purification, to imitate the

Titans when they slew Zagreus, says the myth. This simply implies that in the original play of Zagreus the Titans, like other savages, were disguised in "war-paint," for disguise is essential to protection in the savage mind, it makes a man "someone else," it guards against demons, it impresses the outsider. Again, one verbal interpretation of the Titans is "white-clay-men."

The brutal and savage element in the Bacchic Mysteries was purified by Orpheus. Miss Harrison saw some difficulty in the circumstance that the Orphic cult confounded the sacred bull with the snake; but the bull-snake is merely a variant of the composite dragon-beast known to all mythologies, the horned snake of the American Indians and of China, an animal with the properties and bodily parts of nearly all animals, as De Visser and Elliot Smith have shown.

Miss Harrison, alluding to the *Clouds* of Aristophanes, a dramatic parody of Orphism, believes that it unveiled the actual mystery. She says: "The 'full revelation' . . . of these and all mysteries, was only an intensification, a mysticizing of the old Epiphany rites—the 'Appear, appear' of the Bacchants, the 'summoning' of the Bull-god by the women of Elis. It was this Epiphany, outward and inward, that was the goal of all purification, of all consecration, not the enunciation or elucidation of arcane dogma, but the revelation, the fruition, of the god himself. To what extent these Epiphanies were actualized by pantomimic performances we do not know; that some form of mimetic representation was enacted seems probable."

But for us perhaps the most important point is the existence of the Orphic Tablets, a series of eight

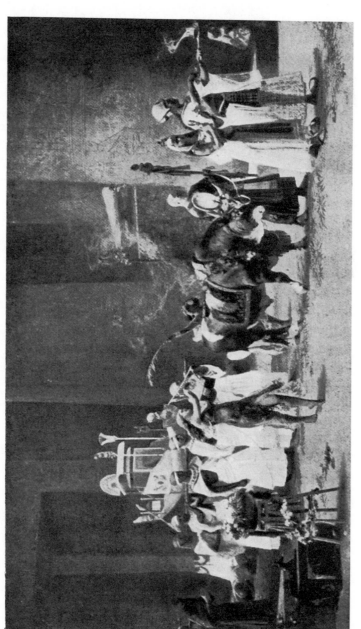

THE FEAST OF THE BULL APIS

After the picture by F. A. Bridgman in the Corcoran Gallery, Washington.

leaflets inscribed on thin gold recovered from tombs in Italy and Crete. These tablets, buried with the dead, contain instructions for their conduct in the Otherworld, formularies to be repeated, and so forth, They compose, indeed, a Book of the Dead.

The Petilia tablet describes how on the left of the House of Hades is a well-spring standing by a white cypress, which must not be approached by the spirit of the dead. There is a better near the Lake of Memory, guarded by spirits, from which the soul should drink, and become one with the heroes of the past. This is a parallel with Osirian belief, and is alluded to in the Book of the Dead,[1] where we also find a " chapter of drinking Water in the Underworld.[2]

The mystic cult of the Cabiri next demands our attention. It is by no means easy to disentangle it from the enormous mass of detail concerning it in the writings of the mystics of the classical age. Pherecides, Herodotus, and Nonnus speak of the Cabiri as sons of Vulcan, Cicero calls them sons of Proserpine, and Jupiter is often named as their father. Dionysius of Halicarnassus, Macrobius, Varro and others consider them the same as the Penates of the Romans, in which, however, the Venetian Altori is opposed to them. According to his opinion and that of Vossius, the Cabiri were nothing more than the ministers of the gods, who were deified after their death, and the Dactyli, the Curetes, and the Corybantes were other names by which they were known. Strabo regards them as the ministers of Hecate. Bochart recognizes in them the three principal infernal deities, Pluto, Proserpine, and Mercury.

The worship of the Cabiri, if the general belief is to be credited, was originally derived from Egypt,

---

[1] Chapter 63.   [2] Chapter 62.

where we find the ancient temple of Memphis consecrated to them. Herodotus supposes that the Pelasgians, the first inhabitants of the Peloponnessus, dwelt first in the isle of Samothrace, where they introduced this worship, and established the famous mysteries into which such heroes as Cadmus, Orpheus, Hercules, Castor, Pollux, Ulysses, Agamemnon, Æneas, and Philip, the father of Alexander, had the honour of being initiated. From their abode in Samothrace the Pelasgi carried these mysteries to Athens, whence they were conveyed to Thebes.

The Cabiri seem to have been worshipped at Memphis in a pigmy form, and are thus represented in the coins of Thessalonica along with the insignia of Vulcan. They also appear in the mythology of the Phœnicians. In the isle of Lemnos and in Tenebros their mystic rites were celebrated. Authorities differ as regards their number, but it is generally accepted that they were twins. In later times they were identified with the twin Dioscuri, Castor and Pollux. Dionysius of Halicarnassus states that they were two " youths armed with spears."

Kenrick, a good authority, in his *Egypt before Herodotus*, stated that the countries in which the Samothracian and Cabiriac worship prevailed were peopled either by the Pelasgi or by the Æolians, who of all the tribes comprehended under the general name of Hellenes approach most nearly in antiquity and language to the Pelasgi.

The name " Cabiri " has been very generally deduced from the Phœnician " mighty," and this etymology is in accordance with the fact that the gods of Samothrace were called " Divi potes." Kenrick believed, however, that the Phœnicians used some other name which the Greeks translated

" Kabeiros," and that it denoted the two elements of fire and wind.

Sanconiathon, the Carthaginian writer, tells us that the cult of the Cabiri was of Carthaginian origin, and was associated with Osiris. The god Thoth ordained that the Cabiri should set down their records of the past. The cult of the Cabiri, indeed, appears to have been brought from North Africa to Egypt and Greece, and it is expressly stated that it was delivered among others to the Egyptian Osiris. The Cabiri are said by Sanconiathon to have been the inventors of boats, of the arts of hunting and fishing, and of building and husbandry. They also invented the art of writing, the use of salt and medicines. Finally, this writer tells us that Poseidon and the Cabiri were settled at Berytus, but not till human sacrifice had been introduced. The Cabiri are in this passage alluded to as husbandmen and fishermen, and the name in this connection seems to apply to a race rather than to a cult.

Rich, in his *Occult Sciences*, summarizing the views of many writers on the subject of the Cabirian Mysteries, says :

" The worship of the Cabiri furnishes the key to the wanderings of Æneas, the foundation of Rome, and the War of Troy itself, as well as the Argonautic expedition. Samothrace and the Troad were so closely connected in this worship, that it is difficult to judge in which of the two it originated, and the gods of Lavinium, the supposed colony from Troy, were Samothracian. Also the Palladium, a pigmy image, was connected at once with Æneas and the Troad, with Rome, Vesta, and the Penates, and the religious belief and traditions of several towns in the south of Italy. Mr. Kenrick also recognizes a

mythical personage in Æneas, whose attributes were
derived from those of the Cabiri, and continues with
some interesting observations on the Homeric fables.
He concludes that the essential part of the War of
Troy originated in the desire to connect together and
explain the traces of an ancient religion. In fine, he
notes one other remarkable circumstance, that the
countries in which the Samothracian and Cabiriac
worship prevailed were peopled either by the Pelasgi
or by the Æolians, who of all the tribes comprehended
under the general name Hellenes, approach the most
nearly in antiquity and language to the Pelasgi. We
seem warranted, then (our author observes), in two
conclusions ; first, that the Pelasgian tribes in Italy,
Greece, and Asia were united in times reaching high
above the commencement of history, by community
of religious ideas and rites, as well as letters, arts, and
language ; and, secondly, that large portions of what
is called the heroic history of Greece, are nothing
else than fictions devised to account for the traces of
this affinity, when time and the ascendancy of other
nations had destroyed the primitive connection, and
rendered the cause of the similarity obscure. The
original derivation of the Cabiriac system from
Phœnicia and Egypt is a less certain, though still
highly probable conclusion. . . . The mysteries of
the Cabiriac worship were celebrated at Thebes and
Lemnos : the time chosen was night. The candidate
for initiation was crowned with a garland of olive,
and wore a purple band around his loins. Thus
attired, and prepared by secret ceremonies, he was
seated on a throne brilliantly lighted, and the
other initiates then danced round him in hieroglyphic
measures. It may be imagined that solemnities of
this nature would easily degenerate into orgies of the

most immoral tendency, as the ancient faith and reverence for sacred things perished, and such was really the case. Still, the primitive institution was pure in form and beautiful in its mystic signification, which passed from one ritual to another, till its last glimmer expired in the freemasonry of a very recent period. The general idea represented was the passage through death to a higher life, and while the outward senses were held in the thrall of magnetism, it is probable that revelations good or evil were made to the high priests of these ceremonies."

In Mexico flourished the cult of the Nagualists, whose priests were the naualli, or master magicians. The cult may, indeed, still survive. It was based on the belief in a personal guardian spirit or familiar. This was known as the nagual, and was attached to each child at its birth. In a History of Guatemala, written about 1690 by Francisco Fuentes y Guzman, the author gives some information regarding a sorcerer who on arrest was examined as to the manner of assigning the proper nagual to a child. When informed of the day of its birth, he presented himself at the house of the parents, and taking the child outside invoked the demon. He then produced a little calendar which had against each day a picture of a certain animal or object. Thus in the Nagualist calendar for January, the first day of the month was represented by a lion, the second by a snake, the eighth by a rabbit, the fourteenth by a toad, the nineteenth by a jaguar, and so on. The invocation over, the nagual of the child would appear under the form of the animal or object set opposite its birthday in the calendar. The sorcerer then addressed certain prayers to the nagual, requesting it to protect the child, and told the mother to take it daily to the same spot, where its nagual would appear to it, and would finally accompany it through life.

Some of the worshippers of this cult had the power of transforming themselves into the nagual. Thomas Gage, an English Catholic who acted as priest among the Maya of Guatemala about 1630, describes in his *New Survey of the West Indies* the supposed metamorphosis of two chiefs of neighbouring tribes, and the mortal combat in which they engaged, which resulted in the death of one of them. But a Nagualist of power was by no means confined to a single transformation, and was capable of taking on many and varied shapes.

Speaking of one of the great magician-kings of the Kiche of Guatemala the Popol Vuh, a native book, states that Gucumatz, the sorcerer-monarch in question, could transform himself into a serpent, an eagle, a tiger, and even into lower forms of life. Many of the confessions of the natives to the Catholic priests remind one forcibly of those which were discovered by the European witch trials of the sixteenth and seventeenth centuries. Thus an old man in his dying confession declared that by diabolical art he had transformed himself into his nagual, and a young girl of twelve confessed that the Nagualists had transformed her into a bird, and that in one of her nocturnal flights she had rested on the roof of the very house in which the parish priest resided.

No sooner had the Mexican aristocracy been accounted for by slaughter or conversion than a significant change took place in the tendency and character of the native faith. The Aztec priesthood, realizing that if its doctrines were to survive at all, it must make a powerful appeal to the mass mind of the nation, threw every ounce of energy into the task of shaping the superstitions of the lower orders into a deadly instrument of vengeance against the whites. In this new movement magic of a repellent kind was joined with political conspiracy against Spanish supremacy, and the extraordinary cult this developed came to be known as Nagualism, whose chief deity was Satan himself, if we are to credit the writings of those who opposed it and laboured untiringly for its destruction.

This mysterious secret society had branches in all parts of the country, and its members were classed in varying degrees, initiation into which was granted only after prolonged and rigorous experience. Local brotherhoods or lodges were organized and there were certain recognized centres of the cult. At each of these places was stationed a high priest or master magician, who had beneath his authority often as many as a thousand lesser priests, and who exercised control over a large district.

The priesthood of this guild was handed down from father to son. The highest grade appears to have been that of Xochimalca or "Flower-weaver," probably because its members possessed the faculty of deceiving the senses of votaries by strange and pleasant visions induced by potent drugs, as, for instance, the peyotl, a plant of the genus cocolia, which resembles garlic. Like the kava of the Polynesians, it was first masticated and then placed in a wooden mortar, where it was left to ferment. Another plant employed by the Nagualists for the purpose of inducing ecstatic visions was the ololiuhqui, from the seeds of which a liniment was crushed and rubbed over the body after being mixed with the ashes of spiders, scorpions, and other noxious insects.

The Nagualists smeared themselves with a magical

ointment by virtue of which they believed they could fly through the air, and engaged in wild and intemperate dances, precisely as did the adherents of Vaulderie in France, or the witches of England ; they met at cross-roads, where they danced to pipe and tabor, and brewed strange potions, love-philtres, and poisons quite in the manner of the Lancashire or Devonshire hags.

But shape-shifting and witchcraft were not the only magical resources of the Nagualists. Their arts were manifold. They could render themselves invisible and walk unseen among their enemies. They could transport themselves to distant places and, returning, report what they had witnessed. Like the fakirs of India, they could create before the eyes of the spectator rivers, trees, houses, animals, and other objects. They would, to all appearances, rip themselves open, cut a limb from the body of another person, and replace it, and pierce themselves with knives without bleeding. They could handle venomous serpents without being bitten, as can their representatives among the Zuñi Indians of Arizona to-day, cause mysterious sounds in the air, hypnotize both men and animals, and invoke spirits who would instantly appear. Of these things the credulous missionary friars believed them fully capable. What wonder, then, that they were regarded by the natives with a mixture of terror and respect ?

The esoteric details of the secret ceremonies and doctrines of Nagualism have never been fully revealed, and it is only from scattered passages in the writings of the Spanish missionary friars that we can throw any light on this mysterious secret society.

The Mysteries of Mithra which seem to have attracted the attention of the West in the later days of the Empire, were, of course, of Persian origin, and so far as their beginnings are concerned only scanty notices are vouchsafed us. Indeed we may say that a couple of lines in Plutarch embrace all that is explicit in this regard. Arising out of the Mithraic religion of sun-worship, and from the very cradle of the Aryan race, they appear to have survived many centuries. Indeed the Mithraic religion became in some respects the military faith of the Roman legions, especially those which were stationed on the Caledonian Wall and on the Rhine. By the second century the Mithraic rites had achieved a strong hold on southern Italy. Its moral sanction was very high, and it had not had to struggle with influences so cosmopolitan as had the faith of Egypt. In its theology the elemental powers and heavenly bodies received divine honours. The fire blazed constantly upon its altars, the sun and moon are nearly always displayed on them. Probably its astrological doctrine had been introduced from Chaldæa, and certainly did nothing to aid its higher aspects, and so far as its divine figures were concerned Mithra seems to have been the only one which profoundly affected the religious imagination of Europe.

His myth was connected with the chase and slaughter of the mystic bull. Where, when, and how this particular incident in Mithraic mythology became associated with the religion of the god it would be difficult to say. It would seem that Mithra is the sun and that the bull is nothing but the earth. In certain bas-reliefs ears of corn are seen shooting from the tail of the dying beast, and his blood gives birth to the vine which yields the sacred juice consecrated in the Mysteries. This appears to have an extraordinary resemblance to a similar Druidic myth which can scarcely be altogether fortuitous. The Isle of Britain was, we know, regarded by the Druids as the enclosure of the sacred white bull, and white bulls were annually sacrificed at the foot of the oak-tree in order that their blood should refresh it. It is significant that the bull symbolized what might be described as " the nettle of the pasture " in Europe as well as in Egypt and Persia. Its slaughter is the allegory of the succession of decay and fructifying power in physical nature, and the guarantee of a final victory over evil and death.

The Mysteries of Mithra could only be experienced after many rites of cleansing and trial. St. Jerome has preserved for us the seven grades through which the neophytes rose to full communion. They were " Corax, Cryphius, Miles, Leo, Perses, Heliodromus, and Pater." According to Porphyry, the first three stages were merely preliminary to complete initiation, and only the Lions were full and real communicants. Admission to each succeeding grade was accompanied by a wealth of symbolism. It was said that the neophyte, blindfold and bound, was obliged to pass through flame, and that he had to take part in an imaginary murder. In any case there seem to have been tests of courage and honour.

I could write at great length of savage mysteries in America, Africa, and Australia, but I have already partly covered this ground in the chapter dealing with " The Origin of the Mysteries," and space will not permit of further elaboration. But for all the practical purposes of analogy those cults which were more nearly germane to that of Egypt have been described, and this must suffice.

CHAPTER IX

THE RITUAL OF THE MYSTERIES

THE Egyptian Mysteries were divided into two phases, the Lesser and the Greater. The first were associated with the cult of Isis, and the second with that of Osiris. In Ptolemaic times there may have been a still further phase, that connected with the cult of Serapis, a god peculiarly sacred to the dynasty of the Ptolemies, and who, from an amalgamation of Osiris and the Bull Apis, came to have an individuality of his own. From Apuleius we know that the Mysteries of Isis constituted the lesser phase, while those of Osiris composed a higher initiation. He also speaks of the third stage, that of Serapis, but whether or not that signified a still loftier plane of knowledge we have no direct means of knowing.

Monsieur Foucart, perhaps the best authority on the Eleusinian Mysteries, believes the Lesser Mysteries to have appertained to Isis and the Greater to Osiris. He shows that in Greece we have the analogy of the Eleusinian Mysteries, one of which was sacred to Demeter, who was merely a Hellenized form of Isis, while the other was associated with Dionysus. Diodorus Siculus, too, remarks upon the resemblance, for he says that the initiation of Osiris is the same with that of Dionysus, while the initiation of Isis is similar to that of Demeter, " only the names have been changed." If this be so, then the Lesser and

Greater Mysteries have changed places in the process. Plutarch also states that Orpheus founded the great feasts of the initiation in Attica, and that he had introduced from Egypt the Mysteries of Isis and Osiris which were the same as those of Demeter and Dionysus.

This gives us a definite basis of fact to proceed from, but before elaborating on the subject it will be well to clear the ground so far as one rather difficult question is concerned. How closely were the mystic dramas which enacted the life and death of Osiris, and the history of Isis actually associated with the Mysteries ? Were they merely ancillary to them, were they the subjects of popular and public representation, or did they form part of the Mysteries ? In the first place we must not gain the impression that these sacred dramas were of the nature of mere theatrical representations, with which, indeed, they had little in common. They were, indeed, more of the type of the Mystery plays of mediæval times. According to Clement of Alexandria, the neophytes of the Eleusinian Mysteries beheld the sacred drama of Persephone and Demeter, their wanderings and their sorrows, by the light of torches in the temple at Eleusis, and Proclus assures us that this representation was secret, just as, remarks M. Foucart, " were those of the Mysteries of Osiris." But we know that certain of the Egyptian dramatic representations, according to Herodotus, were not confined to an audience of neophytes alone, but were publicly performed. As we shall see, the researches of M. Moret have established the existence of a secret Osirian drama also.

In this chapter the endeavour is to glean from the various sources available to us the data concerning

the ritual of the Egyptian Mysteries, while in the
tenth and eleventh chapters I hope to digest this in
more orderly form so far as the Lesser and Greater
Mysteries are concerned respectively. M. Foucart is of
opinion that the religion of Osiris was more or less an
allegory of the wheat plant which had a religious
value. He quotes M. George Foucart as saying that
a certain series of monuments which have not so far
drawn a great deal of attention to themselves throw
much light upon this allegory. "In the oldest
catalogue of the British Museum," he says, " Arundale
draws attention to a series figuring the ear of the
wheat. None of the examples which do so are older than
the New Empire, although more primitive forms are to
be found in the Museum at Leyden and elsewhere."

Commenting on this, M. Paul Foucart tells us that
in the texts of the Theban Book known as the *Hours
of the Night* a deity is shown holding in his hand two
beautiful ears of corn called respectively the seed and
the grain, and he believes this to be an allegory of the
life and death of Osiris. I have already pointed out
the connection of Osiris with the grain, and it is
unnecessary to labour the question further. But it is
significant that M. Foucart believes the Osirian grain
allegory to have been associated with the rites and
ceremonies of the second or Osirian degree of
initiation.

The initiation of the Isiacs, he says, is almost
identical with that of Eleusis. In the Romance of
Apuleius, Lucius, after being initiated into the
Mysteries of Isis, does not propose to go further,
until about a year later it is ordained that he be
initiated into the rites of Osiris. He then recognizes
that although the nature and the religion of the two
divinities were so intimately bound up, there was

still a very considerable difference between the two
initiations, just as in the case of the separate but
allied cults of Demeter and Dionysus, although in
this instance the rites of Demeter were regarded as
the Greater.

Let us examine generally the statements of Apuleius.
Lucius, his hero, freed from the magical form of an
ass, and once more enjoying human shape, promises
to devote his life to the goddess Isis. He rents a cell
in the precincts of the temple and becomes a strict
attendant at the daily rites of the goddess. After
a while he is initiated, but not until the goddess herself has called him at the appointed time. It is clear
that the whole act of initiation was regarded as the
death of the Old Man and the birth of the New. After
the morning service the High Priest shows Lucius a
sacred book written in hieroglyphs, from which he
instructs him. He is then baptized by complete
immersion in a bath, and led back to the temple,
where he supplicates the goddess. The High Priest
then acquaints him with certain words of power and
enjoins simple living without butcher meat or wine.
He spends ten days in meditation, after which he
returns to the temple at eventide and receives gifts
from the initiates. Clothed in a linen robe, he is
introduced into the inner part of the temple. More he
refuses to tell us of the Isiac Mysteries, except that
he drew near to the confines of death, was borne
through all the elements and returned to earth again ;
that he saw the sun gleaming at dead of night, that he
approached the superior and inferior gods and
worshipped them face to face ; yet, having said so
much, he assures us that although we have heard
these things we must yet know nothing of them.

Are we then to infer from Apuleius' statement that

he has been speaking to us in the terms of allegory ?
I do not think so. I rather believe that what he does
intend to convey is that he underwent the initiatory
process which he outlines and precisely as he outlines
it, but that no one who has not had a similar experience can comprehend the exact nature of what he
actually saw and passed through ; that just as it has
always been impossible for the religious mystic or the
adept in magic to convey the significance or purport
of his own experiences to others, simply because of
their unique character, Apuleius feels himself in a
similar difficulty, his vow of secrecy notwithstanding.
He tells us, as a traveller might tell us, that he has
passed through certain spheres and seen and heard
certain sights and sounds, but just as that traveller's
lips might be sealed concerning the facts of a visit to a
sacred city, so the lips of Apuleius are similarly dumb
concerning his journey " through all the elements."
In short, he is trying to make us understand that the
Mysteries can only be understood by apprehension.

But it is possible for us to glean something in the
way of information about his journey from the
analogical data concerning the Mysteries of Demeter
at Eleusis, which, we have seen, was nothing more
or less than the Mystery of Isis in a Greek form. He
says, for example, that he " trod the threshold of
Proserpine." This is precisely what the Eleusinian
initiate also did. The Underworld adventures of
Demeter and Kore, which is merely another name for
Proserpine or Persephone, were given dramatic
representation in this Mystery. Says Plutarch :
" The soul at the moment of death receives the same
impression as do those who are initiated into the
Mysteries." He proceeds to say that it must travel
many avenues of hazard, of painful detours through

the shadow-world, until at last a marvellous light appears before it and it approaches a higher sphere.

Dion Chrysostom, Aristides, Himerius, and Proclus all allude to the apparitions which struck the imagination of the initiates in these ceremonies. These mysterious visions, terrifying in their portent, stalked the footsteps of the mystes through the shrine. Elsewhere I have given some indication of how these apparitions may have been induced, either by drugs or by mechanical means. But there is this to add, that as nearly all writers on the Mysteries strongly aver, there was little or no space or equipment for the provision of mechanical or phantasmagorical aids in the Temple of Eleusis, although certain excavators, whom I have quoted, have provided data of a very different nature. I rather prefer to believe that the apparitions seen may have been generated by the long fasting and high state of excitement of the initiate, aided perhaps by the allegorical drama which was proceeding around them, although I am not indisposed to believe in their supernatural origin.

Plato himself has alluded to these apparitions seen in the mystic progress. In a celebrated passage in his *Phœdra* he brings forward the theory of Ideas or of Essences which the soul has contemplated during a former life, and which permit her to preserve the memory of past events. To illustrate what he means, he mentions the apparitions of the Mysteries, and for doing so he has been blamed for revealing that which he should not have done. The passage is taken to mean that the apparitions seen during initiation were of a spiritual character, although appearing in corporeal shape, and that they had reference to the

MYSTERIES BY TORCHLIGHT

The Tyskiewicks Vase, showing the Eleusinian Mysteries.
Demeter (*seated*) and Kore (*with torches*).

mystics' past lives. They were, thinks Foucart, introduced for the purpose of giving to man a direct knowledge of the divine realities, and were imaginary rather than realistic.

There is, perhaps, another allusion to the initiatory rites in Plato's *Phædo*, where he mentions the path taken by the soul descending into the infernal regions as one so highly complicated as to necessitate a guide. I have already mentioned the Orphic tablets, in which the journey of the soul after death is outlined, and the perils of its passage stressed. But to sum up the evidence regarding this, it would seem that the initiates were thought to traverse the lower regions, that they presented themselves before their dark rulers and finally gained the light of more delectable regions. We are strengthened in this assumption by a dialogue which occurs in Lucian, in which one of two deceased persons descending into the shadows of Hades, addresses his fellow-traveller as follows: " Tell me, Cyniscus, thou who hast been initiated into the Mysteries of Eleusis, do you not find that things here resemble those yonder?—Entirely, but see how a woman with torches who advances with a strange and menacing air appears like a Fury." This would seem to make it plain that the first steps of initiation into the Mysteries of Eleusis were mimetic of the passage of the soul through Hades, and that these were based on the Egyptian tradition there is indeed no good reason to doubt.

M. Foucart lays some stress on the similarity of the details vouchsafed by Apuleius regarding the Mysteries of Isis and those of Eleusis, which he states emphatically were derived from Egypt. At the same time, he remarks that differences exist and that these are very considerable. For example, the initiation of the Isiac confraternity does not seem to have taken place at fixed dates, nor were its initiates prepared for their experience in batches. On the contrary, the individual awaited the good pleasure of the goddess to undergo his ordeal. These are highly important differences, and should make us cautious in drawing too free an analogy between the practice of Egypt and that of Eleusis. At the same time it is obvious that Apuleius' mystic hero, Lucius, was by no means an ordinary initiate. His sacerdotal vocation was determined by a formal order from Isis, received during the hours of sleep. M. Foucart stresses the great fervour of Lucius and his prolonged watching and ascetic life; but, frankly, I must admit that I have some doubts as to whether the story actually illustrates the true career of an initiate. The former rather profligate life of Lucius, who certainly seems to have been one of the " bloods " of his day, and the comparatively short period of preparation he underwent seem to me scarcely in consonance with what I believe to have been the very rigid requirements of the exacting priesthood of the Isiac Mysteries. This notwithstand- ing, it may be that the worship of Isis transplanted may not have been of a character so rigid as in its place of origin, that a difficulty may have been experienced in securing the services of likely sup- porters and adherents, and that the obvious repent- ance of Lucius, whose ass-form must surely be regarded as allegorical of the stupidity of the wild career of a boisterous young man, may have struck the priests of Isis as the sign of hopefulness for better things in him. Or the ass-form may be typical of the enemy—Set. In short, where propagandists were required with some urgency personal selection might readily have been of a less rigorous kind, and that the propaganda was forthcoming is proved by the popularity of Apuleius' pseudo-novel.

In his monumental work on *The Cults of the Greek States*, Sir Lewis Farnell has certain objections to offer regarding the supposition that the Eleusinian mystæ proved the terrors of the Underworld. At this period, he remarks, the Greeks were not subject to such terrors. But this is scarcely borne out by the references of Polygnotus and Plato. Again, if they were not general, and accepted, the Mysteries did much to make them so. Mr. Farnell, as most students of Folklore would, reduces the whole process to something resembling the mere " dancing-out " of a myth, and dismisses the allusions to infernal horrors, nor does he believe that stage-machinery was employed or that mystical paintings of the initiation ceremony existed. But it is possible to rebut the first contention on historical grounds, as M. Foucart has done on page 404 of his work, and the vases reproduced in this work and in his own dispose of the second.

From the infernal regions, mimetic or imaginary, the mystæ passed to the fields of light to view those things which the two goddesses had promised to the faithful. Among these were the sacred objects, regarding which, very naturally, we have only a scanty selection of notices. Of these the statues of the two goddesses were an important part. Clement tells us that the password of the Eleusinian Mysteries is as follows : " I have fasted, I have drunk the barley-drink, I have taken things from the sacred chest, having tasted the rock I have placed them into the Kalathos and again from the Kalathos into the chest." The knowledge of this formula seems to have distinguished the initiated. It seems to imply that the mystæ drank of the selfsame cup as Demeter drank

from when breaking her long fast, and the eating by
the communicant of some sacred food, probably
cereals and fruits.

Says Farnell : " When we have weighed all the
evidence and remember the extraordinary fascination
a spectacle exercised upon the Greek temperament,
the solution of the problem is not so remote or so
perplexing. The solemn fast and preparation, the
mystic food eaten and drunk, the moving passion-
play, the extreme sanctity of the objects revealed,
all these influences could induce in the worshipper,
not indeed the sense of absolute union with the divine
nature, such as the Christian sacrament or the
hermit's reverie or the Mænad's frenzy might give,
but at least the feeling of intimacy and friendship
with the deities, and a strong current of sympathy
was established by the mystic contact. But these
deities, the mother and the daughter and the dark
god in the background, were the powers that governed
the world beyond the grave : those who had won their
friendship by initiation in this life would by the
simple logic of faith regard themselves as certain to
win blessing at their hands in the next. And this, as
far as we can discern, was the ground on which
flourished the Eleusinian hope."

This is eloquent, if it be true, of a certain amount
of haziness as to the whole purport of the Mysteries on
the part of the Greek " initiates," and M. Foucart
would seem to agree with this supposition when he
quotes Synesius as saying that Aristotle believed that
the initiates were not obliged to understand but merely
received impressions, and that this resulted in a
certain disposition or mental bias towards mystical
obfuscation. A passage in Plutarch gives a similar
impression.

But it seems to me that most writers on the subject have scarcely realized an important consideration with reference to the Eleusinian Mysteries : to wit, that they were by no means the perfect reflection of the Egyptian Mysteries. As such they must be judged, and the whole atmosphere of dubiety thus surrounding them, the mere statement that it was not necessary to apprehend them, is thus explained away in a word. We observe in this transplanted recension of what was well understood in Egypt a debased and confused general idea of the whole Egyptian process. We observe, too, that here the rites of the god are of less importance and primary to those of the goddess, which is merely the Egyptian practice reversed. If there was doubt in Eleusis there was certainly none at Sais, or elsewhere in Egypt, for dubiety was assuredly not one of the shortcomings of the precise priesthood of Egypt. We must remember, too, that the passage of time, besides having an eroding influence upon those pristine principles which had been originally imported, not to say a distorting influence, would scarcely be friendly to clarity of motive. It is notorious that a priesthood finding itself in difficulties so far as interpretation and elucidation are concerned, falls back either on explanatory myth or on the even less virtuous expedient of plunging intention into the darkness of pseudo-mysticism. That, in my way of thinking, affords a perfect explanation of the haziness which surrounded the significance of the Mysteries at Eleusis, but that it is in any sense true of Egyptian mystical doctrine, I certainly do not believe, having reference, as I have said, to the impeccable character of Egyptian practice. If further proof were needed to buttress this contention, it would be forthcoming most readily from the fragmentary nature of the

Orphic tablets and their merely partial relationship to the material of the Book of the Dead and other Egyptian texts. The fact that the literary reflections of Egyptian mysticism in Greece and Hellenized Sicily are so comparatively obscure is perhaps the best proof we possess that both the ritual and "theological" notions of Eleusis regarding Egyptian thought and practice were equally hazy and fragmentary.

But surely for us Theo of Smyrna's statement that there were five parts of initiation into the Mysteries of Greece will help us in establishing the necessary analogical resemblances with Egypt, if these actually exist. These were Purgation, the Tradition of the Sacred rites, Inspection, the Binding of the Head and Fixing of the Crown, and Friendship with Divinity. But we can see at a glance that this does not carry us far. Of course Theo obviously omits Contemplation, which undoubtedly preceded Purgation, in Greece, as in Egypt.

Previous Contemplation and Purgation can be accepted as unquestioned in the case of both the Greek and Egyptian Mysteries. We may associate with the third part Tradition, a dramatic representation of the life-history or myth of the god. Subsequently sacred objects were revealed, sacred food was eaten, and at the call of the heralds the mystæ underwent ceremonial ablution in the sea or the River Nile. The journey through Hades to the Elysian Fields (or through Amenti to Aalu in the case of the Egyptian Mysteries) then took place, after which the rebirth of Dionysus or Osiris was enacted symbolically, and union with Osiris was achieved by the neophyte.

How, then, does our reconstruction of the " programme " of the Egyptian Mysteries compare with the account of Apuleius ? It will have been seen to consist of : (1) contemplation, (2) purgation, (3) representation of the myth of the god, (4) revelation of the sacred objects, (5) eating of the sacred food, (6) ablution, (7) the journey through Amenti to Aalu, (8) the rebirth of Osiris, (9) and the Union with Osiris.

In the case of " Lucius " we find : (1) contemplation, (2) instruction, (3) purgation by ablution, (4) initiation into words of power, (5) further meditation, (6) passage through the infernal regions, (7) then through the elements, (8) rebirth, (9) communion with the gods.

Our " reconstruction," then, does not altogether agree with the account of Apuleius so far as the incidence of the several phases is concerned. We find certain phases common to both, however : contemplation, purgation, journey through the lower and higher regions, rebirth, communion with the gods. Of the exactitude of these, then, we may feel pretty well assured.

But we have no good reason to doubt that representation of the myth of the god, and the eating of sacred food, also took place, in the later Mysteries at least. Indeed we have the evidence of Herodotus for the first of these. And the evidence of Apuleius as to the initiation into knowledge of words of power is so much in consonance with what we know of Egyptian practice that we can scarcely doubt it.

It seems to me, then, that by a combination of both formulæ we may arrive at the truth. But what the precise incidence of this was and how the several phases were divided between the Lesser and Greater Mysteries of Egypt I must leave for the chapters which deal with these especially, and which now follow.

NOTE.—Heckethorn, in his none too precise book,

Secret Societies, gives an account of initiation into the Mysteries of Isis. From what source he compiled it it is impossible for me to state, but I append it, not so much for what it is worth, as for the sake of completeness and comparison, though there is little or nothing, it seems to me, of probability in its terms : " The candidate, conducted by a guide, was led to a deep, dark well or shaft in the pyramid, and, provided with a torch, he descended into it by means of a ladder affixed to the side. Arrived at the bottom, he saw two doors—one of them barred, the other yielding to the touch of his hand. Passing through it, he beheld a winding gallery, whilst the door behind him shut with a clang that reverberated through the vaults. Inscriptions like the following met his eye : ' Whoso shall pass along this road alone, and without looking back, shall be purified by fire, water, and air ; and overcoming the fear of death, shall issue from the bowels of the earth to the light of day, preparing his soul to receive the mysteries of Isis.' Proceeding onward, the candidate arrived at another iron gate, guarded by three armed men whose shining helmets were surmounted by emblematic animals, the Cerberus of Orpheus. Here the candidate had offered to him the last chance of returning, if so inclined. Electing to go forward, he underwent the trial by fire, by passing through a hall filled with inflammable substances in a state of combustion, and forming a bower of fire. The floor was covered with a grating of red-hot iron bars, leaving, however, narrow interstices where he might safely place his foot. Having surmounted this obstacle, he has to encounter the trial by water. A wide and dark canal, fed by the waters of the Nile, arrests his progress. Placing the flickering lamp upon the head, he plunges into the canal, and swims to the opposite bank, where the greatest trial, that by air, awaits him. He lands upon a platform leading to an ivory door, bounded by two walls of brass, into each of which is inserted an immense wheel of the same metal. He in vain attempts to open the door, when, espying two large iron rings affixed to it, he takes hold of them, but suddenly the platform sinks from under him, a chilling blast of wind extinguishes his lamp, the two brazen wheels revolve with formidable rapidity and stunning noise, whilst he remains suspended by two rings over the fathomless abyss. But ere he is exhausted the platform returns, the ivory door opens, and he sees before him a magnificent temple, brilliantly illuminated, and filled with the priests of Isis clothed in the mystic insignia of their offices, the hierophant at their head. But the ceremonies of initiation do not cease here. The candidate is subject to a series of fastings which gradually increase for nine times nine days. During this period a rigorous silence is imposed upon him, which if he preserve inviolate, he is at length fully initiated into the esoteric doctrines of Isis. He is led before the triple statue of Isis, Osiris, and Horus—another symbol of the sun—where he swears never to publish the things revealed to him in the sanctuary, and first drinks the water of Lethe presented to him by the High priest, to forget all he ever heard in his unregenerate state, and afterwards the water of Mnemosyne, to remember all the lessons of wisdom imparted to him in the mysteries. He is next introduced into the most sacred part of the secret edifice, where a priest instructs him in the application of the symbols found therein. He is then publicly announced as a person who has been initiated into the mysteries of Isis—the first degree of the Egyptian rites."

CHAPTER X

THE RITUAL OF REBIRTH

WE are now far from all analogies, bent, indeed, on recovering the actual formulæ and essence, the rite and thought, of the Mysteries of Egypt.

Here we may receive much assistance from the admirable essay of Professor Alexandre Moret of the Collège de France, whose book, *Mystrès Égyptiens*,[1] has done much to make the ritual of the Mysteries known to us, if it has not effected a great deal in discovering the spirit which animated them. But Professor Moret's method in disclosing the ritual of the Mysteries, which he has pieced together from the merest hints and the baldest references, is so remarkably ingenious and admirably clear that I cannot do better than provide the reader with a brief précis of it.

The Egyptian Mysteries, he believes, were reserved to a body of élite priests and spectators and celebrated in isolated buildings on certain dates. The Egyptians referred to their ceremonies as *Seshtaou* and *Akhout*, which in a vague sense mean " things sacred, glorious, or profitable." The rites were associated with words and gestures, with things said and acted. As Iamblichus has it, things were done which it is impossible to describe in words, and others represented allegorically, as nature expresses visible reasons through

[1] *Mystères Égyptiens*, new edition, Paris, 1927.

visible forms—symbolic acts, more efficacious than
prayer or the recital of formulated dogmas. It is the
inexplicable power of symbols which conveys the
intelligence of divine things.

That is to say, certain mimetic acts and allegories,
by dint of sympathetic magic, are more efficacious
than prayer or dogma.[1]

" Isis," says Plutarch, " did not desire that the
combats and trials which she had suffered, and in
which all the signs of her courage and wisdom
appeared, should be forgotten in silence. She therefore instituted the most holy Mysteries in which the
scenes and representations of her sufferings were
mimetically presented, in order that they might serve
as a lesson of piety and consolation to men and women
who might pass through the same tests." In effect, the
death and resurrection of Osiris were enacted partly
in open air and before the public, partly in the
interior of the temples, the chapels of Osiris. There
were thus two species of Mysteries, the public,
resembling the Mystery Plays of European
mediæval times, and those which were secret or
arcane.

The drama of the death of Osiris was celebrated on
the first of the month Pachons. The Pharaoh took
the part of Osiris, god of vegetation. He cut a branch
of herbs, and sacrificed a white bull, sacred to Min,
god of fecund energy. This bull was a form of Osiris,

---

[1] There is, of course, a perfectly sound anthropological as well as
a mystical reason for this. The mimetic or symbolical act, arising
out of the tribal dance or totemic (or pre-totemic) rite is of greatly
older sanction than prayer or dogma, and is therefore more powerful.
Mere rite precedes myth, and its outward meaning is usually lost,
therefore it becomes " mystical." Vague " powers," of which it is
impossible to posit any myth, precede gods in human belief, and
when " the gods arrive " in the full panoply of historical mythology
the mythless " powers " and their storyless symbolism come to
possess all the sanctity of mystery.—L. S.

and in the 22nd Thot another mystery was enacted descriptive of that god's resurrection.[1]

But in the intervals of these public ceremonies were enacted the secret Mysteries. All that had been celebrated in public described the life-history of Osiris. There followed in private, and in the interior of the sanctuary, the rites which assured the resurrection of the god. In the times of the Ancient Empire they were known as " the sacred rites, celebrated in conformity with the secret book of the acts of the officiants," the *Herj Seshta,* or the Chief of the Mysteries *par excellence.*[2]

Each god and cult had its own " mystery," but the funeral mysteries were described as " the things of Abydos," as Iamblichus states.

In the great Ptolemaic temples, at Edfu, Dendereh, and Philæ, the very chambers in which the Mysteries were enacted have been found. They are placed in a part of the temple to which entrance was difficult or forbidden to the public. At Philæ, for example, there was a little temple of Osiris composed of two chambers on the roof of the edifice, yet the rites are inscribed in hieroglyphs on the architrave of the pronaos.

Usually the sculptured scene shows a statue of Osiris enveloped in a funeral shroud, a bed on which the divine mummy is extended, and various accessories, crowns, sceptres, arms, vases full of holy water for the libations, jars of incense and myrrh for fumigations. The dramatis personæ is composed of priests who play the parts of the Osirian family, Shou and Geb, the father and grandfather of Osiris, Horus, his son, Anubis and Thoth, his brothers, the children of

---

[1] This was the drama as described elsewhere in allusion to the *stele* of the priest Ikhernofret.

[2] He appears to have worn the dog-headed mask of Anubis.

Horus, the goddesses Isis and Nephthys, wife and sister of Osiris, and other goddesses, who play the parts of mourners. Beside them stand officiating priests who recite the formula, the " chorus," so to speak—the officiant, who recites the texts, the servitor who performs the rites of libation and fumigation and who employs the magical instruments, the prophet who attends to the libations and the Great Seer, the acknowledged visionary of the god.

The texts lay stress on the fact that during the twelve hours of the day and twelve hours of the night a separate guard is maintained. The holy corpse is guarded both by night and day, in order that nothing evil may approach. The secret drama is composed of twenty-four scenes, one for each hour of the day, and it commences on the first hour of the night (six o'clock according to our computation) and concludes on the last hour of the day following (five to six o'clock). It advances by stages to the resurrection of the god. Each hour was treated separately as containing a complete and self-contained drama.[1]

At the beginning of each hour the guardian god of the hour enters with his train, and enacts his appropriate rite. In the middle of the hour he cries : " Rise, Osiris, thou art triumphant over thine enemies." Despite this cry of victory Isis is unceasing in her lamentations. The acts, as a whole, may be briefly described as follows, so far as we are acquainted with them :

Isis and Nephthys lament the death of Osiris in eloquent terms, the former recounting how she has traversed land and sea and Hades to find him. She entreats the gods and goddesses to join with her in

---

[1] The appropriate references for these ceremonies are given by M. Moret throughout.

mourning, as described in the Berlin Papyrus. The gods then enter the Ouabt or " Pure place," where Osiris lies dead. Horus, Anubis, and Thoth are the principal actors in this scene. They bear the magical instruments, and the vases of fresh water, incense, and unguents. The rite commences with libations and fumigations. At the sixth hour a Vase of Nile Water, the Noun, or essence of Osiris, intended to recreate him in the name of Ra, the Creator of all things, is sprinkled on his supposed body.

Osiris then passes to heaven, accompanied by his Ka or double, and the officiant exclaims : " the heaven is reunited with the earth," to the accompaniment of a joyful noise on the sistrum of Isis. In the following hour " the Water of earth " is poured in a libation, and in the third hour of the drama the appropriate libation has the effect of making the spirit of the god pass over his country, the place of his birth. " Take the water that thou mayest come to thy country." The subsequent libation of the fourth hour, from Elephantine, refreshes the hearts of the gods. As regards the libations and purgations which follow, research has not as yet confirmed them.

These preliminary rites accomplished, the gods execute on the body of Osiris a series of miracles. The first is the reconstitution of the body of the god, who has been dismembered by Set. Isis and Nephthys have recovered each divine fragment, they place in order the skeleton, they purify the flesh, they reunite the separate members. The head is reconnected with the body. Isis and Horus perform magnetic passes to recall the soul.

The mystery following is that of the revivified body, restored by the holy water which gives life and strength, with oils and ointments one by one. The

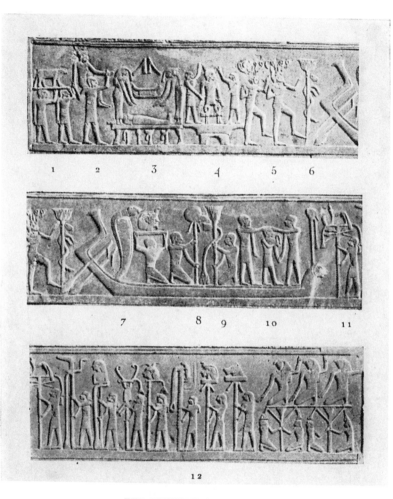

THE MYSTERY OF REBIRTH

From Stele C. 15. in the Louvre.

(1) Animal to be sacrificed. (2) The Tikenou. (3) Isis and Nephthys making incantations. (4) Reconstitution of the body. (5) Crowned dancers. (6) Flaying of the sacrificed animal. (7) The uræus (?) crown in the barque. (8) The Symbol of the Tikenou under the skin. (9) The skin exhibited. (10) The dead Osirian reborn. (11) Anubis (?) and the *shedshed*. (12) The gods hail the reborn Osiris.

Great Magician touches each organ with the magical instruments. At the fourth hour of the day it is supposed that the mummified Osiris is interred at Busiris. In this act is depicted the mystery of his vegetal rebirth, that is to say, the rebirth of the god in the sense of his annual reappearance as the corn-plant. In the same hour it is announced that Osiris has another grade of rebirth, the animal. Animal victims are sacrificed at the gate of the *Ouabt*. Their skin is regarded as that of Set, the enemy, which serves as a shroud in which to wrap Osiris. It is the " cradle " of skin (*Meskhent*) in or through which the god is reborn as a child or an animal.

" I salute thee," cries Isis, " behold thy meskhent, the house where the divine Ka renews its life." The skin is that of a cow, and Nut, the cow-goddess of the heavens, mother of Osiris, is thus evoked. Osiris is extended on the skin and his mother Nut comes to speak with him, and conjures him to arise.

The god who presides over these rites is Anubis, who bears the symbol of the nebride, the skin of a beast attached to a stake. Anubis " passes over " the holy couch or skin. He assumes the attitude of the fœtus in the womb, thus hoping by sympathetic magic to render efficacious the simulacrum of gestation in the case of the god. Horus follows him, in the name of his father, upon another skin-cradle, the *Shedshed.*[1]

On the sixth hour of the day it is announced that " the mother Nut has conceived," and to attest the resurrection a pillar is erected, the dad, the " fetish " of Osiris, as described in the ceremony of Ikhernofret.

At midday Osiris is resuscitated, that is, at the time when the sun is at its height. The Pharaoh then

---

[1] In the later formulæ only, not in those of the Old Kingdom.

approaches in person, bearing offerings. At the twelfth hour (five to six) the rites conclude. Lamps are lit to drive away evil spirits, and the doors are opened, with pæans of joy. Osiris has regained the holy word, the ma-khrou, of the demiurgos, which is capable of protecting him against all evil, all dangers, all difficulties. He sojourns in peace in his arcane temple.

Very great importance, thinks M. Moret, attaches to the rite of animal rebirth. Here, indeed, we can display one of the most mysterious " secrets " of the Egyptian rites, and one of which the monuments tell us but little. In theory it is the dead himself who renews his life in passing through the skin of the victim. The monuments show the dead, or the initiate himself, performing this rite. Ordinarily, throughout the ages, the passage through the skin is confined to the officiants, or to human victims or animals.

There were, indeed, several varieties of this ceremonial episode. The original theme appears to have been on the following lines : a human victim or victims were strangled in order that their spirits might restore the dead to life. In the earliest period the human victims were actually regarded as the representatives of Set, the enemy of Osiris. Later, prisoners of war, Ethiopians generally, were substituted as the victims, and, at a period more civilized, animals were substituted for men—bulls, gazelles, or the pig, which was the beast symbolic of Set, although the ceremony was invariably carried out in imitation of a human sacrifice. Indeed, they caused men or dwarfs to pass through the skin of the sacrificed bull or gazelle.

In these ceremonies there was always one salient human figure, the Tikenou, who was dragged on a

THE TIKENOU

Above—Isis draping the Tikenou.
Below—The Tikenou leaving the naos.

wooden sledge before the skin of the sacrificed beast.
A hole was dug in the earth, and the skin, the thigh,
and the heart of the bull, as well as the hair of the
Tikenou were cast into it and burned, as a sacrifice
of the part for the whole.   Through the flame the
simulacrum of the man and the skin of the victim rose
to heaven.

It was believed to be Anubis who had revealed to
gods and men the means of rebirth defined by the
rituals as " the passing through the skin-cradle " for
the benefit of Osiris.   This rite appears to have been
in use in the period of the Old Kingdom.   In that
period the Tikenou shares the solar barque with the
corpse.   Under the New Empire the Tikenou is found
occupying the victim's sledge.   He is now no longer
covered with a skin, but by a long sheet or shroud,
which is sometimes speckled like a beast's skin.   In
some scenes even Isis wears the painted shroud of the
Tikenou in the funeral cortège.[1]   The figure is, indeed,
the simulacrum of the foetus resting in the womb.

Arrived at the tomb, the Tikenou took part in a
rite which consisted of lying on a low bed in the
attitude alluded to above.   This, then, is the magical
process invented by Anubis, the substitution of an
act of sympathetic magic for the act of sacrifice.
The Tikenou, acting the part of a human embryo,
issues from the painted skin-sheet as an infant
newly born.

At a still later time the rôle of the Tikenou dis-
appears and is taken by one of the officiants.   The
rite was simplified by that person merely lying on a
couch, clothed in the shroud, and appearing to sleep.
But the effects of this slumber were not less miracu-

[1] The shrouded figure of the Tikenou resembles too closely that
of the initiate as given in the vase paintings of Eleusis for the likeness to be fortuitous. Compare pictures facing pages 214 and 220.

lous, for, on awaking, the officiant spoke the words :
" I have seen my father (Osiris) in all his transformations." The transformations in question were
into locusts, bees, and lastly into a shadow. When
the officiant rose he was believed to bring back with
him " the shadow of the skin-shroud," that is to say,
the reborn soul of the dead, and also of the locusts
and the bees, which bear witness, as in the legend of
Aristæus, that the skin has been fecundated, gener-
ating living beings which fly away with a new life.
As to the body, it does not die any more. Soul and
body are reborn for the life eternal.[1]

All this, thinks M. Moret, is of exceedingly ancient
origin, indeed he believes it to be prehistoric. The
shroud Osiris wears is a development of that of the
Tikenou. Rebirth, too, came to be associated with
an object known as the *shedshed*, which seems to have
been a vehicle by which the soul mounted to heaven,
and which was in some manner associated with the
skin-cradle, as was the *meskhent* if, indeed, it was not
the skin-cradle. Many other skins, besides that of the
cow, also did duty as skin-cradles, for example that
of the cynocephalus ape and the panther or leopard.
The dead man is pictured in the solar barque in
juvenile form as a reborn youth with an inflated skin
floating behind. In this picture M. Moret believes
the artist to have represented the rites of the Mysteries
in a manner so discreet that they might not be
divulged to the profane. " These figures," he says,
" give, to the eye alone, the ancient processes of
initiation of which the texts say nothing."

---

[1] The bee is also found in the Greek Mysteries. The Thriæ,
nurses of Apollo, had the properties of bees, and honey was part of
the sacred diet of the initiates. The priestesses of Demeter are
alluded to as " bees," and a bee-woman, wearing an Egyptian wig,
is pictured on an embossed plate from Camiros. The bee in Medi-
terranean lore is the arisen soul, as is the butterfly in Celtic legend.

CHAPTER XI

RECONSTRUCTION OF THE MYSTERIES

BUT, M. Moret asks, were the living unable to profit by the Mysteries for their earthly good and to safeguard their future life ? The answer, he thinks, is not easy to find. The rites of the Mysteries applied in the main to the Pharaoh.

The name of the jubilee called *Sed* signifies " Feast of the queue." The Pharaoh wore a false queue attached to his waist-belt. This was the remnant, so to speak, of the skin-cradle, and the *sed* is merely a corruption of *seshed* or *shedshed*, the vehicle of the soul's transportation to heaven. The royal jubilee was then the celebration of the mystery of the skin, the sign of the initiate after he had perfected the rites, a symbol of initiation.

An example of much the same kind is to be found in the Hindu Vedic rituals. At the ceremony of the Diksa, or deification of a human being celebrated by the Vedic priests, a shed was built for the use of the sacrificiant, and he was given the skin of a black antelope. The shed symbolized the matrix, the skin the fœtal membrane, and a belt the umbilical cord. Lustrations of water symbolized the seminal fluid, and a ceremony resembling that of the reborn Osiris, in which unguents and oils were applied to the several membranes, was gone through. The Diksa is, indeed, the drama of a second birth, a regeneration which makes the man a god, a last initiation.

Now in the feast of the *Sed* we find the same formulæ, the construction of an edifice, the applications of lustration, unction, passage through a skin, and so forth. But was this rite exclusively the privilege of the King ? Was it after death only that the initiate underwent the rites which assured rebirth ? We know that one Oupouatouaa " passed through the skin " by the especial favour of his royal master at Abydos. The official in question was alive at the time of his initiation, but it was obvious that, at the period he speaks of, the rite was very rarely administered. Was his initiation complete ? Were there indeed, degrees of initiation ? The circumstance that in the Græco-Roman period complete initiation was granted in the Mysteries of Isis and that these included rites of a simulated death and rebirth render it most probable that Oupouatouaa had been admitted to the last degrees of initiation then known. Perhaps we may consider as " perfect initiates " those few men who vaunt in their epitaphs the fact that they are " a perfect *akhou,* one fortified, knowing the formulas," or " who knows all the secret magic of the Court." Those were initiates while living. The others did not become so until after death and the funeral rites of Osiris had made them so. One phrase frequently found in inscriptions of the New Empire is *ouhem ankh,* " He who renews his life," that is, the reborn through initiation.

The rebirth after death by means of magical rites, the most important of which is that of the skin, is, thinks M. Moret, the *raison d'être* of the Osirian Mysteries. The certainty of eternal survival is the result of initiation. The monuments of the Ancient Empire reveal to us the process of initiation conferred on the living king in the *Sed* festival and on the dead

king in the funeral rites. The secret rites are epitom-
ized in the " mystery of the skin." Guided by the
dog-deities Sed, Anubis, and Ouapouatou (the two
latter the gods of the skin), the king, or an officiant
called *Iounmoutef*, who is dressed in a skin, passes
from rebirth to the heavens on an object, the *shedshed*, which was a skin, become by fashion or conven-
tion a vestment, a shroud or a fillet, once the skin of
the sacred Nut cow, the symbol of the Great Mother
of birth. The very skins themselves, in the end,
became the heavenly cities of Out, Meska, Kenemt,
and Shedt !

Let us now review M. Moret's interesting description
of the Mysteries. Not only will this give us grounds
for the consideration of the views of the official
Egyptologist, but it will provide us with an excellent
means of comparison with our own conclusions.

Summarized, M. Moret's conclusions are as follows :

The Egyptian Mysteries were the preserve of a
body of priests specially set apart for the purpose of
their celebration.

They were rites associated, some with words and
gestures impossible of description in words, while
others were of the nature of acted allegory, the death
and resurrection of Osiris.

The spirit which governed them was that of
sympathetic magic. They were celebrated, in conformity with the secret Book of the Acts of the
Officiants, in the most secluded part of the
temple.

Priests played the part of the Osirian family, and
were assisted by a priestly chorus and other officials
who recited the texts and undertook the magical acts,
libations, and fumigations.

The sacred drama was composed of twenty-four

scenes, each of which was acted at a special hour of the night or day set apart for it.

These acts were gradually directed to the restoration of life of the god Osiris, and consisted of refreshment by libation and asperging, fumigation to drive off evil influences, the restoration of the body by placing its several members together, the treatment of them by magical instruments, the purification of the flesh, and magnetic passes to recall the soul.

Then followed the mysteries of the rebirth of Osiris in his vegetal and animal forms. In the latter phase cows are sacrificed and their skins serve as shrouds or " skin-cradles " through which the god may be reborn as the son of his mother Nut, the cow-goddess of the sky.

Anubis stretches himself on the skin in the hope that by example, or sympathetic magic, he may induce Osiris to do likewise and thus undergo rebirth. The mother Nut, in the form of the " skin-cradle," then conceives, and to attest the resurrection of the god the *dad* or pillar-symbol of Osiris is raised up.

At an early period of Egyptian history the victim was evidently a human being, and somewhat later his place was taken by the Tikenou, a man or dwarf wrapped in a shroud painted like a cow-skin. This person enacted the part of a human embryo or fœtus, issuing from the skin-shroud as an infant newly born. Still later, the part of the Tikenou was taken by the officiant, who slept and awakened, bringing back with him the shadow or reborn soul of the dead Osiris.

Rebirth was also associated with an object known as the *shedshed*, a vehicle by which the soul of Osiris mounted to heaven, and which was connected with the *meskhent* or skin-cradle.

ASPECTS OF THE TIKENOU

Above—The Tikenou being drawn in procession.
Below—(*left*) The simulacrum enveloped in its shroud.
(*right*) The attitude of the Tikenou and the animal victim compared.

At the royal jubilee of the *Sed*, a similar ceremony was gone through, a hut representing the matrix of Nut, and rebirth taking place therefrom. An example of a similar ceremony is discovered in Vedic ritual.

It is certain that these rites were applied to the living as well as to the dead. Those who underwent them while living were the initiates of the Mysteries. The initiate was thus the lineal descendant of the early victim.

Now how far do these conclusions agree with those already put forward in the ninth chapter? We find nothing here of contemplation or purgation, although these may reasonably be inferred. Nor do we discover the phases of revelation of the sacred objects or eating of the sacred food. The journey through Amenti to Aalu is awanting, although we find the representation of the myth of the god, and the ceremony of rebirth.

Nor do they altogether agree with the ceremonial as described by Apuleius, where initiation into words of power and meditation and passage through the infernal regions and the elements are distinctly referred to. Again, they do not in any way allude to the spectacle of Osiris displayed, or communion with the gods. In a word, the most " spiritual " portion of the Mysteries is ignored.

I believe these discrepancies to have arisen from two considerations. In the first place, M. Moret has undoubtedly given us a restoration of the Mysteries as they were celebrated at a comparatively early period. Indeed he makes that plain. There is nothing here much later than the Eighteenth Dynasty, or about 1600 years prior to the account of Apuleius. From this it must be manifest that the Mysteries had generations to develop from the early forms he describes to those formulated by Apuleius.

Again it is clear that the one actual rite of the Mysteries to which M. Moret refers at all is that of rebirth. This, according to Apuleius, was included in the Lesser Mysteries, and we have seen that the Lesser Mysteries of Eleusis consisted almost entirely of a representation of the death and rebirth of Dionysus, the Greek form of Osiris. These facts make it clear, to me at least, that at the comparatively early period of which M. Moret writes only that phase of the Mysteries which dealt with rebirth had as yet been invented. The Greater Mysteries had yet to be developed, and as for those of Serapis, or the third phase, we know these were deliberately invented by Ptolemy with the aid of Greek and Egyptian priests. It is thus obvious that it is merely with a rite of rebirth that M. Moret has been dealing.

A point of some difficulty here presents itself, and it is complicated by the relatively late nature of the information we possess. Were the Lesser Mysteries actually those of Isis and the Greater those of Osiris ? The rite of rebirth, as we have seen, was the one mystery known in early times, associated, at least, with Osiris and Isis. It circles almost exclusively round the figure of Osiris, yet, we know, it came to be in later ages regarded as the Lesser Mystery, and the Lesser Mystery is invariably identified with the name and cult of Isis.

My own opinion is that as time proceeded the personality of Isis began to bulk so largely that it overshadowed, so far as this rite was concerned, that of Osiris. He lay silent and recumbent on his couch, a passive actor, while she carried out the principal part and by her loud lamentations attracted most attention, drawing, too, most interest and affection to herself as the pious wife and mother. Plutarch makes it plain that in his day she was regarded as the chief protagonist of the Mysteries, their institutor and instructress.

Again, when, at a later date, a more spiritual ideal of the Mysteries came to be adopted, that would unquestionably be associated with Osiris, the great lord of the Otherworld, the place of souls. From the consideration of this more exalted outlook, the Greater Mysteries, in my opinion, arose.

We therefore know very much more, from Egyptian sources, and through the researches of M. Moret, regarding the Lesser, or what afterwards came to be known as the Isiac Mysteries, than we do regarding the Greater or Osirian Mysteries.

What, precisely, do we know about the Greater Mysteries of Egypt ? The Coffin Texts and the Book of the Dead obviously refer merely to variants of the rebirth formula ; the passage of the King over the Lily Lake and his subsequent arrival in the City of the Sun are clearly associated with the Osirian rebirth and the " skin-cradle," although they do not allude to it. It seems, indeed, to have been in itself associated with the solar barque, wherein we see it, and it may be that it was the *shedshed,* a species of flying-carpet, magically aspiring to the sky, as the skin of the sky-dwelling cow-mother well might aspire by dint of sympathetic magic.

I believe we glean more concerning the Greater or Osirian Mysteries from comparison with those of Eleusis than from any other source. Hades and Persephone are, in reality, none but Osiris and Isis in another form. It matters little that Demeter, the great mother, plays the chief part here, for, after all, hers was a local myth associated with the imported and older one. Besides, the interpolation of the

" Iacchos " incident renders the whole atmosphere doubly Osirian. From the complex and obscure mass it is not indeed very difficult to restore the outlines of the Osirian myth and therefore of the Greater Mysteries. Here, indeed, we have the shadow of the myth of Osiris and Isis much more veridically projected than in the early rite of rebirth as reconstructed by M. Moret, which, indeed, reflects little of the myth of these deities as Plutarch has bequeathed it to us. The wanderings of Demeter in search of Persephone are merely those of Isis in search of Osiris, the birth of the holy child Bromios is that of Horus. Moreover, the whole had the same " agricultural " significance as did the myth of Osiris.

I believe, therefore, that we can reconstruct the Egyptian Mysteries as they were known in later times somewhat after the following manner.

The Lesser Mysteries, or the Mysteries of Isis :

These consisted in :

(1) Preparation.

(2) Instruction by the high priest in the secrets of " the Secret Book of the Acts of the Officiants," containing the " words of power."[1]

(3) The rite of baptism.

(4) Ten days spent in ascetic meditation outwith the temples.

(5) Introduction into the heart of the sanctuary, clothed in the linen robe, " evolved " in course of time from the skin-shroud.

(6) The performance of the Osirian drama during twenty-four hours, 6 p.m. to 5 p.m. on the following day, during which the neophyte experienced the

---

[1] See Virey, *Religion*, p. 278 ; Moret, *Au temps de Pharaons*, p. 218.

various rites associated with the mimic birth of Osiris. The later stage of this at the period of Apuleius, included a progress through Amenti to Aalu and " through the elements," and the vision of the gods Osiris and Isis face to face, that is, union with the gods.

M. Moret, in his *Kings and Gods of Egypt*, has a passage concerning the Mysteries which is so pregnant with significance that I make no apology for quoting it in full.

" Was the descent into Hell in the Holy Vigil interpreted in the same way as by the Egyptian ?[1] Was the neophyte, like the Egyptian dead, called before an Osirian tribunal, and was his conscience weighed in the balance against Justice and Truth ? The texts suggest no answer, but the tribunal in the Nether World was a theme often treated by the Roman poets, especially Virgil, Horace, and Ovid. It must also have been familiar to the Isiacs, be it only through the Roman channel. Besides the megarum of Pompeii affords, in favour of this hypothesis, a valuable testimony : the presence, among the plaster reliefs found there, of the " Devourer," the Egyptian monster, which devours the guilty cast out by the Osirian Justice. May we not infer that the tribunal of Osiris was one of the scenes or pictures shown to the initiate ? As to the secrets confided to him by the priest, they were perhaps the powerful formulæ which facilitated the deceased Egyptian in his justification. Furthermore, the ethical standard of the worshippers of Isis, according to Plutarch and Apuleius, their observance of a temperate life, their love of fair dealing, their thirst for truth, are all merits likewise advanced by the deceased Egyptian

---

[1] That is, in Roman times.

as claims to a favourable verdict from the Osirian tribunal.

" The neophyte, exalted by ten days of fasting and meditation, was probably less sensitive to the puerile mimicry or the conventional stagery of the rites, than amazed and impressed by the sublime significance of the Osirian death, instrument of redemption, promise of immortality. Besides, the surroundings now become more cheerful. Leaving the dismal crypt, where he had experienced the pangs of death, he was introduced to another chamber, where Isis, clad in white raiment, sparkling with jewels, welcomed him maternally. Suddenly a disc of beaming rays illuminated the room. Lucius ' saw at dead of night the sun glowing with splendour.' It is indeed in the bosom of the Sun Ra, in the Solar Barge that the Egyptians located their supreme Paradise. Osiris himself, united with the sun, became one with the star whose daily death and rebirth are another symbol of human destiny. At this stage of the initiation, the neophyte, first identified with Osiris, then with Ra, ' was borne through all the elements and approached the gods above and the gods below.' So did the blessed Egyptian, who in the other world ' adored the morning sun, the moon, the air, the water, and fire.' Perhaps the initiate was shown, from the Sacred Books, the journeyings of the Solar Barge ; perhaps he was supposed to wander through the twelve Elysian reigons that correspond to the twelve hours of the night. This would explain the twelve sacerdotal robes that he puts on during the course of his initiation. We learn from Porphyrius that ' the souls in passing through the spheres of the planets put on, like successive tunics, the qualities of those stars.' Be that as it may, the neophyte, his initiation over, is supposed to be absorbed into the Sun Ra as was Osiris, as were all the Egyptian dead ; when he reappears before the people, his head is crowned with a halo of rays, like unto the Sun Ra."

The Greater Mysteries, or the Mysteries of Osiris :

I believe these, from the analogy of the Greater Mysteries of Eleusis, and because of the decidedly agricultural character of the drama of the passion of Osiris, as enacted at Sais, to have been associated with the allegory of the corn-plant. St. Hippolytus, we will remember, refers to the exhibition of an ear of wheat in silence. The myth of Iacchos or Bacchus (" the stranger ") in the Greater Mysteries at Eleusis is, indeed, the transported myth of Osiris as celebrated at Sais. Accepting this, then, and comparing the two rituals, we get the following progression of events :

(1) The wanderings and lamentations of Isis (like those of Demeter for Persephone).

(2) The finding of the body of Osiris.

(3) The " reconstitution " or rebirth of the god as the corn-plant.

Round these particular ideas I believe the Greater Mysteries to have been crystallized. The myth or allegory of Osiris in the Greater Mysteries was the basis of a still greater comprehension of the nature of the god, of his creation, of the fact that he sustained man, that man's flesh was mystically his, made so through communion by the material link of the pabulum of corn or wheat. The ancient Mexicans called their maize-god " Maize-god—*of our flesh*." In such a manner did the Egyptians regard Osiris. But the Greater Mysteries did not possess a merely material aspect only. Their central and fundamental lesson was that just as the body existed and was nurtured by the god, so was the soul. They composed, like the Christian rite of Holy Communion, an admission and comprehension that there existed a mystical and spiritual bread greater and more efficacious than all earthly pabulum, the bread of the spirit. This and this alone was the central idea of the Greater Mysteries of Egypt.

CHAPTER XII

ILLUSION AND PHANTASMAGORIA IN THE MYSTERIES

THE most extraordinary statements are encountered in the pages of the writers of
antiquity regarding the marvels, mechanical
and otherwise, which the exponents of the Egyptian
and other mysteries are said to have introduced into
their ceremonies with the object of heightening the
atmosphere of occult terror which they inspired. The
initiate, we are told, after undergoing a preliminary
course of instruction and preparation found himself
in a region of obscurity as profound as that of the
infernal regions, broken only by occasional flashes of
light, by the aid of which he caught glimpses of
monstrous phantoms and awful spectres. From
gloomy corners proceeded the hissing of serpents and
the howling of wild beasts, prolonged and rendered
more horrid by reverberating echoes.[1]

Suddenly the scene was brilliantly illuminated, the
earth trembled, shook as if in earthquake, and the
pictures and statues by which the novice was surrounded became animated, speaking and admonishing
him. The spirits of the dead approached him, but
shrank from his touch, thunder rolled, lightnings
flashed, and scenes of terror multiplied themselves
before the eyes of the horror-stricken neophyte. At

[1] Salverté, *The Philosophy of Magic*, Vol. I, p. 238.

last the gods appeared and he bent in fear and trembling before their awful presence.

How much of truth and what proportion of imagination is combined in these accounts it is of course now impossible to say. But that the protagonists of the mysteries employed mechanical and other adventitious aids to enhance the effect of the secrets they propounded and the dramatic allegories they unveiled is certain enough. The drama, the theatric sense, is unquestionably one of the most fitting channels for the appropriate presentation of mystical and symbolical truth. This is a circumstance so little understood and appreciated by the uninitiated that it is frequently confounded with mere charlatanism. Yet many of the most adept among the mystics were educated to its use and have from time to time employed the thespian art for the purposes of occult explication. If it does not rank among the higher instruments of arcane science, it is still, when devoutly employed, by no means an unworthy one, and it is a narrow and illiberal attitude which seeks in a shallow spirit of mere levity to scoff at the employment of scenic or theatrical aids to the presentation of mystic truth, and to confuse them with the crudities of empirical hallucination designed towards an unworthy end.

Cassiodorus, a statesman and scholar of the sixth century A.D., refers in his writings to " the science of constructing wonderful machines whose effects seem to overthrow the whole order of nature." Salverté remarks that as his period (1846) was incapable of placing an Egyptian monolith on a pedestal without incredible difficulty, he inferred that the Egyptians were its superiors in mechanical science. He states that in order to descend into the cave of Trophonius

those who came to consult the oracle placed themselves before an aperture apparently too narrow to
admit a middle-sized man, yet as soon as the knees
had entered it, the whole body was rapidly drawn in by
some invisible power. The mechanism used for this
purpose was connected with other machinery which
at the same time enlarged the entrance to the grotto.[1]

Philostratus, in his *Life of Apollonius of Tyana*,
narrates that when the sages of India conducted
Apollonius to the temple of their god, singing hymns
and forming a sacred march, the earth, which they
struck with their staves in cadence, was agitated
like a boisterous sea, and raised them up nearly two
feet, then calmed itself and resumed its usual level.

The Unedited Antiquities of Attica, by the Society
of Dilettanti (London, 1817), contains a curious
passage concerning the remains of mechanism discovered in the temple of Ceres at Eleusis, the theatre
of the celebrated mysteries associated with the name
of that place. Some English travellers who visited
it observed that the pavement of the sanctuary is
rough and unpolished, and much lower than that of the
adjacent portico. They thought, therefore, that it
was probable that a wooden floor, on a level with the
portico, covered the present floor, and concealed a
vault destined to admit of the action of machinery
beneath the sanctuary for moving the floor. In the
soil of an interior vestibule they observed two deeply
indented grooves, or ruts, and as no carriage could
possibly be drawn into this place, the travellers
conjectured that these were grooves intended to
receive the pullies which served in the mysteries
to raise a heavy body, " perhaps," said they, " a
moving floor." In confirmation of their opinion they

[1] Op. cit., Vol. I, p. 248.

perceived further on other grooves, which might have served for the counter-balances to raise the floor; and they also detected places for wedges to fix it and render it immovable at the desired height.   These were eight holes fixed in blocks of marble and raised above the ground, four on the right, and four on the left, adapted to receive pegs of large dimensions.

" Imposture," says Salverté, " always betrays itself. However much the mind of the candidate might have been preoccupied, the creaking of the pullies, the coiling of cordage, the clicking of wheels, and the noise of the machines, must necessarily have struck upon his ear, and disclosed the weak hand of man in those exhibitions which were intended to excite admiration as the work of supernatural powers.   This danger was felt and foreseen, but far from seeking to deaden the sound of the machines, those who worked them studied to augment it, sure of increasing the terror intended to be excited.   The tremendous thunder accompanied with lightning was regarded by the vulgar as the arm of the avenging gods, and the Thaumaturgists were careful to make it heard when they spoke in the name of the gods.

" The labyrinth of Egypt enclosed many palaces so constructed that their doors could not be opened without the most terrific report of thunder resounding from within.   When Darius, the son of Hystaspes, mounted the throne, his new subjects fell prostrate before him, and worshipped him as the elect of the Gods, and as a God himself, and at the same moment, thunder rolled and they saw the lightning flash."

Maimonides, a Spanish-Jewish rabbi of the early thirteenth century, alludes to buildings in which the oracular Teraphim, or angelic images were kept by the Jews.   These, by artificial means, were made to speak, and similar images are mentioned in the writings of the so-called Hermes Trismegistus as being employed by the Egyptians. Casselius, in his *Dissertation sur les pierres vocales ou parlantes*, quotes the scholiast of Juvenal who described the statue of the Memnon as speaking by means of machinery, and this seems to have been derived from the authority of ancient tradition.

In an illuminating chapter in his *New Light on Ancient Egypt*, Sir Gaston Maspero provides us with some interesting details concerning "Egyptian Animated Statues." Nothing, he says, was done without first consulting the gods, and the god, represented by his image, heard the request and tendered his advice by sound, action, or sign. "Their statues especially were privileged to give the answers asked of them, not any sort of statue, but idols made and prepared expressly for that duty. To my knowledge we do not possess any specimen of them ; as far as we can conjecture, they were most often of wood, painted or gilded like the ordinary statues, but made of jointed pieces which could be moved. The arm could lift itself as high as the shoulder or elbow, so that the hand could place itself on an object and hold it or let it go. The head moved on the neck, it bent back and fell again to its place. The legs do not seem to have been jointed, and it is improbable that the complicated business of walking was exacted of them. The statue, now finished in the image of the divinity for whom it provided corporeal form, had to be animated ; the being of whom it was the portrait was evoked for that purpose, and by means of operations still imperfectly known a portion of himself was projected into the wood, a soul, a double, a power which never left it. In this way terrestrial gods were constructed, exact counterparts of the celestial gods, their ambassadors on earth, as it were, capable of protecting, punishing, and teaching mankind, of sending them dreams, of speaking in oracle. When they were addressed, they had recourse to one of two methods, gesture or voice. They took up the word, and pronounced the verdict suitable to the business in hand either in a few words or in a long speech. They moved arms and head to an invariable rhythm. It was not considered miraculous, it was part of every-day life, and consultation of the gods belonged to the usual functions of the chiefs of the state, kings or queens. The monuments present numberless examples, in the great Theban epoch and in the time that followed it."

The images nodded their heads twice to imply agreement, or spoke " in a loud and intelligible voice." In fact priests were set apart for this duty. Their function was not secret, they performed it openly in the sight and with the knowledge of all. " They had their place in the sacerdotal hierarchy, and all the people knew that they pulled the wires so that he (the god) nodded his head at the right moment. It was none of those pious frauds such as we generally suspect in like circumstances."

How, then could such counsels be regarded with confidence ? Simply because the people were brought up to believe that divine souls animated the statues. The priests believed that the hand which made the statues move was itself inspired and animated by a divine and higher power.

" From the nature of some optical wonders displayed in the assumed miracles of the Thaumaturgists," says Salverté, " and in the pompous and terrible representations of mysteries and initiations, we were authorized to conclude that the aid of scientific resources was requisite for carrying them into effect. The ancients were acquainted with the mode of fabricating mirrors, which presented the images multiplied or reversed, and, what is remarkable, in certain positions lost entirely the property of reflecting. It is unimportant whether the latter peculiarity depended solely on sleight-of-hand, or was analogous to polarized light, which reaching the reflecting body, under a certain angle, is absorbed without producing any image. It is very evident that, in either case, the employment of such mirrors was well fitted to give birth to numerous apparent miracles. Aulus Gellius, quoting Varro, informs us of these facts, at the same time he considers the study of such curious phenomena as unworthy the attention of a philosopher. From whatever may have given rise to an opinion so unreasonable, yet so universal, even among the enlightened classes of the ancients, and held by Archimedes himself, its vast advantage to the Thaumaturgists is easily perceived. Had those who, under the enlightened influence of increasing civilization, were the reformers of science, devoted their efforts to the experimental elucidation of phenomena, instead of confining themselves to theoretical inquiries, the miraculous secrets of the charlatan could no longer have merited the name of magic.

" The luxurious gardens, the magnificent palaces, which in the initiations suddenly appeared, from the depths of obscurity, brilliantly illuminated by magic light, or, as it were, by a sun of their own, are reproduced for us in the justly-admired modern invention of the Diorama. The principal artifice lies in the manner of throwing light upon the objects, while the spectator is kept in darkness. This was not difficult, as the initiated hurried from one subterraneous apartment to another, and, being now elevated in the air, and again suddenly precipitated, he might easily imagine himself to be still in the bowels of the earth, from the obscurity of the place that inclosed him, although on the level of the ground. And how, we may enquire, could it happen that the Thaumaturgist, whose whole aim was to discover means of multiplying his wonders, could remain unacquainted with this invention ? Observation was sufficient to reveal it, without any effort of art. If a long gallery was terminated by an arbour of umbrageous trees, and the gallery lighted at one extremity only, the landscape, beyond the arbour, would appear nearer, and display itself to the eye of a spectator like the picture in a Diorama."

Apparitions occasionally appeared in the course of the mysteries. Kircher, in his *Œdipus*, says that: " In a manifestation which must not be revealed . . . there appeared on the wall of the temple a diffusive mass of light, which in becoming concentrated, assumed the appearance of a face evidently divine and supernatural, severe of aspect, but with a touch of gentleness, and very beautiful to look upon. According to the dictation of their mysterious religion, the Alexandrians honoured it as Osiris and Adonis."

" The end of magic," says Iamblichus, " is not to create beings, but to cause images resembling them to appear and soon again to vanish without leaving the slightest trace behind them,"[1] but elsewhere in his essays he censures the employment of such phantasmagoria.

St. Epiphanius, in his *Epistle against the Heretics*,

---

[1] *De Mysteriis.*

accuses the Thaumaturgists of employing powerful drugs to bewitch the senses of the initiates in the mysteries. Plutarch has preserved to us a description of the mysteries of Trophonius, related by a man who had passed two nights and a day in the grotto. They appear to be rather the dreams of a person intoxicated by a powerful narcotic than the description of a real spectacle. Timarches, the bewildered initiate, experienced a violent headache, when the apparitions commenced; that is to say, when the drugs began to affect the senses, and when the apparitions vanished and he awoke from this delirious slumber, the same pain was as keenly felt.

There can be little doubt that belladonna, hemp, opium, and other drugs were employed in the mysteries to heighten their effect on the novice, as is proved by the circumstance that he was frequently plunged into a profound sleep. Such a draught, too, seems to have been that taken by Pausanius when he was initiated into the mysteries at Trophonius. The priests first made him drink from the well of Oblivion, to banish his past thoughts; and then from the well of Recollection, that he might remember the vision he was about to behold. He was then shown a mysterious representation of Trophonius, and forced to worship it. He was next dressed in linen vestments, with girdles around his body, and led into the sanctuary, where was the cave into which he descended by a ladder: at its bottom, in the side of the cave, there was an opening, and having placed his foot in it internally, his whole body was drawn into it by some invisible power. He returned through the same opening by which he had entered, and being placed on the throne of Mnemosyne, the priests inquired what he had seen, and finally led him back to the sanctuary of the Good

Spirit. As soon as he recovered his self-command, he was obliged to write the vision he had seen on a little tablet, which was hung up in the temple.[1]

Indeed there seems to have been no end to the varieties of drugs administered to the initiates in the course of the Mysteries. The Water of Lethe and the Water of Mnemosyne mentioned above could certainly not have been *aqua pura*. Many of those who consulted the oracles seem to have undergone in a lesser degree much the same experiences as those who were initiated into the Mysteries, and indeed some oracles seem only to have been open to consultation by initiates, but yet to have required a species of initiation of their own. Such an oracle seems to have been that of Trophonius, alluded to above, and of which Plutarch writes. He tells us that a certain Timarches, who passed two nights and a day in the grotto, experienced a violent headache when the scenes and apparitions conjured up by the drugs he had taken began to manifest themselves, and when he came out of the visionary state the keen discomfort he felt was in no way abated. Indeed three months after his visit to the grotto of Trophonius he died. Probably the awful experience may have proved too much of a shock for his nervous system, as initiation not infrequently does, or again, the powerful drugs employed may have shattered his health. However this may be, Suidas tells us that those who consulted this particular oracle acquired a melancholy which lasted all their lives. Their visionary sleep ended, they were carried to the gate of the grotto and allowed to regain their senses gradually, when they were presented with a draught in the nature of a restorative.

<hr>

[1] Pausanius, Lib. IX, cap. 39.

The famous hashish which was used by the cult of the Assassins to give their initiates a foretaste of Paradise, is, as most people know, merely an extract of hemp still used in the East to induce pleasing visions. But Salverté seems to think that the Assassins could not have been ignorant of a secret drug which they might have borrowed from Egypt, and which may have been used in the Egyptian mysteries. This was the Stone of Memphis, which is described as a round body of a sparkling colour, about the size of a small pebble. Salverté believes it to have been artificial, and its purpose was to deaden pain.

But perfumes of a powerful odour and penetrative effect seem also to have been employed in some of the Mysteries. In the Orphic Mysteries, for example, a separate perfume was assigned to accompany the invocation of each deity. Indeed the physical and moral action of odours was a very especial study of the ancient Thaumaturgists. Ointments and liniments, too, were certainly employed. In the romance of Achilles Tatius, an Egyptian physician, the cure of Leucippus from an attack of frenzy is mentioned as having been effected by the application of a liniment to the head, and before consulting the oracle of Trophonius the body was rubbed with oil. This was also certainly done in connection with the rites of the Mexican Indians.

Salverté's editor, Dr. A. T. Thomson, adds a curious note on the effect of such ointments, which may or may not have a bearing on certain of the visions seen in the course of the Mysteries. He tells us that when a person is wrapped in sleep induced by such an ointment his dreams are highly coloured by the most adventitious physical circumstances. " If a light is suddenly brought into a room where a person is in this kind of sleep, he will either dream of being under the Equator or in a tropical landscape, or of wandering in the fields in a clear summer's day, or of fire. If a door is slammed, but not so loud as to awake the sleeper, he will dream of thunder ; and if his palm be gently tickled his dreams will be one of ecstatic pleasure. If some particular idea completely occupies the mind during the waking state it will recur in dreams during sleep . . . the only frictions said to have been employed by the sorcerers must have had narcotic properties ; but independent of these, whatever gently stimulates the skin operates sympathetically on the sensorium and favours sleep and dreaming." Wierius, the well-known writer on witchcraft, says that the ointment used by the witches to effect this purpose consisted of human fat mixed with the juice of parsley, aconite, solanum, pentaphylum, and soot.

Possibly some such ointment was employed by the bacchantes. That the imagination was influenced in certain of the initiatory rites by mortifications and fasts can scarcely be questioned. This was increased by solitude and darkness, and perhaps by an intoxication produced by the sacred food and drinks, and was also stimulated by the use of certain herbs. In Egypt the care of the different parts of the human body was divided among the thirty-six genii of the air, and the priests practised a separate invocation for each genius, as Origen informs us.

CHAPTER XIII

TEMPLES AND SITES OF THE
MYSTERIES

THE Egyptian sites chiefly associated with the Mysteries were Sais and Philæ. According to Herodotus, Sais, now practically demolished, was certainly a site of the Mysteries, and we know that at Philæ there stood a great temple of Isis, still standing in ruins, though fast crumbling away beneath the force of the water with which modern engineering necessities have flooded the country.

In Chapter I of the Book of the Dead, too, we find a passage which seems to point to another site. " I look upon the hidden things in Re-stau." These typified the birth and death of the sun-god, as performed in the sanctuary of Seker, the god of death, at Saqqara, celebrated between midnight and dawn. Again, in Chapter CXXV of the Book of the Dead (Papyrus of Ani), we read : " I have entered into Re-Stau (the otherworld of Seker, near Memphis) and I have seen the Hidden One (or mystery) who is therein." Chapter CXLVIII (Saite Recension) is to be recited " on the day of the new moon, on the sixth-day festival, on the fifteenth-day festival, on the festival of Uag, on the festival of Thoth, on the birthday of Osiris, on the festival of Menu, on the night of Heker, during the mysteries of Maat, during the celebration of the mysteries of Akertet," so that there were not only other mysteries than those of Osiris and Isis, but several sites at which they were celebrated.

The earliest form of Egyptian temple was a mere hut of plaited wickerwork, serving as a shrine for the symbols of the god; the altar but a mat of reeds. The earliest temples were developed from a wall built round the name-stela, which was afterward roofed in. With the advent of the New Empire the temple-building became of a much more complicated character, though the essential plan from the earliest period to the latest remained practically unchanged. The simplest form was a surrounding wall, the pylon or entrance gateway with flanking towers, before which were generally placed two colossal statues of the king and two obelisks, then the innermost sanctuary, the *naos*, which held the divine symbols. This was elaborated by various additions, such as three pylons, divided by three avenues of sphinxes, then columned courts, and a hypostyle or columnar hall. In this way many of the Egyptian kings enlarged the buildings of their predecessors.

These temples stood in the midst of populous cities, the huge surrounding wall shutting out the noise and bustle of the narrow streets. Leading up to the great pylon, the chief gateway, was a broad road carried right through the inhabited quarter and guarded on each side by rows of lions, rams, or other sacred animals. In front of the gateway were two obelisks, likewise statues of the king who founded the temple, as protector of the sanctuary. On either side of the entrance stood a high tower, square in shape, with the sides sloping inward. These were, of course, originally designed for defensive purposes, and the passage through the pylon could thus be successfully barred against all foes, while from postern-gates in the wall sorties could be made. Tall masts were fixed in sockets at the foot of the pylon. From these gaily coloured streamers waved to keep afar all menace of evil, as did the symbol of the sun, the Winged Disk, over the great doors. These were often made of wood, a valuable material in Egypt, and covered with a sheathing of glittering gold. The outer walls were decorated with brightly coloured reliefs and inscriptions, depicting the deeds of the founder, for the temple was as much a personal monument as a shrine to the tutelary deity. Inside the pylon was a great court, open to the sky, usually only colonnaded on either side, but in larger temples, as that of Karnak, a series of columns ran the length of the centre. Here the great festivals were held, in which a large number of citizens had the right to take part. By a low door-way from this the hypostyle was entered, the windows of which were near the roof, so that the light was dim, while the sanctuary was in complete and profound darkness.

This, the Holy Place, was the chief room of the temple. Here stood the *naos*, a box-like structure, rectangular in shape and open in front, often with a latticework door. This served as the receptacle of the divine symbols or in some cases as the cage of the sacred animal. On either side of the sanctuary were dark chambers, used as the store-rooms for the sacred vestments, the processional standards and sacred barque, the temple furniture, and so on. It is to be noted that as the progression was from the blazing light of the first great court to the complete darkness of the Holy of Holies, so the roofs grew less lofty. The inside walls and columns were decorated with reliefs in brilliant colours depicting the rites and worship connected with the presiding deity in ceremonial order. It is obvious, therefore, that if the Mysteries were actually performed in the temples (as we know from Apuleius that they must have been) the progression of their various stages or phases must have been made from the pro-naos to the inner sanctuary, and, indeed, the whole of mystical tradition assures us that this was so, by its language and terminology ; thus we speak of the neophyte as standing " at the gate of the temple," or " before the pro-naos," and at a later stage, of " the secrets of the inner shrine."

Surrounding the temple was the *temenos*, enveloped by a wall in which were situated other and smaller temples, with groves of sacred trees and birds, lakes on which the sacred barque floated, the dwellings of the priests, and sometimes palaces amid the gardens. Outside again were sacred ways that led in different directions, some branching from temple to temple ; through cities, villages, and fields, while, at the side, steps sloped down to the Nile, where boats were anchored. Along these ways went the sacred processions, bearing the images of the gods ; by them came the monarch in royal state to make offerings to the gods ; and here the dead were carried to their tombs across the Nile.

Greece has frequently been alluded to as the " Land of Temples." The appellation might with greater justice be applied to Egypt, where fanes of Cyclopean magnitude rose in every nome ere yet Hellas could boast knowledge of the mason's art.

Still they stand, those giant shrines, wellnigh as perfect as when fresh from the chisels of the old hierophants who shaped and designed them. And so long as a fostering love of the past dwells in the heart of man so long shall they remain.

Nothing, perhaps, in the entire volume of ancient mystery inspires in the mind of modern man a feeling of such eerie wonder as the idea of the labyrinth. He visions it as a subterranean maze winding its serpentine way through the recesses of a mountain or a path beset by occult dangers in the bowels of some ancient temple. It is a little disappointing at first to find that the word labyrinth means merely " a passage." But what collection of sounds or letters could better convey an atmosphere of mystic wonder or provide a better mental picture of shadowy fear ? The word lab-y-rinth in itself is a legend, a weird fable of ancient and magical associations.

The most famous of all the sites known by this name was certainly the great Labyrinth of Egypt, which formerly stood near the pyramid of Hawara in the Fayyoum, and which was so graphically described by Pliny, Herodotus, and Strabo at different periods, though considerable doubt exists that any of them actually explored its recesses. In his *Natural History* Pliny tells us that it was constructed by King Pete-suchis or Tithoes, although Herodotus assures us that at least twelve Egyptian monarchs laboured at building and extending the structure. The entrance, says Pliny, was of Parian marble, while the remainder was built of granite, and the huge mass was constructed with such solidity that the lapse of ages could not destroy it.

It contained thirty " regions and perfections " with

a vast palace assigned to each, and in addition temples of all the gods of Egypt and forty statues of Nemesis in as many sacred shrines, besides numerous pyramids forty ells in height. The many galleries which traversed it formed crossings so inextricable that the visitor was certain to grow perplexed and lose his way. Pliny waxes eloquent on the porticoes and banqueting halls approached by broad flights of steps, the vast columns, the statues of gods and kings which littered the length and breadth of the enormous place. Some of the palaces, he writes, obviously holding his breath as he does so, were equipped with doors, which when opened, emitted a dreadful sound like the reverberations of thunder, and the whole Stygian vicinity had perforce to be traversed in utter darkness.

Professor Sir William Flinders Petrie, who examined the site in 1887, found that it covered an area about 1000 feet long and 800 feet broad, sufficient space, indeed, to accommodate " all of the temples on the east of Thebes." This he was able to identify as the Labyrinth mentioned by Herodotus near Crocodil-opolis and Lake Moeris. The site was covered by a thick deposit of limestone chips, the remains of the vast building which was destroyed by the people of Heracleopolitis " because they held it in abhorrence." Disregarding the account of Pliny, which he found by personal examination of the site to be inaccurate, Sir William suggested as a " restoration " of the Labyrinth a structure containing nine shrines, each situated in a pillared court, the whole opening upon a great hall, on the other side of which a similar series of courts was ranged. This, again, bounded a second hall, which led to still another group of courts. Sir

William also discovered the mummies of many of the sacred crocodiles which, tradition alleged, had been buried in the building, besides many fragments of statues, mostly of Sebek, the crocodile god, the remains of fluted and painted columns and fire altars, and limestone models of pyramids, perhaps those to which Pliny referred.

It is impossible to say whether any Mysteries were celebrated in the Labyrinth or not, but the probability is that there were. The place seems the prototype of the Labyrinth at Knossos in Crete where the Mysteries of Dionysus were performed, and there can be little doubt that one was the model of the other. Another link seems to exist between them: both were places where monsters were placated—the crocodile and the Minotaur. Now the Minotaur in certain of his representations much more resembles a crocodile than a bull. On a seal found at Knossos he has a strong resemblance to the Egyptian portraits of Sebek, the crocodile-god of the dead. " That he is a bull-god," says Miss Harrison, " is not so certain." For those and other reasons, then, I believe that the Labyrinth in the Fayyoum was a site of the Mysteries, perhaps their chief and original site.

One of the chief later temples of the Mysteries was the famous Serapeum at Alexandria, built by Ptolemy Soter. Rufinius, who visited the latter temple at the end of the fourth century, describes it as follows: " The mount on which it has been built was formed, not by nature, but by the hand of man. It towers above a mass of buildings and is reached by more than one hundred steps. It extends on all sides in a square of great dimensions. All the lower part, up to the level of the pavement, is vaulted. This basement, which receives the light from above through openings, is divided into secret chambers, separated from one another and serving divers mysterious functions. The circuit of the upper story is occupied by conference halls, cells for the pastophori and a very high building, generally inhabited by the guardians of the temple, and the priests who have taken vows of chastity. Behind these buildings, on the inside, cloisters run along the four sides in a square. In the centre rises the temple, decorated with columns of precious material and built of magnificent marbles, employed in profusion. It contains a statue of Serapis, of such proportions that it can touch one wall with the right and the other with the left hand. It is affirmed that all kinds of metals and woods enter into the composition of this colossal figure. The walls of the sanctuary are reputed to be covered first with plates of gold, then with plates of silver, and on the outside is a third layer of bronze for the purpose of protecting the two others."

M. Moret, describing the ruins of the Iseum, or shrine of Isis at Pompeii, says : " The Iseum of Pompeii did not have these colossal dimensions. As we know to-day, it occupies the site of an older temple, destroyed by the earthquake of 63, rebuilt before any other in Pompeii by a zealous community and already in use when there occurred the final catastrophe of the year 79.

" In the centre of a square court (*area*) surrounded by the ruins of a colonnade, was the sanctuary (*cella*), decorated by a pediment upborne by seven columns and reached by a flight of seven steps. Within the sanctuary is seen a base which served at one and the same time as a pedestal for the statue of Isis and a

THE TEMPLE OF ISIS AT POMPEII

closet for the storing of the articles used in the service of worship. On the left of the court a large altar and a few smaller ones for sacrifices have been discovered ; near at hand is a small square building with a narrow underground passage where two benches are cut in the masonry. This is supposed to have been the *megarum* or probation-hall where the aspirants to initiation slept at night, to be visited by Isis in prophetic dreams. Behind the sanctuary, the outside wall is pierced by five large openings giving access to a larger hall, which is believed to have been the *schola*, a place for meetings, banquets, and the lectures attended by the Isiacs. Adjoining the *schola* was a vestry with a fountain for the purposes of purification. Lastly, between the temple and the neighbouring municipal theatre can be traced the lodgings of the priests, in the remains of a suite of five rooms."

As regards the temple where the Eleusinian Mysteries were celebrated, the wall which enveloped the sacred edifices at Eleusis, was part of the fortifications of the town. The temple of Demeter itself, like that at Athens, was known as the Eleusinion. In a small shrine to the right of the flanking propylons have been found two bas-reliefs representing the god and the goddess. Near-by was the temple of Demeter, elevated on a rocky eminence, and corner to corner with it, the very much larger Telesterion, or Hall of Initiation, with its forty-two pillars.

" It suffices to cast the eye over the plan," remarks Foucart, " to see how little the Telesterion resembles a Greek temple." It is, he says, essentially not a temple, but a hall of initiation, of these faithful to the secret Mysteries. The superficies of the hall is 2717 metres, there are eight ranks of accommodation which would accommodate about 3000 persons when seated. It seems obvious, says M. Foucart, that the building was designed in accordance with the models of Persian architecture. The plan is the same, even if the proportions are considerably smaller, and indeed, the general aspect is not unlike that of the pillared hall of Persepolis.

CHAPTER XIV

THE SURVIVAL OF THE MYSTERIES

THAT the essence of the Egyptian Mysteries, their secrets and philosophy, was carried into the countries of Europe and Asia by the Egyptian priests on the break-up of the old Egyptian religion and the foundation of Christianity in the Nileland, is scarcely possible of challenge. Just as the Magi were in communication with the Greek philosophers, as Plato tells us the Magus Gobry was with Socrates, so immigrant Egyptian priests driven from their country travelled to Greece and Rome and interpenetrated the beliefs of the inhabitants of these lands with their own philosophy. Moreover, the schools of mysticism situated in Alexandria sent forth scores of their initiates to Byzantium and Rome. As we have already seen, the worship of Serapis and of Isis penetrated to the farthest bounds of the Roman Empire, even to Britain, for the native Druidism was most certainly affected by it. " We suspect," says Salverté, " that sorcery was founded by those Egyptian priests of the last order, who, from the commencement of the Roman Empire had wandered in every direction, and who, although they were publicly despised, yet were consulted in secret, and continued to make proselytes amongst the lowest classes of society." He proceeds to say that the worship of the cat and the goat occurring in European witchcraft probably had an Egyptian origin, a notion which students of the witch-cult may or may not accept, and to this he adds : " It is also well known of what importance another agent, the key, was in the tricks of witchcraft, how many cures the Key of St. John and the Key of St. Hubert performed. The handled cross, *crux ansata*, so frequently observed on the Egyptian monuments, was a key, and from the religious ideas which placed it in the hand of the principal gods of Egypt we discover in the key the hieroglyphic of sovereign power." But that it had another and more basic and primeval symbolism even the dabbler in things Egyptian is aware.

But Salverté (although he is always to be followed with caution) provides us with data of a more useful kind when he suggests that the magical book known as the *Pseudo-monarchia Demonum* appears to have had an Egyptian origin, and that the names which this volume contains are reproduced with but little alteration in certain pamphlets respecting witchcraft. " Among the genii of the Pseudo-monarchia one is a mermaid, a figure peculiar to the planispheres, another a venerable old man mounted on a crocodile and carrying a hawk upon his wrist. A third is represented under the form of a camel, which bespeaks its Egyptian origin . . . whilst another appears partly a wolf, and partly man, displaying like Anubis the jawbones of a dog ; and the fifth is Ammon or Hammon whose name reveals its origin."

When Octavius the Roman Emperor conquered Egypt about the beginning of the Christian era, the first great blow to the Egyptian religion in its own native seat was given. But it underwent a renaissance in Italy and the western Roman Empire, making thus a second visitation to the shores of Europe, where indeed the Cult of Isis was erected to a position at least equal to that it had enjoyed in Egypt. It awakened interest in all classes and grew extremely fashionable in Italy.

In Italy an Iseum, that is, a temple of Isis, was built at Pompeii as early as 105 B.C., and in A.D. 38 a great temple to Isis Campensis was built by Caligula on the Field of Mars at Rome. The worship of the goddess reached its apogee at Rome in the time of the Antonines, and flourished exceedingly for nearly five hundred years. From the various classes of the priesthood attached to the Isiac temples we glean some knowledge of the analogous types of hierophant who must have ministered to the Mysteries of Osiris and Isis in Egypt. There was first a high priest, who was supported by three other grades : prophets, whose duties it appears to have been to maintain intercourse with the gods, stolists, both men and women, whose office it was to clothe the statues of the deities in garments either of bright or darksome hues, to symbolize the half-knowledge which mankind possessed regarding divinity, and pastophori, the guardians of the holy doctrines. These were clad in long, light-coloured robes, their breasts and arms were bare, and their heads shaven after the Egyptian fashion. The priestesses wore long, transparent gowns and fringed scarfs knotted upon the breast like a gypsy's kerchief. They carried the sistrum of Isis, a rattle which gave forth a noisy tintinabulation, an instrument which I believe was developed from a species of corn-crake used to scare away birds from the standing corn, but which was thought to have the property of scaring Set, the evil principle.

But it was scarcely the pure worship of Osiris and Isis which gained such an ascendancy over Europe.

Passing through the alembic of Alexandria, it naturally brought in its train much of the influence of the arcane schools of that mysterious city in which the philosophies of Greece were mingled with the theology of Egypt.

The first king of the Ptolemaic Dynasty made a great effort to bring about a good understanding between his Greek and Egyptian subjects, by founding at Alexandria a religion containing the elements of both the Greek and Egyptian faiths. He called to his counsels the skilful mythographer Manetho and the Greek Timotheus, a member of the sacred family of the Eumolpidæ of Eleusis. By this method he united the Eleusinian faith to that of Isis, and even invented a new deity to preside over the composite cult he had created. This was Serapis, whose precise origin is a little obscure, and which may or may not be found in a compound of Osiris and the Bull, Apis. Some traditions bring him even from Asia Minor or Babylon. Be this as it may, Serapis took the place of Osiris, and with Isis and Harpocrates formed the Egyptian trinity in Greece and Rome. But they were usually accompanied by Anubis, the dog-headed god, who was identified with Hermes.

Extraordinary efforts on the part of a small army of mystics at Alexandria succeeded in launching this synthetic cultus on the Western world. Those Italian ports which traded with Alexandria appear to have been the places of entry of the new-old religion, and the foreign merchants, sailors, and slaves who arrived there almost daily doubtless acted as the earliest missionaries of the faith of Isis in Italy. At first it met with fierce opposition, but the popularity of the Pythagorean system, combining so many influences of philosophy and religion in East and

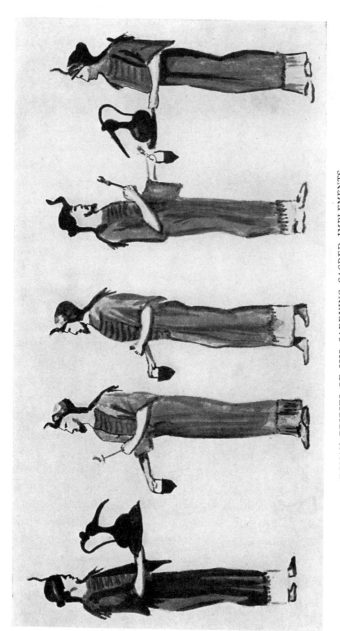

ROMAN PRIESTS OF ISIS CARRYING SACRED IMPLEMENTS

West, greatly assisted the new cult. Thousands gathered to the worship of Isis, which held out to them not only the promise of life and aid in the future after death, but the consideration of a present human comfort. The pitiful and emotional tale of the dead Osiris, and the maternal anxiety of Isis seem to have made an irresistible appeal to thousands of those whose worldly circumstances were not of the happiest, and especially did it appeal to women.

For ten years, between 58 and 48 B.C., a terrific struggle was waged between the protagonists of the older Roman religion and those of the new cult, until at length Isis took her place beside the ancient gods. When Egypt became a Roman province, the power of the Isiac cult was greatly strengthened, and soon the emperors themselves posed as the servants of the goddess, especially Domitian, who rebuilt the Temple of Isis in the Campus Martius in A.D. 92 on a magnificent scale. The rites of Isis extended to Spain, Gaul, and Britain, as well as to North Africa, as did those of Serapis. The remains of her temples are to be found in Holland and at Cologne, the Sixth Legion raised her altars at York, and in many places in France and Switzerland her shrines have been explored.

It was not merely the pomp and circumstance of the Egyptian rites which captured the Roman world. The Europeans of that period had long been accustomed to a mythology which might almost be described as Continental. That is, its deities in Gaul and Britain strongly resembled similar divinities in Greece and Rome, and it is now certain that the more important of them at least had a common origin. But the faiths which surrounded them were inchoate, lacking in moral sense and fixity of outlook, and the introduction of a novel cult which supplied these wants and assured its worshippers of existence after death was therefore hailed with gratification. But characteristically, perhaps, the European mind did not accept the animal cult of Egypt to any great extent, for the very simple reason, probably, that it had long outgrown its own totemism, at least so far as that had been official. It is significant that Apuleius scarcely mentions it, so that we are perhaps justified in thinking that the reactions of Europe on the ancient faith of Egypt were, to say the least of it, wholesome and " modern."

The great object of Alexandrian propaganda, as expressed, for example, in the writings of Plutarch, was to assert the essential unity of the Divine nature. It combined Platonism with a trinitarian mono-theism. It brought to its aid all the scientific and philosophical wisdom of the age in order to recover the arcane significance which it believed ancient wisdom had handed down in the veiled forms of legend and tradition. Still the hand of the deliberate myth-ographer is a little too obvious in its composition, and it certainly entertained the grossest superstitions side by side with the most sublime ideas, yet the ideals of ascetic purity, of good living, and its vision of a life to come constituted a distinct advance on the old popular religions of Europe, and that it paved the way for the acceptance of Christianity we cannot doubt. In short, it aroused an extraordinary spiritual energy, which in the early centuries of our era was struggling for self-expression, and its effects were profound and elevating.

The motto of the faith of Isis, " Be of good courage," is found inscribed on many tombs of the period, and indicated that the human soul, although it might have to pass through many bodies and mortal lives, would yet reach the Life Eternal. The outstanding festivals of the Egyptian worship in Europe were the Blessing of the Sacred Barque on the fifth of March, and the Celebration of the quest and finding of Osiris in November, when a banquet of the initiated was held. These festivals abounded in pomp and many-coloured display, and must have retained much of the ancient Egyptian symbolism.

There can be little doubt, however, that the purity of the Egyptian Mysteries suffered considerably from its European associations. It was transformed by Greek philosophy more than it was able to inspire the same. If it retained its broad outlines, its doctrines certainly underwent a considerable change. Degeneration set in. The precision of the rite, the manner in which it was carried out, came to be considered of more importance than the theology which inspired it.[1] This, of course, is strictly speaking not so much of the nature of degeneration as a return to early practice, where ritual has its origins in beliefs so vague that they can hardly be termed myths, and requires the creation of a secondary myth to explain it. In fact the original impulse has frequently been of a character so shadowy that many expert students of comparative religion like Robertson Smith have even insisted that ritual is prior in origin to myth. It may be, in the sense that I have indicated, but it is surely equally manifest that it cannot be prior to mythic idea or imagination.

So the magical part of the Mysteries now began to bulk more largely than before in the transplanted Egyptian Mysteries, as is obvious from the Roman writings of the period. The wise and (shall I say)

---

[1] In reality it was actually more important, as we have seen elsewhere, at least so far as apprehension goes.

almost " Calvinistic " priests of Thebes and Memphis had employed the magical or compulsory forces at their disposal with admirable discretion and reserve, and had surrounded them with that prudent secrecy which the true professors of the Great Art have invariably observed. But in a Europe almost childishly crazed for marvel the solemn purport of magic was lost. Cosmopolitan Rome, athirst for novelty, too often regarded the temples of Isis and Serapis as the shrines of superstition, and too often did the priests who should have guarded their secrets and reserved their magical formulæ place these at the disposal of persons who sought their assistance on the most frivolous of pretexts.

In Strabo's time the Temple of Serapis at Canopus was thronged by patients of the noblest rank and was famous for its miraculous cures, and the Temples of Isis were equally celebrated for their interpreters of dreams.

So far as the survival of the Greek Mysteries is concerned, Pythagoras, who seems to have been initiated at Sidon, travelled throughout the ancient world in the quest of knowledge, and was initiated into the mysteries of all the countries he visited. From his knowledge of the whole he developed a new system of his own. This necessitated a probation in the first place of five years' abstinence and silence. The candidate was rejected if found to be passionate or intemperate, contentious or ambitious in the worldly sense. His personal courage and insensibility to pain were also severely tried, and if found worthy he was initiated into the first degree, that of the Acousmatici. After the lapse of another considerable space of time he might be admitted to the second degree, that of the Mathematici, and, latterly, into the third and last, the degree of the Pythagoreans.

Under the system of Pythagoras, grammar, rhetoric, and logic were taught to cultivate and improve reason, and mathematics, because he conceived that the ultimate benefit of humanity consisted in the arcane science of numbers. Geometry, music, and astronomy were also inculcated, and a system of symbols was developed to illustrate the higher meanings of his system. Thus the equilateral triangle was eloquent of the perfection of the deity, the right angle the union of the celestial and terrestrial capacities, and the perfect square the divine mind, and so forth.

The Latin authors who write on the Mysteries lived in the time of transition and reveal its effects. Virgil, in his *Æneid,* speaks of the gate of ivory through which he and his guide were dismissed after their journey through the infernal regions. But there was another gate of horn through which the aspirant entered ; for all caverns of initiation had two gates, one called the descent to hell, the other the ascent of the just. The ancient poets said that through the gate of horn issued true visions, and through the gate of ivory, false. Now from this, and the fact that Æneas and his guide issued through it, it has been inferred by some critics that Virgil meant to intimate that all he had said concerning the infernal regions was to be considered a fable. But such could not be the poet's intention ; what he really implied was that a future state was a real state, whilst the representations thereof in the mysteries were only shadows. The ivory gate itself was no other than the sumptuous door of the temple through which the initiated came out when the ceremony was over.

It is, of course, impossible to trace the " genealogy "

of the Mysteries throughout the history of Mediæval Europe step by step, but it must be obvious that their influence lasted in an unbroken line. It can be perceived in the Alexandrian schools and in their Moorish and Spanish offshoots, in the writings of the mystical fathers of the mediæval Christian Church, as well as in those of the alchemists, the Rosicrucians, and the later Illuminati, as well as in those of Saint Martin and Martinez Pasqually. It is also to be found in a more individual sense in the philosophy of Jacob Boehme, in the works of Swedenborg, and in the mystical writings of Blake. In Britain, France, and Germany the Legend of the Holy Grail mingled Christian with Egyptian symbolism, but how far the Coptic church of Egypt maintained the spirit of the ancient sodalities it would be difficult to say.

In more modern times there are evidences and traces that the Mysteries, or at least a recension of them, have survived in Europe, although in an arcane sense. The rituals and beliefs of all the churches are eloquent of their influence, and as more than one writer has shown, the entire machinery for the celebration of their rites in a psychical sense is to be found therein for those who seek it.

This takes no account of the quite artificial survival of the cult of Isis in certain circles in Paris and in America. The cult in question appears to have been re-established by persons only dimly acquainted with the ancient ritual and inspired by very different intentions from those who originally founded it. It will be more profitable to endeavour to trace the survival of the tenets of the Mysteries in certain other arcane orders, especially in those of the Assassins and the Rosicrucians.

The history of the secret society known as Assassins,

a distorted remnant of Alexandrianism, and therefore of Egyptian mystic philosophy, chiefly because of the romantic circumstances surrounding it, has scarcely received its proper perspective in the dazzling picture of Near Eastern chronicle. In the minds of the majority, and even in those of certain specialists who have been carried away by the glamour of tradition, this strange fraternity, perched on its mountain fastness at Alamut, was little more than a nest of fanatical slayers, whose sole purpose was to kill wantonly at the behest of a shadowy tyrant, " the Old Man of the Mountain." The later character of the sect readily lends itself to such an interpretation. But in reality its origins were Alexandrian, and therefore Egyptian, as well as mystical and philosophical, although its beliefs were based on the higher principles of Islam, and the mountain community which gave them a merely murderous significance had little in common with the first principles and exalted mysteries of its parent body.

Traced to its source, the Society of the Assassins is now known through recent German researches to have originated in that sect of Mohammedans known as Ismaelites and was founded in the latter part of the eleventh century by Hassan Sabah, who disseminated its doctrines throughout Syria and Persia. It was actually an offshoot from the Western Lodge of the Ismaelites at Cairo, which, like the other affiliated lodges of the Order, recognized the Caliph as its supreme head, and comprised a large membership of both sexes. In the reign of the Caliph Haken-bi-emr-illah it gained an increased importance from the extraordinary munificence of that insane monarch, who established it in a stately palace at Cairo known as the House of Wisdom, which he furnished with an elaborate library and equipped with a wealth of mathematical and astrological instruments. This institution developed into a species of popular university, professors of law, logic, and medicine were appointed to give free lectures within its walls to all who cared to receive their instruction, and it is said that the caftans worn by these teachers were the prototypes of the official robes in use to-day in our British universities.

But underlying the popular instruction afforded by the House of Wisdom was a mystical teaching of much deeper import. It consisted of nine degrees of progressive initiation into the higher tenets of the Ismaelite sect, from the first, which strove to bring the student wholly under the influence of his teachers, to the concluding stage, where he was taught that " nothing was to believed, but that everything might be accomplished." The intermediate steps conducted him through the labyrinth of Islamic mysticism, in which the actual nature of the hidden truths contained in the Koran, the occult significance of septenary numbers, the lives of the seven great lawgivers and the systems of Plato and Aristotle were inculcated. But in the last degree the veil was torn from the eyes of the aspirant, and he was cynically informed that prophets and teachers, heaven and hell, religion and philosophy, were idle dreams and that all actions were permissible in a world which was merely a remnant of chaos. Such a philosophy, or negation of philosophy, is outlined in The Rubáiyát of Omar Khayyám, who was an early intimate of Hassan, the founder of the Assassin cult, and who not only swore blood-brothership with him, but engaged with the Old Man of the Mountain that whoever was the more successful should share his fortune with the other. But the author of *The Rubáiyát* later placed himself under the protection of his friend Nizam-al-melk, another comrade of Hassan's, and seems to have forsworn his early fealty to the Order, although his great poem reveals his adherence to the Assassin philosophy of pleasure.

But Hassan, then an ambitious leader of the Ismaelite sect, clearly perceived that the plan of the society at Cairo was defective as a means of acquiring the temporal power he desired, and he resolved to give the anarchical philosophy of that body a more practical turn, and to put its tenets into actual force. He recognized, however, that if his policy was to have any real sanction behind it, it must ostensibly have a religious basis, and when in 1090 he settled in the mountain fastness of Alamut in Persia, he impressed upon his followers the most rigid obedience to the precepts of Islam. He reduced the nine degrees of the Ismaelites to seven, laying stress upon the necessity for admitting to the Order only those persons who had a sound knowledge of human nature. The aspirant was taught that allegory was the true path to religion, and that by its means any desired significance might be drawn from the pages of the Koran.

The philosophy of the Assassin cult was, indeed, the parent of Sufism, that mystic Pantheism which envisages deity as possessing the qualities of both good and evil, and which, in its original form, presupposed the equal status of both and the freedom of man to employ them without restriction. An extraordinary conviction of the absolute infallibility of its tenets rendered the faith of the Assassins extremely hostile to all other religions and temporal powers, and in order that it might gradually extend its sway over the whole of Islam, and indeed beyond it, it embarked on a policy of terrorising its opponents by the assassination of their rulers and political leaders. In order to carry out his designs with certainty and despatch, Hassan instituted the grade of the Fedavi, or Devoted Ones, who were to become the ministers of his wrath against authority. These were, for the most part, sturdy male children, purchased from their parents as slaves, and brought up in his mountain stronghold in habits of severe discipline and the most implicit obedience. They were carefully instructed in several languages, so that they might travel wherever the Sheik commanded them, and that they were habitually drugged with the hashish from which they afterwards took their name seems indisputable.

The most romantic yet still the most credible account of the manner in which the Fedavi or Assassins proper were inspired and incited to their gruesome task is to be found in an Arabic work known as the *Siret-el-Haken*, or *Memoirs of Haken*, an historical romance written shortly after the fall of Alamut. It tells how the Old Man of the Mountain caused a vast pleasure-garden to be laid out, in the midst of which he built a kiosk joined by four arches, and in the sides of which were set four richly ornamented windows, painted with stars of gold and silver. This bijou palace he plenished with roses, porcelain, and drinking-vessels of gold and filled it with servants, male and female, clad in Persian silks. Its columns were overlaid with musk and amber. The garden was divided into four parts, in each of which grew the choicest fruits and flowers, and it was intersected by refreshing canals and reservoirs, and stocked with game and birds of bright plumage.

Into this little paradise the Fedavi selected for the

duty of assassination was brought after having been heavily drugged with hashish or benjeh. On regaining his senses, he found himself in an environment such as surpassed all his imaginings, and was informed by the slaves of the kiosk that this was indeed Paradise, and that they only awaited his death to make him free of its delights. He was then approached by the Sheik in person, who corroborated the statement of the slaves, and entertained him to a sumptuous banquet. But the wines he partook of had also been drugged with hashish, and when he had once more succumbed to its fumes, he was carried back to the place whence he came. He was then told by the Sheik that he had been in Paradise and that if he carried out his commands and assassinated a certain person of note, he would, if slain in the enterprise, immediately be transported to the delightful sphere he had lately visited through supernatural agency. The hope of such a destiny, acting on a plastic mind inured to discipline, had its due effect, and the Fedavi set forth on his mission in the fanatical assurance of immortal bliss.

The Assassins soon began to make themselves felt as a power in Persia and Syria. Their first victim was the Nizam-el-melk, with whom Hassan and Omar had been fellow-students. His son speedily followed him, as did the Sultan of Persia. That monarch's successor made war with the Assassins, but was so terror-stricken by their murderous tactics, that he speedily cemented a peace. Hassan died at an advanced age in 1124, having assassinated both his sons, and left as his successor his chief prior, Hiabusurg-Omid, during whose reign the Order was far from fortunate. The list of its victims had by this time become a long and illustrious one. The fourth Sheik of the Mountain—another Hassan—made public

the secret doctrines of the society, announcing that
the religion of Islam was abolished and that all men
might give themselves up to feasting and pleasure.
He further announced that he was the promised Caliph
of God upon Earth, but some four years later he himself was assassinated and succeeded by his son
Mahomed II, whose rule of forty-six years was marked
by deeds of revolting cruelty. But Mahomed had
several implacable enemies, the chief of whom was
the famous Saladin, and the Syrian branch of the
society seceded from his sway, and became independent. This branch it was with whom the Crusaders
came so much into contact, and whose emissaries slew
Raymond of Tripoli, and Conrad of Montferrat.
Mahomed's son, Hassan III, restored the old form of
Ismaelite doctrine—that is, the people were strictly
confined to the practice of Islam, whilst the initiates
were as before mystical and agnostic. His was the
only reign in which no assassinations occurred and he
was regarded with friendship by his neighbours. But
after a rule of twelve years he was poisoned, and
during the minority of his son Mahomed II assassination was greatly in vogue. After a reign of thirty years
he too was slain by his successor, Rukneddin ; but
vengeance quickly followed, for only a year later the
Tartars swept into Persia, took Alamut and other
Assassin strongholds, and slew the reigning monarch.
Over 12,000 Assassins were massacred, and their
power was completely broken. A like fate overtook
the Syrian branch, which was nearly extirpated by
the Egyptian Mamelukes. But in the more isolated
valleys of Syria, many of them lingered and are
believed still to exist there. At all events, doctrines
similar in character to theirs are occasionally to be met
with in Northern Syria, and it does not seem at all

unlikely that, if the official philosophy of the Order be extinct, its ideas may survive in a debased form and account for many a deed of fanatical violence in that still isolated region.

We see, then, that the cult of the Assassins was to a large extent merely of the nature of an Alexandrian or neo-Egyptian rite perverted to the purposes of a dynasty of degenerate tyrants. Of certainly greater purity was the Order of the Rosicrucians, which also may have had a distant Egyptian origin.

Of late years the controversy regarding the former existence of the Rosicrucians has languished somewhat, but it has never wholly withered, and the question is still posed : Did such an Order as the Rosicrucians formerly flourish, and, if so, what were its tenets and its main objects ? Those are still to be found who reply to the first part of this question affirmatively, although all close students of mystical literature are aware that from De Quincey's time to our own a quite extraordinary amount of proof has been brought to buttress the negative position. Indeed, De Quincey, in his crushing essay, and Mr. A. E. Waite in his no less authoritative *True History of the Rosicrucians*, seemed to have given the *coup de grâce* to what many believe to have been one of the most extraordinary hoaxes in the records of human credulity. But none of those whose aim it has been to shatter the arguments of the pro-Rosicrucians appears to have sufficiently allowed for the fact that the fraternity of the Rosy Cross may have had affiliations with still older mystical societies, and its present-day protagonists point triumphantly to the circumstance that a Rosicrucian Brotherhood still flourishes.

It is now generally agreed that the first public

revelation of the Rosicrucian Order, real or imaginary, was closely connected with Lutheran propaganda. In the second decade of the seventeenth century there appeared in succession three works, obviously from the same pen, *The Universal Reformation, Fama Fraternitatis,* and the *Confessio Fraternitatis,* the expressed intention of which was the purification of an unrighteous and worldly age by the foundation of a society composed of the learned and the enlightened. The spirit of the time was pro-mystical, and the projector of the proposed brotherhood tempered his invitation to the world's wisdom with more than a hint of the mysterious. It was in the *Fama Fraternitatis* particularly that arcane suggestions were thrown out. It speaks of the Order of the Rosy Cross as already instituted, and narrates its inception and history.

Christian Rosenkreuz, it informs us, a man of noble descent, travelled widely in the East, and acquired its occult lore. Upon his return to Germany he established a secret society, composed first of four and afterwards of eight members, who dwelt together in " the House of the Holy Ghost," the location of which is not specified. Having instructed his disciples in the arcane tenets he had acquired during his Eastern travels, he despatched them on a mission of healing throughout Europe, but commanded them to fore-gather at the central institution annually on a given day, the word " Rosy-Cross " to be their watchword, and its pictured representation their sign or hiero-glyph. They were, furthermore, to preserve the secret of the society's existence for 100 years. Christian Rosenkreuz died at the age of 106 years, and not even his disciples knew the whereabouts of his place of burial. But when the Order had existed for 120 years a door was discovered in the House of the Holy Ghost leading to a sepulchral vault, where were discovered the secret books of the Order, the *Vocabularium* of Paracelsus, and a quantity of mystical apparatus. Under the altar was found the body of Rosenkreuz himself, without taint or corruption, holding in his right hand a book written on vellum in golden letters. Immediately after this narrative follows a declaration of its mysteries addressed by the Order to the world. It professed itself to be of the Protestant faith, and stated that the art of gold-making was but " a slight object " with its members. The House of the Holy Spirit, it says, " though a hundred thousand men should have looked upon it, is yet destined to remain untouched, imperturbable, out of sight and unrevealed to the whole godless world for ever."

The *Confessio* contains little more than general explanations upon the objects and traditions of the Order, which is therein described as having several degrees. Not only princes, nobles, and the wealthy, but " mean and inconsiderable persons " were admitted to its ranks, provided their intentions were pure and disinterested. The Order, we are told, possessed an esoteric language, and had accumulated more gold and silver than the whole world beside could yield. It was not, however, the mere gathering of wealth which concerned it, but philosophy and the inculcation of altruistic sentiment.

The spirit of the Order is, indeed, well illustrated by a passage from the writings of Robert Fludd, the English Rosicrucian : " We of the secret knowledge," he says, " do wrap ourselves in mystery, to avoid the objurgation and importunity of those who conceive that we cannot be philosohpers unless we put our knowledge to some worldly use. There is scarcely one who thinks about us who does not believe that our society has no existence ; because, as he truly declares, he never met any of us. And he concludes that there is no such brotherhood, because, in his vanity, we seek not him to be our fellow. We do not come, as he assuredly expects, to that conspicuous stage upon which, like himself, as he desires the gaze of the vulgar, every fool may enter ; winning wonder, if the man's appetite be that empty way : and, when he has obtained it, crying out : ' Lo, this is also vanity ! ' "

Naturally, in a credulous and mystery-ridden age, such a proclamation as the *Fama Fraternitatis* created an enormous sensation. Hundreds of scholars offered themselves, by pamphlet and otherwise, to the service of the Order, though no address appeared in its public declarations. But to none of these was any answer vouchsafed. Seemingly reliable evidence has been discovered that the author of the Rosicrucian treatises was John Valentine Andrea, a celebrated theologian of Würtemburg, known also as a satirist and poet, and the suggestion has been made that his reason for the publication of them was that he sincerely deplored the wretchedness of his country consequent upon the Thirty Years' War, and hoped to remove it by the institution of such an Order as the *Fama* describes, holding out the intellectual foible of the age, the hope of occult knowledge as a lure to the learned. That he did not avow the books as his own, or make any answer to the hundreds of applicants who desired to join this Order has been critically explained as averse from his scheme.

But this " explanation," on the face of it, is insufficient, and unlikely, and takes no notice of the facts that not only did Andrea disown the writings in question, but actually joined the party who ridiculed the Rosicrucian Order as a chimera. Moreover, he confessedly wrote *The Chemical Nuptials of Christian Rosycross*, a comic extravaganza, designed to satirize and discredit the entire Rosicrucian position. It is also manifest that the *Universal Reformation* was borrowed wholesale from the *Raguaglio di Parnasso* of Bocalini, who suffered for his faith in 1613.

The work of Bocalini, of which the *Universal Reformation* is merely a reflection, is, though penetrated by a spirit of the fabulous, unquestionably in the direct line of mystical profession and tradition, and is manifestly inspired by older arcane writings, Byzantine, Gnostic, and Kabbalistic. Although Lutheran in spirit, it exhibits little or no Teutonic influence, and it therefore remains for the opponents of the reality of Rosicrucianism to show, not that its obvious German imitation has no traditional arcane authority, but that the Italian model was not so inspired. Rome was the uncompromising foe of all occult learning, an attitude which drove the professors of the mystical into the opposing camp of Lutheranism. Nor can the serious intentions of Bocalini and his standing as a protagonist of occult lore be challenged, and although his work differs slightly from the German Rosicrucian writings, internal evidence is not wanting to show that it was founded on circumstances of fact much more ancient than the Milanese himself actually appreciated. This, indeed, reopens the whole Rosicrucian question. But not only are Kabbalistic and Gnostic influences obvious in the writings of Bocalini, but others are apparent which I believe have a more or less direct bearing on the Mysteries of Egypt, and that he was in the direct line

of succession as regards this particular tradition seems
to me more than probable.

Regarding the decay of the Mysteries, Heckethorn
says : " In the mysteries all was astronomical, but a
deeper meaning lay hid under the astronomical
symbols. While bewailing the loss of the sun the
epopts were in reality mourning the loss of that light
whose influence is life ; whilst the working of the
elements according to the laws of elective affinity
produces only phenomena of decay and death. The
initiated strove to pass from under the dominion of
the bond-woman Night into the glorious liberty of
the free-woman Sophia ; to be mentally absorbed
into the Deity, i.e. into the Light. The dogmas of
ancient nature-wisdom were set before the pupil, but
their understanding had to arise as inspiration in his
soul. It was not the dead body of science that was
surrendered to the epopt, leaving it to chance whether
it quickened or not, but the living spirit itself was
infused into him. But for this reason, because more
had to be apprehended from within by inspiration
than from without by oral instruction, the Mysteries
gradually decayed ; the ideal yielded to the realistic,
and the merely physical elements—Sabaeism and
Arkism—became their leading features. The frequent
emblems and mementoes in the sanctuary of death
and resurrection, pointing to the mystery that
the moments of highest psychical enjoyment are the
most destructive to bodily existence—i.e. that the
most intense delight is a glimpse of paradise—these
emblems and mementoes were eventually applied to
outward nature only, and their misapprehension led
to all the creeds or superstitions that have filled the
earth with crime and woe, sanguinary wars, interne-
cine cruelty, and persecution of every kind."

There are obvious blunders and inconsistencies in the above statement, but I quote it at the conclusion of this chapter as providing on the whole a useful summary of the facts which accompanied the evanishment of the Mysteries from the public view into hidden secrecy. Truth certainly resides in the main argument that inspiration rather than oral instruction was the veridical genius of the Mysteries, and that the non-apprehension of this truth hastened their disappearance and subsequent withdrawal from public knowledge.

CHAPTER XV

THE SIGNIFICANCE OF INITIATION

IT is now essential that we should attempt to arrive at conclusions regarding the utility of the Mysteries and of the lessons they hold for the mystic to-day. It must be obvious, even to the wayfaring man, that although it is veiled by the outward doctrines and official systems of the world's various religions, the true doctrine has been perpetuated and is still capable of being recovered by him who seeks it earnestly, for the essence of the Mysteries is only to be enjoyed by those prepared to receive it. Even the " personal " and individual way is ever open.

If anything in particular has been stressed in this book, it is the obvious fact that the externals of initiation constitute merely the portals to the true knowledge of the spirit. Ritual of itself is naught compared with this knowledge any more than " table manners " are in respect of eating. These symbolize the process and lend dignity to it, and that is all. Rite and symbol, apart from high intention and spiritual significance, can even be degrading, yet, they often express much more than mere words are capable of expressing, that is, they are efficacious as supplementing the imperfect medium of human speech in the conveyance of subliminal ideas, although they must not be regarded as actually achieving any act which will have magical or supernatural repercussions upon the spirit of the initiate. Again, initiation by itself can never reveal the truth in its entirety. The degree of truth unveiled is in ratio of the mystic's own psychic potentialities.

The nature of the doctrine revealed to their initiates by the several official Mystic orders throughout the ages is assuredly capable of expression in one formula, despite the variety of rite and ceremony which has characterized them. It is the entrance into a new life, or, rather, the return to an old one, that is, to that "paradise" from which man fell, to that divine communion from which he, by his own acts, has been excluded. The central doctrine of all the Mysteries is that of pre-existence, and occasionally, a pre-existence associated with reincarnation. Initiation is, thus, the instinctive as well as intellectual aspiration of the higher man towards restoration to the divine communion, unity, or absorption. The initiate is equipped with the knowledge of how he came into the material world, and how he must reascend. In certain Mysteries he is instructed that he has taken on this mortal coil through his own volition, in others that his initiation is really the first step in his spiritual progress.

The several grades of initiation, although they differ considerably in respect of the various orders which have existed in the history of mankind, may actually be reduced to three, or perhaps four, the nascent grade, or rebirth, the stationary, or that of spiritual "hovering," or juvenility, the third, the new life proper, and, lastly, and more occasionally, its sequel, symbolical of the experience of the new condition. There may even, as we have seen regarding

the Mysteries of Isis, be a preparatory stage typical
of the soul's incubation prior to rebirth. Some, such
as the Druidical, were symbolical of no less than three
births, the natural, that from the cell of the neophyte,
that from the coracle, but in reality the difference is
more apparent than real. It is only when the material
life is left behind and supernatural rebirth is achieved
that initiation has taken place. The three great
degrees may roughly be described as purification,
consecration, and illumination.

Does initiation in itself suffice for actual illumination ? That real knowledge was passed on to the
Egyptian and Greek epopts we cannot doubt. Even
so, it must have been insufficient of itself without a
spiritual transformation in the soul of the neophyte.
Indeed, the genuine neophyte is himself the true
hierophant, nor can the hierophant be other than a
demonstrator, adviser and inspiring force. He cannot
by any word or act transform the neophyte into the
perfected initiate unless there be already in the heart
of the latter a supreme intention and responsive desire.
Initiation is, indeed, an inward act of the soul, a
" magical " act of the psychical entity in man, free,
unfettered, determined, responsive, yet wholly self-
inspired in the ultimate. It resembles Christian
salvation in this, that, no matter how long or how
ardently the Supreme Power, the God made Man, may
knock at the human heart, rescue is not consummated before the door is opened wide by the dweller
within.

But it may well be said that, having accomplished
initiation, it is impossible for the epopt to convey its
full significance to those outside of the portals even
if he would. Words and forms he can reveal if he be so
minded, and if he break his oath, but these would hold

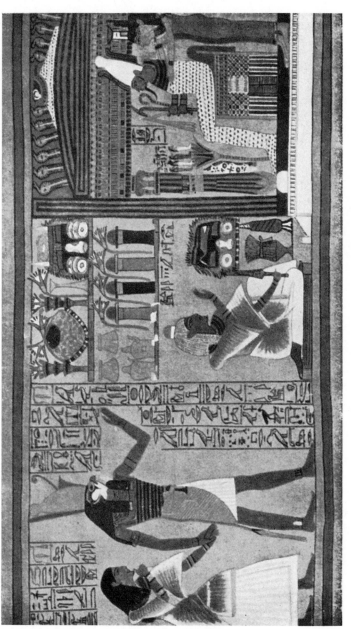

THE PRESENTATION OF THE INITIATE TO OSIRIS

Papyrus of Ani.

no meaning for the uninitiated, simply because he would be confronted with matters unterrestrial and outwith the scope and vocabulary or mundane knowledge and apprehension. Indeed, such secrets as are unveiled to him are and were conveyed to his spirit through the voiceless message of symbols and not through words. And they are actually apprehended as often as not through subsequent reflection and contemplation rather than through immediate illumination.

There is, to be sure, nothing in the Mysteries which the born mystic may not excogitate for himself by dint of his own genius, just as the born poet invariably discovers for himself those fundamental truths regarding his inspirational art which appear almost as of a semi-supernatural order to workaday men. He will shortly find, for example, that of itself the human soul is imperfect, that, lacking the quality of receptivity, the essential of communication with the supernatural, the act of marriage and union with the divine, the spirit is powerless—and other and equally cogent illuminations will rapidly present themselves to the veridical mystic. It follows that self-initiation is perfectly possible, has been attained in hundreds of instances by the exceptional, who, it may be, are souls who have undergone more than one experience of incarnation.

The descent of the soul into matter is one of the most profound mysteries of human existence, as is its converse, the ascent of the spirit into the realms immaterial. These twain constitute symbolic death and rebirth, and were bodied forth in the Mysteries. It is a legend of ages untold, embraced by all the mystical orders. It is, indeed, the intellectual and psychic discernment of the divine, when the soul, making not a mythos for herself, but through sheer sleight of awakened and instinctive spirituality, arrives at a knowledge of the truth concerning her actual origin and the " realities " of her existence. It is a novel, or rather, a reawakened sense of perception, and initiation is merely its drama, the symbolic gesture of its aroused consciousness of the need for reunion with divinity.

By initiation nothing can be gained but that which has to be gained. The seeming crudity of such a statement includes a truth so obvious yet so deep as to appear as needless as profundity frequently appears to persons of material tendency, for there is but one way : the Egyptian, the Greek, the Christian mysteries may seem to differ from each other by an entire heaven, still they are the same, mere rituals of slightly various types encasing the truth enshrined in the temple which was founded before the beginning of the world. The way is well trodden, the stones are deeply worn. There are no unessentials of power, of magic, of mere romantic potentialities won for the adept—wealth, charm, long life, the ability to wield occult powers. These are, indeed, the insignia of the slight and fatuous soul dallying in the purlieus of the temple, vain and degenerate in essence. The true secrets are those of grace, understanding, perfect apprehension and joy in the knowledge of the abounding life unrolled before the spirit, rhythmic delight, the sovereign poise of certainty.

Out of the dimness of his own native faith, whatsoever it be, the mystic rises and transcends to the comprehension of the higher knowledge of the Divine, just as Proclus assures us that the ancient Mysteries at first trod the paths of the popular mythologies until their epopts at the last were brought face to face with essential Deity. The Soul, he tells us, first beholds the shadows and images of things, but "returning into herself" she slowly comprehends and beholds her own essence. She sees the mind, and later the divine substance, with which she at last becomes joined. This, certain writers believe, necessitates the intense natural introspection of trance, that profound self-hypnotism known to all true poets, when "thought" becomes unforced and therefore instinctive and genuine.

The initial purification of the neophyte is said by some to induce such a condition, and we may believe that the mystic bath contained essences inductive of a semi-somnolent or trance-like condition. This was followed by the descent into Hades, which symbolized the terror of the novel state in the mystic, and this again preceded the more blessed condition of release to the Elysian Fields. I believe, from the evidence set forth above and gathered from other sources, that both hypnotic and medicinal aids were employed in certain of the Mysteries as regards the grades alluded to, but I will not stress this point, as it must be obvious that practice would differ in the case of individuals whose idiosyncrasies and needs would be well known to the hierophants.

But these were associated with the Lesser Mysteries only. The core of the revelation in the Greater Mysteries lay in Intellection, in which the archetypal image of universal nature was revealed. The contemplation and union with the Highest supervened. Thus it will be seen that ritual and drama had little to do with the higher stages, which were almost purely of a supernormal and spiritual character. But to express this adequately mere language fails. These things are apprehended, neither seen nor heard. Here thought ends, and the true Magic, as a direct act of mind, begins. For Magic, the true Magic, is, indeed, the very heart of the philosophy of the Mysteries. The life is mystical, the way is mystical, as are the life and way of Magic, the Magic of enchantment, of that " unreal " which is more real to the mystic than the real, of that ecstasy which is the higher music of the universe, that rapture which is translation and life in the Divine. The true poet, who is invariably a mystic, and who cleaves to that higher and loftier apprehension which beggars " thought," and the mystic, who must after all be a poet, penetrate these realms to the confusion, jealousy, and dismay of lesser men simply because they hold the sesame to rapture which the world seeks through the betinselled and shoddy pageantry of " pleasure " instead of in the wast tapestries of spiritual space and in these sphery heights that are the true abiding places of the soul of man.

For what is there to learn in this apprenticeship of life other than the essential poise and approach to Otherwhere ? This world is, indeed, an aerodrome in which man is building, fitting, and testing those winged pinnaces which shall bear him to immortality. If he fail in his 'prentice task then must he assuredly return to the scene of his toil. The process is wrongly described as of the nature of punishment or retribution. It is merely the self-discipline of the Divine endeavouring at great distances to justify itself by various experiments in the depths of time and space, sending out its colonist particles to replenish the spheres and to triumph ere they return to the Fatherland to gain new strength from the sources of the Ultimate.

So that it becomes essential to cultivate toward this

end a particular psychic state through steady contemplation of the Divine, the Afar, that Distance, that
Wonder of Aloofness which is the Heart of Paradise.
Intellection, Inspection, the reduction of the mental
and psychical chaos, the worldly confusion of the
heart, mind, and soul, to the orderly through rapt
comprehension of the one simple truth and necessity
—union with God. This is the sole and only " way "
of the adept. It is open to him through many paths
besides that of the Mysteries or the world's religions,
but these are at least beaten paths, although some
of them are assuredly dark and obscure. It is
unquestionably the religion of the future, the core and
essence of all the vitality which is behind the creeds
and dogmas of all religions. The man who faithfully
follows his native creed and church is well enough
accommodated, only, to put it baldly, he gets all the
smoke of the sacred torch and little of the light and
the joy of the light, and too often he misses the
rapture of knowledge and certainty, tormented as he
is in that reek of doubt, which is the fuliginous vapour
of the lamp of faith.

Moreover, the true significance of the divine union
is too frequently misapprehended, especially by those
who dread it as being peradventure of the nature of
individual psychic extinction. In one sense the
human soul is never entirely out of communication
with the Divine, indeed its native character renders
it more easy to aspire than to grovel, the doctrine of
its native wickedness notwithstanding. The wretched
and truly damnable doctrine that the heart of man is
" desperately wicked " has, I contend, wrought
mischief untold, and has probably wrecked more lives
than it has helped to ways of grace. It is a dark
saying of hierophantic superiority based on a

degenerate assumption of universal and widespread human depravity which could only have been engendered in some hypersensitive and cloistered mentality unused to human converse and aloof from the true nobility of the common mind which shows visibly in the neighbourhood of each and every one of us.

The Soul of man is tired of being told it is wicked, when, on the whole, it is good and is essaying most admirably to find its way through the fogs to the sun. And who can blame it if it is equally tired of religions in which the truth that eternal life must inevitably end in ecstasy (if its laws be adequately fulfilled) is occluded by a ministry, which, with all its virtues, is prone to lay stress on the gloomy side of things, and is certainly unvisited of the spirit of rapture ?

The consciousness of fellowship with God is the first significant token that union with the Divine has commenced. But of this I am very sure, that it does not imply the full achievement of unity. It is, I believe, an expression prior and preparatory to initiation, for union with God grows and advances as comprehension and expression and intuition grow through successive acts of the spirit. The wings strengthen and the flight grows longer. The lamp is constantly burning and it behoves man to make use of the light. There must be continuous and ever-extended explorations in the Otherwhere, and the experience gained therein must be garnered and hoarded as supplying new force for fresh and farther flight.

The neophyte must, however, be given to understand that the Mysteries, as we know them, must assuredly be described as the Mysteries of Earth. Their whole intent is a stepping from this mortality to immortality, consequently they cannot in any way be related to the Mysteries of the Divine, of which man has rumours, but cannot even conceive the nature or the felicity thereof. Mystery, in short, reveals on its unveiling, fresh mystery, and so must the progression proceed far past the human ken.

Can we attach importance to Mysteries founded on mythologies the significance of which has grown effete ? It has been said that we cannot, any more than we can look for aid to systems of ceremonial which inculcate simple or admitted truths. But I would enter a caveat here, for assuredly the two things are not capable of comparison or analogy. Mysteries founded on dead mythologies may not be effete simply because that on which they were based is dead, for the very obvious reason that they are the flower and fruit of the ancient systems of thought which produced them, the essence of them, their spiritual improvement. They are not only in the direct line of tradition but (and this is the point) they are part of that tradition, the very rock on which it is builded, and it is about as wise to ignore or attempt to displace them as it would be to forget or try to hack away the subaqueous foundations of a coral island.

That is why I believe the Mysteries of Egypt, in so far as it has been given me to understand and describe them, are of much avail to the modern mystic, as constituting for the first time in the history of man a reasoned and official body of mystical belief and practice. The purpose of initiation is a conventional attempt to realize man's place in the universe and in the divine scheme of things, and this, I believe, the Egyptian Mystical System achieved for the first time in an orderly and philosophical manner.

Its significance and its lesson are therefore fundamental, nor can they be waived.

*   *   *   *   *

The peculiarly insensible attitude of the greater
part of European humanity toward the deeper
mysteries of spiritual existence constitutes a grave
danger to that section of the race which scientists
have dubbed Aryan or Caucasian. Avidly seizing
upon the husks of the material, it has permitted itself
to forget the inestimable treasures of the spirit; its
attitude of impatience with affairs spiritual and of
the utmost importance to its own racial and individual
welfare must undoubtedly arouse the gravest unrest
in men and women of serious and exalted character.
Still, at no time, perhaps, have these beloved islands
of ours, has our vast American cousinship, been so
deeply stirred to the extraordinary need for the
contemplation of subjects which signify so much for
the behoof of a weary and passion-exhausted world.

The countless centuries of experience hoarded and
preserved by an ancient world which knew little of
the hectic haste and unrest of ours, its extraordinary
earnestness regarding things divine, make it manifest
that the lessons it inculcated should be profoundly
considered by that English-speaking race which is so
particularly involved in the cause of world-peace and
in the administration of the affairs of the older
nations of the East which have long ago inherited and
comprehended the wisdom of Egypt. Do we not
realize that for lack of consideration, for the pitiful
sake of immediate material emolument, we are
throwing away the greatest and richest treasure the
world has to give us ?

These are plain, and perhaps poorly expressed, but

serious words. A country, an empire which cannot afford to examine and to grapple with the great problems of psychic existence, which is wrapt up in things material and pleasurable, which is not established on the rock of indubitable truth, whose people believe all wisdom to be based on material fact, which has, in short, no strain or desire toward spiritual ascension, is indeed in a perilous position. It is beside the question to argue that at no time has any country been able to boast of other than a comparatively small proportion of exalted spirits within its body politic, for the simple reason that our race has now greatly increased opportunities for cultivating that very wisdom of the higher things which it professes to despise or to ignore.

" Where there is no vision the people perish." I quote once again the well-worn saying, because none other so peculiarly expresses our national situation. Just as I am well assured that no individual can lead a life of psychic security without at least a minimum of contemplation upon things hidden and divine, so am I equally persuaded that no nation which in the main ignores them can be secure in justice and in loftiness of ideal. How serene was Egypt in her five thousand years of empire, calm, dignified, aye, and prosperous and happy in her rapt contemplation of the Divine. No people were ever at once so pious and so contented as were her people, and not until a European hegemony of admittedly inferior type, the Ptolemaic, interrupted her visionary quietism was she confounded. Have we no lesson to learn from Egypt ? Aye, the greatest in the world, the knowledge of that divine introspection which alone can give man the likeness of the Divine.

A CATALOG OF SELECTED DOVER
BOOKS IN ALL FIELDS OF INTEREST

CONCERNING THE SPIRITUAL IN ART, Wassily Kandinsky. Pioneering work by father of abstract art. Thoughts on color theory, nature of art. Analysis of earlier masters. 12 illustrations. 80pp. of text. 5⅜ x 8½.   23411-8

ANIMALS: 1,419 Copyright-Free Illustrations of Mammals, Birds, Fish, Insects, etc., Jim Harter (ed.). Clear wood engravings present, in extremely lifelike poses, over 1,000 species of animals. One of the most extensive pictorial sourcebooks of its kind. Captions. Index. 284pp. 9 x 12.   23766-4

CELTIC ART: The Methods of Construction, George Bain. Simple geometric techniques for making Celtic interlacements, spirals, Kells-type initials, animals, humans, etc. Over 500 illustrations. 160pp. 9 x 12. (Available in U.S. only.)   22923-8

AN ATLAS OF ANATOMY FOR ARTISTS, Fritz Schider. Most thorough reference work on art anatomy in the world. Hundreds of illustrations, including selections from works by Vesalius, Leonardo, Goya, Ingres, Michelangelo, others. 593 illustrations. 192pp. 7⅛ x 10¼.   20241-0

CELTIC HAND STROKE-BY-STROKE (Irish Half-Uncial from "The Book of Kells"): An Arthur Baker Calligraphy Manual, Arthur Baker. Complete guide to creating each letter of the alphabet in distinctive Celtic manner. Covers hand position, strokes, pens, inks, paper, more. Illustrated. 48pp. 8¼ x 11.   24336-2

EASY ORIGAMI, John Montroll. Charming collection of 32 projects (hat, cup, pelican, piano, swan, many more) specially designed for the novice origami hobbyist. Clearly illustrated easy-to-follow instructions insure that even beginning papercrafters will achieve successful results. 48pp. 8¼ x 11.   27298-2

THE COMPLETE BOOK OF BIRDHOUSE CONSTRUCTION FOR WOOD-WORKERS, Scott D. Campbell. Detailed instructions, illustrations, tables. Also data on bird habitat and instinct patterns. Bibliography. 3 tables. 63 illustrations in 15 figures. 48pp. 5¼ x 8½.   24407-5

BLOOMINGDALE'S ILLUSTRATED 1886 CATALOG: Fashions, Dry Goods and Housewares, Bloomingdale Brothers. Famed merchants' extremely rare catalog depicting about 1,700 products: clothing, housewares, firearms, dry goods, jewelry, more. Invaluable for dating, identifying vintage items. Also, copyright-free graphics for artists, designers. Co-published with Henry Ford Museum & Greenfield Village. 160pp. 8¼ x 11.   25780-0

HISTORIC COSTUME IN PICTURES, Braun & Schneider. Over 1,450 costumed figures in clearly detailed engravings–from dawn of civilization to end of 19th century. Captions. Many folk costumes. 256pp. 8⅜ x 11¾.   23150-X

CATALOG OF DOVER BOOKS

STICKLEY CRAFTSMAN FURNITURE CATALOGS, Gustav Stickley and L. & J. G. Stickley. Beautiful, functional furniture in two authentic catalogs from 1910. 594 illustrations, including 277 photos, show settles, rockers, armchairs, reclining chairs, bookcases, desks, tables. 183pp. 6½ x 9¼. 23838-5

AMERICAN LOCOMOTIVES IN HISTORIC PHOTOGRAPHS: 1858 to 1949, Ron Ziel (ed.). A rare collection of 126 meticulously detailed official photographs, called "builder portraits," of American locomotives that majestically chronicle the rise of steam locomotive power in America. Introduction. Detailed captions. xi+ 129pp. 9 x 12. 27393-8

AMERICA'S LIGHTHOUSES: An Illustrated History, Francis Ross Holland, Jr. Delightfully written, profusely illustrated fact-filled survey of over 200 American lighthouses since 1716. History, anecdotes, technological advances, more. 240pp. 8 x 10¾. 25576-X

TOWARDS A NEW ARCHITECTURE, Le Corbusier. Pioneering manifesto by founder of "International School." Technical and aesthetic theories, views of industry, economics, relation of form to function, "mass-production split" and much more. Profusely illustrated. 320pp. 6⅛ x 9¼. (Available in U.S. only.) 25023-7

HOW THE OTHER HALF LIVES, Jacob Riis. Famous journalistic record, exposing poverty and degradation of New York slums around 1900, by major social reformer. 100 striking and influential photographs. 233pp. 10 x 7⅞. 22012-5

FRUIT KEY AND TWIG KEY TO TREES AND SHRUBS, William M. Harlow. One of the handiest and most widely used identification aids. Fruit key covers 120 deciduous and evergreen species; twig key 160 deciduous species. Easily used. Over 300 photographs. 126pp. 5⅜ x 8½. 20511-8

COMMON BIRD SONGS, Dr. Donald J. Borror. Songs of 60 most common U.S. birds: robins, sparrows, cardinals, bluejays, finches, more–arranged in order of increasing complexity. Up to 9 variations of songs of each species.
Cassette and manual 99911-4

ORCHIDS AS HOUSE PLANTS, Rebecca Tyson Northen. Grow cattleyas and many other kinds of orchids–in a window, in a case, or under artificial light. 63 illustrations. 148pp. 5⅜ x 8½. 23261-1

MONSTER MAZES, Dave Phillips. Masterful mazes at four levels of difficulty. Avoid deadly perils and evil creatures to find magical treasures. Solutions for all 32 exciting illustrated puzzles. 48pp. 8¼ x 11. 26005-4

MOZART'S DON GIOVANNI (DOVER OPERA LIBRETTO SERIES), Wolfgang Amadeus Mozart. Introduced and translated by Ellen H. Bleiler. Standard Italian libretto, with complete English translation. Convenient and thoroughly portable–an ideal companion for reading along with a recording or the performance itself. Introduction. List of characters. Plot summary. 121pp. 5¼ x 8½. 24944-1

TECHNICAL MANUAL AND DICTIONARY OF CLASSICAL BALLET, Gail Grant. Defines, explains, comments on steps, movements, poses and concepts. 15-page pictorial section. Basic book for student, viewer. 127pp. 5⅜ x 8½. 21843-0

THE CLARINET AND CLARINET PLAYING, David Pino. Lively, comprehensive work features suggestions about technique, musicianship, and musical interpretation, as well as guidelines for teaching, making your own reeds, and preparing for public performance. Includes an intriguing look at clarinet history. "A godsend," *The Clarinet,* Journal of the International Clarinet Society. Appendixes. 7 illus. 320pp. 5⅜ x 8½. 40270-3

HOLLYWOOD GLAMOR PORTRAITS, John Kobal (ed.). 145 photos from 1926-49. Harlow, Gable, Bogart, Bacall; 94 stars in all. Full background on photographers, technical aspects. 160pp. 8⅜ x 11¼. 23352-9

THE ANNOTATED CASEY AT THE BAT: A Collection of Ballads about the Mighty Casey/Third, Revised Edition, Martin Gardner (ed.). Amusing sequels and parodies of one of America's best-loved poems: Casey's Revenge, Why Casey Whiffed, Casey's Sister at the Bat, others. 256pp. 5⅜ x 8½. 28598-7

THE RAVEN AND OTHER FAVORITE POEMS, Edgar Allan Poe. Over 40 of the author's most memorable poems: "The Bells," "Ulalume," "Israfel," "To Helen," "The Conqueror Worm," "Eldorado," "Annabel Lee," many more. Alphabetic lists of titles and first lines. 64pp. 5$\frac{3}{16}$ x 8¼. 26685-0

PERSONAL MEMOIRS OF U. S. GRANT, Ulysses Simpson Grant. Intelligent, deeply moving firsthand account of Civil War campaigns, considered by many the finest military memoirs ever written. Includes letters, historic photographs, maps and more. 528pp. 6⅛ x 9¼. 28587-1

ANCIENT EGYPTIAN MATERIALS AND INDUSTRIES, A. Lucas and J. Harris. Fascinating, comprehensive, thoroughly documented text describes this ancient civilization's vast resources and the processes that incorporated them in daily life, including the use of animal products, building materials, cosmetics, perfumes and incense, fibers, glazed ware, glass and its manufacture, materials used in the mummification process, and much more. 544pp. 6⅛ x 9¼. (Available in U.S. only.) 40446-3

RUSSIAN STORIES/RUSSKIE RASSKAZY: A Dual-Language Book, edited by Gleb Struve. Twelve tales by such masters as Chekhov, Tolstoy, Dostoevsky, Pushkin, others. Excellent word-for-word English translations on facing pages, plus teaching and study aids, Russian/English vocabulary, biographical/critical introductions, more. 416pp. 5⅜ x 8½. 26244-8

PHILADELPHIA THEN AND NOW: 60 Sites Photographed in the Past and Present, Kenneth Finkel and Susan Oyama. Rare photographs of City Hall, Logan Square, Independence Hall, Betsy Ross House, other landmarks juxtaposed with contemporary views. Captures changing face of historic city. Introduction. Captions. 128pp. 8¼ x 11. 25790-8

AIA ARCHITECTURAL GUIDE TO NASSAU AND SUFFOLK COUNTIES, LONG ISLAND, The American Institute of Architects, Long Island Chapter, and the Society for the Preservation of Long Island Antiquities. Comprehensive, well-researched and generously illustrated volume brings to life over three centuries of Long Island's great architectural heritage. More than 240 photographs with authoritative, extensively detailed captions. 176pp. 8¼ x 11. 26946-9

NORTH AMERICAN INDIAN LIFE: Customs and Traditions of 23 Tribes, Elsie Clews Parsons (ed.). 27 fictionalized essays by noted anthropologists examine religion, customs, government, additional facets of life among the Winnebago, Crow, Zuni, Eskimo, other tribes. 480pp. 6⅛ x 9¼. 27377-6

FRANK LLOYD WRIGHT'S DANA HOUSE, Donald Hoffmann. Pictorial essay of residential masterpiece with over 160 interior and exterior photos, plans, elevations, sketches and studies. 128pp. 9¼ x 10¾. 29120-0

THE MALE AND FEMALE FIGURE IN MOTION: 60 Classic Photographic Sequences, Eadweard Muybridge. 60 true-action photographs of men and women walking, running, climbing, bending, turning, etc., reproduced from rare 19th-century masterpiece. vi + 121pp. 9 x 12. 24745-7

1001 QUESTIONS ANSWERED ABOUT THE SEASHORE, N. J. Berrill and Jacquelyn Berrill. Queries answered about dolphins, sea snails, sponges, starfish, fishes, shore birds, many others. Covers appearance, breeding, growth, feeding, much more. 305pp. 5¼ x 8¼. 23366-9

ATTRACTING BIRDS TO YOUR YARD, William J. Weber. Easy-to-follow guide offers advice on how to attract the greatest diversity of birds: birdhouses, feeders, water and waterers, much more. 96pp. 5³⁄₁₆ x 8¼. 28927-3

MEDICINAL AND OTHER USES OF NORTH AMERICAN PLANTS: A Historical Survey with Special Reference to the Eastern Indian Tribes, Charlotte Erichsen-Brown. Chronological historical citations document 500 years of usage of plants, trees, shrubs native to eastern Canada, northeastern U.S. Also complete identifying information. 343 illustrations. 544pp. 6½ x 9¼. 25951-X

STORYBOOK MAZES, Dave Phillips. 23 stories and mazes on two-page spreads: Wizard of Oz, Treasure Island, Robin Hood, etc. Solutions. 64pp. 8¼ x 11. 23628-5

AMERICAN NEGRO SONGS: 230 Folk Songs and Spirituals, Religious and Secular, John W. Work. This authoritative study traces the African influences of songs sung and played by black Americans at work, in church, and as entertainment. The author discusses the lyric significance of such songs as "Swing Low, Sweet Chariot," "John Henry," and others and offers the words and music for 230 songs. Bibliography. Index of Song Titles. 272pp. 6½ x 9¼. 40271-1

MOVIE-STAR PORTRAITS OF THE FORTIES, John Kobal (ed.). 163 glamor, studio photos of 106 stars of the 1940s: Rita Hayworth, Ava Gardner, Marlon Brando, Clark Gable, many more. 176pp. 8⅜ x 11¼. 23546-7

BENCHLEY LOST AND FOUND, Robert Benchley. Finest humor from early 30s, about pet peeves, child psychologists, post office and others. Mostly unavailable elsewhere. 73 illustrations by Peter Arno and others. 183pp. 5⅜ x 8½. 22410-4

YEKL and THE IMPORTED BRIDEGROOM AND OTHER STORIES OF YIDDISH NEW YORK, Abraham Cahan. Film Hester Street based on *Yekl* (1896). Novel, other stories among first about Jewish immigrants on N.Y.'s East Side. 240pp. 5⅜ x 8½. 22427-9

SELECTED POEMS, Walt Whitman. Generous sampling from *Leaves of Grass*. Twenty-four poems include "I Hear America Singing," "Song of the Open Road," "I Sing the Body Electric," "When Lilacs Last in the Dooryard Bloom'd," "O Captain! My Captain!"—all reprinted from an authoritative edition. Lists of titles and first lines. 128pp. 5³⁄₁₆ x 8¼. 26878-0

THE BEST TALES OF HOFFMANN, E. T. A. Hoffmann. 10 of Hoffmann's most important stories: "Nutcracker and the King of Mice," "The Golden Flowerpot," etc. 458pp. 5⅜ x 8½. 21793-0

FROM FETISH TO GOD IN ANCIENT EGYPT, E. A. Wallis Budge. Rich detailed survey of Egyptian conception of "God" and gods, magic, cult of animals, Osiris, more. Also, superb English translations of hymns and legends. 240 illustrations. 545pp. 5⅜ x 8½. 25803-3

FRENCH STORIES/CONTES FRANÇAIS: A Dual-Language Book, Wallace Fowlie. Ten stories by French masters, Voltaire to Camus: "Micromegas" by Voltaire; "The Atheist's Mass" by Balzac; "Minuet" by de Maupassant; "The Guest" by Camus, six more. Excellent English translations on facing pages. Also French-English vocabulary list, exercises, more. 352pp. 5⅜ x 8½. 26443-2

CHICAGO AT THE TURN OF THE CENTURY IN PHOTOGRAPHS: 122 Historic Views from the Collections of the Chicago Historical Society, Larry A. Viskochil. Rare large-format prints offer detailed views of City Hall, State Street, the Loop, Hull House, Union Station, many other landmarks, circa 1904-1913. Introduction. Captions. Maps. 144pp. 9⅜ x 12¼. 24656-6

OLD BROOKLYN IN EARLY PHOTOGRAPHS, 1865-1929, William Lee Younger. Luna Park, Gravesend race track, construction of Grand Army Plaza, moving of Hotel Brighton, etc. 157 previously unpublished photographs. 165pp. 8⅞ x 11¾. 23587-4

THE MYTHS OF THE NORTH AMERICAN INDIANS, Lewis Spence. Rich anthology of the myths and legends of the Algonquins, Iroquois, Pawnees and Sioux, prefaced by an extensive historical and ethnological commentary. 36 illustrations. 480pp. 5⅜ x 8½. 25967-6

AN ENCYCLOPEDIA OF BATTLES: Accounts of Over 1,560 Battles from 1479 B.C. to the Present, David Eggenberger. Essential details of every major battle in recorded history from the first battle of Megiddo in 1479 B.C. to Grenada in 1984. List of Battle Maps. New Appendix covering the years 1967-1984. Index. 99 illustrations. 544pp. 6½ x 9¼. 24913-1

SAILING ALONE AROUND THE WORLD, Captain Joshua Slocum. First man to sail around the world, alone, in small boat. One of great feats of seamanship told in delightful manner. 67 illustrations. 294pp. 5⅜ x 8½. 20326-3

ANARCHISM AND OTHER ESSAYS, Emma Goldman. Powerful, penetrating, prophetic essays on direct action, role of minorities, prison reform, puritan hypocrisy, violence, etc. 271pp. 5⅜ x 8½. 22484-8

MYTHS OF THE HINDUS AND BUDDHISTS, Ananda K. Coomaraswamy and Sister Nivedita. Great stories of the epics; deeds of Krishna, Shiva, taken from puranas, Vedas, folk tales; etc. 32 illustrations. 400pp. 5⅜ x 8½. 21759-0

THE TRAUMA OF BIRTH, Otto Rank. Rank's controversial thesis that anxiety neurosis is caused by profound psychological trauma which occurs at birth. 256pp. 5⅜ x 8½. 27974-X

A THEOLOGICO-POLITICAL TREATISE, Benedict Spinoza. Also contains unfinished Political Treatise. Great classic on religious liberty, theory of government on common consent. R. Elwes translation. Total of 421pp. 5⅜ x 8½. 20249-6

MY BONDAGE AND MY FREEDOM, Frederick Douglass. Born a slave, Douglass became outspoken force in antislavery movement. The best of Douglass' autobiographies. Graphic description of slave life. 464pp. 5⅜ x 8½.   22457-0

FOLLOWING THE EQUATOR: A Journey Around the World, Mark Twain. Fascinating humorous account of 1897 voyage to Hawaii, Australia, India, New Zealand, etc. Ironic, bemused reports on peoples, customs, climate, flora and fauna, politics, much more. 197 illustrations. 720pp. 5⅜ x 8½.   26113-1

THE PEOPLE CALLED SHAKERS, Edward D. Andrews. Definitive study of Shakers: origins, beliefs, practices, dances, social organization, furniture and crafts, etc. 33 illustrations. 351pp. 5⅜ x 8½.   21081-2

THE MYTHS OF GREECE AND ROME, H. A. Guerber. A classic of mythology, generously illustrated, long prized for its simple, graphic, accurate retelling of the principal myths of Greece and Rome, and for its commentary on their origins and significance. With 64 illustrations by Michelangelo, Raphael, Titian, Rubens, Canova, Bernini and others. 480pp. 5⅜ x 8½.   27584-1

PSYCHOLOGY OF MUSIC, Carl E. Seashore. Classic work discusses music as a medium from psychological viewpoint. Clear treatment of physical acoustics, auditory apparatus, sound perception, development of musical skills, nature of musical feeling, host of other topics. 88 figures. 408pp. 5⅜ x 8½.   21851-1

THE PHILOSOPHY OF HISTORY, Georg W. Hegel. Great classic of Western thought develops concept that history is not chance but rational process, the evolution of freedom. 457pp. 5⅜ x 8½.   20112-0

THE BOOK OF TEA, Kakuzo Okakura. Minor classic of the Orient: entertaining, charming explanation, interpretation of traditional Japanese culture in terms of tea ceremony. 94pp. 5⅜ x 8½.   20070-1

LIFE IN ANCIENT EGYPT, Adolf Erman. Fullest, most thorough, detailed older account with much not in more recent books, domestic life, religion, magic, medicine, commerce, much more. Many illustrations reproduce tomb paintings, carvings, hieroglyphs, etc. 597pp. 5⅜ x 8½.   22632-8

SUNDIALS, Their Theory and Construction, Albert Waugh. Far and away the best, most thorough coverage of ideas, mathematics concerned, types, construction, adjusting anywhere. Simple, nontechnical treatment allows even children to build several of these dials. Over 100 illustrations. 230pp. 5⅜ x 8½.   22947-5

THEORETICAL HYDRODYNAMICS, L. M. Milne-Thomson. Classic exposition of the mathematical theory of fluid motion, applicable to both hydrodynamics and aerodynamics. Over 600 exercises. 768pp. 6⅛ x 9¼.   68970-0

SONGS OF EXPERIENCE: Facsimile Reproduction with 26 Plates in Full Color, William Blake. 26 full-color plates from a rare 1826 edition. Includes "The Tyger," "London," "Holy Thursday," and other poems. Printed text of poems. 48pp. 5¼ x 7.
        24636-1

OLD-TIME VIGNETTES IN FULL COLOR, Carol Belanger Grafton (ed.). Over 390 charming, often sentimental illustrations, selected from archives of Victorian graphics—pretty women posing, children playing, food, flowers, kittens and puppies, smiling cherubs, birds and butterflies, much more. All copyright-free. 48pp. 9¼ x 12¼.
        27269-9

PERSPECTIVE FOR ARTISTS, Rex Vicat Cole. Depth, perspective of sky and sea, shadows, much more, not usually covered. 391 diagrams, 81 reproductions of drawings and paintings. 279pp. 5⅜ x 8½. 22487-2

DRAWING THE LIVING FIGURE, Joseph Sheppard. Innovative approach to artistic anatomy focuses on specifics of surface anatomy, rather than muscles and bones. Over 170 drawings of live models in front, back and side views, and in widely varying poses. Accompanying diagrams. 177 illustrations. Introduction. Index. 144pp. 8⅜ x11¼. 26723-7

GOTHIC AND OLD ENGLISH ALPHABETS: 100 Complete Fonts, Dan X. Solo. Add power, elegance to posters, signs, other graphics with 100 stunning copyright-free alphabets: Blackstone, Dolbey, Germania, 97 more–including many lower-case, numerals, punctuation marks. 104pp. 8⅛ x 11. 24695-7

HOW TO DO BEADWORK, Mary White. Fundamental book on craft from simple projects to five-bead chains and woven works. 106 illustrations. 142pp. 5⅜ x 8. 20697-1

THE BOOK OF WOOD CARVING, Charles Marshall Sayers. Finest book for beginners discusses fundamentals and offers 34 designs. "Absolutely first rate . . . well thought out and well executed."–E. J. Tangerman. 118pp. 7¾ x 10⅝. 23654-4

ILLUSTRATED CATALOG OF CIVIL WAR MILITARY GOODS: Union Army Weapons, Insignia, Uniform Accessories, and Other Equipment, Schuyler, Hartley, and Graham. Rare, profusely illustrated 1846 catalog includes Union Army uniform and dress regulations, arms and ammunition, coats, insignia, flags, swords, rifles, etc. 226 illustrations. 160pp. 9 x 12. 24939-5

WOMEN'S FASHIONS OF THE EARLY 1900s: An Unabridged Republication of "New York Fashions, 1909," National Cloak & Suit Co. Rare catalog of mail-order fashions documents women's and children's clothing styles shortly after the turn of the century. Captions offer full descriptions, prices. Invaluable resource for fashion, costume historians. Approximately 725 illustrations. 128pp. 8⅜ x 11¼. 27276-1

THE 1912 AND 1915 GUSTAV STICKLEY FURNITURE CATALOGS, Gustav Stickley. With over 200 detailed illustrations and descriptions, these two catalogs are essential reading and reference materials and identification guides for Stickley furniture. Captions cite materials, dimensions and prices. 112pp. 6½ x 9¼. 26676-1

EARLY AMERICAN LOCOMOTIVES, John H. White, Jr. Finest locomotive engravings from early 19th century: historical (1804–74), main-line (after 1870), special, foreign, etc. 147 plates. 142pp. 11⅜ x 8¼. 22772-3

THE TALL SHIPS OF TODAY IN PHOTOGRAPHS, Frank O. Braynard. Lavishly illustrated tribute to nearly 100 majestic contemporary sailing vessels: Amerigo Vespucci, Clearwater, Constitution, Eagle, Mayflower, Sea Cloud, Victory, many more. Authoritative captions provide statistics, background on each ship. 190 black-and-white photographs and illustrations. Introduction. 128pp. 8⅞ x 11¾. 27163-3

LITTLE BOOK OF EARLY AMERICAN CRAFTS AND TRADES, Peter Stockham (ed.). 1807 children's book explains crafts and trades: baker, hatter, cooper, potter, and many others. 23 copperplate illustrations. 140pp. 4⅝ x 6.   23336-7

VICTORIAN FASHIONS AND COSTUMES FROM HARPER'S BAZAR, 1867–1898, Stella Blum (ed.). Day costumes, evening wear, sports clothes, shoes, hats, other accessories in over 1,000 detailed engravings. 320pp. 9⅜ x 12¼. 22990-4

GUSTAV STICKLEY, THE CRAFTSMAN, Mary Ann Smith. Superb study surveys broad scope of Stickley's achievement, especially in architecture. Design philosophy, rise and fall of the Craftsman empire, descriptions and floor plans for many Craftsman houses, more. 86 black-and-white halftones. 31 line illustrations. Introduction 208pp. 6½ x 9¼.   27210-9

THE LONG ISLAND RAIL ROAD IN EARLY PHOTOGRAPHS, Ron Ziel. Over 220 rare photos, informative text document origin (1844) and development of rail service on Long Island. Vintage views of early trains, locomotives, stations, passengers, crews, much more. Captions. 8⅞ x 11¾.   26301-0

VOYAGE OF THE LIBERDADE, Joshua Slocum. Great 19th-century mariner's thrilling, first-hand account of the wreck of his ship off South America, the 35-foot boat he built from the wreckage, and its remarkable voyage home. 128pp. 5⅜ x 8½.
40022-0

TEN BOOKS ON ARCHITECTURE, Vitruvius. The most important book ever written on architecture. Early Roman aesthetics, technology, classical orders, site selection, all other aspects. Morgan translation. 331pp. 5⅜ x 8½.   20645-9

THE HUMAN FIGURE IN MOTION, Eadweard Muybridge. More than 4,500 stopped-action photos, in action series, showing undraped men, women, children jumping, lying down, throwing, sitting, wrestling, carrying, etc. 390pp. 7⅞ x 10⅝.
20204-6 Clothbd.

TREES OF THE EASTERN AND CENTRAL UNITED STATES AND CANADA, William M. Harlow. Best one-volume guide to 140 trees. Full descriptions, woodlore, range, etc. Over 600 illustrations. Handy size. 288pp. 4½ x 6⅜.   20395-6

SONGS OF WESTERN BIRDS, Dr. Donald J. Borror. Complete song and call repertoire of 60 western species, including flycatchers, juncoes, cactus wrens, many more—includes fully illustrated booklet.   Cassette and manual 99913-0

GROWING AND USING HERBS AND SPICES, Milo Miloradovich. Versatile handbook provides all the information needed for cultivation and use of all the herbs and spices available in North America. 4 illustrations. Index. Glossary. 236pp. 5⅜ x 8½.
25058-X

BIG BOOK OF MAZES AND LABYRINTHS, Walter Shepherd. 50 mazes and labyrinths in all—classical, solid, ripple, and more—in one great volume. Perfect inexpensive puzzler for clever youngsters. Full solutions. 112pp. 8⅛ x 11.   22951-3

PIANO TUNING, J. Cree Fischer. Clearest, best book for beginner, amateur. Simple repairs, raising dropped notes, tuning by easy method of flattened fifths. No previous skills needed. 4 illustrations. 201pp. 5⅜ x 8½. 23267-0

HINTS TO SINGERS, Lillian Nordica. Selecting the right teacher, developing confidence, overcoming stage fright, and many other important skills receive thoughtful discussion in this indispensible guide, written by a world-famous diva of four decades' experience. 96pp. 5⅜ x 8½. 40094-8

THE COMPLETE NONSENSE OF EDWARD LEAR, Edward Lear. All nonsense limericks, zany alphabets, Owl and Pussycat, songs, nonsense botany, etc., illustrated by Lear. Total of 320pp. 5⅜ x 8½. (Available in U.S. only.) 20167-8

VICTORIAN PARLOUR POETRY: An Annotated Anthology, Michael R. Turner. 117 gems by Longfellow, Tennyson, Browning, many lesser-known poets. "The Village Blacksmith," "Curfew Must Not Ring Tonight," "Only a Baby Small," dozens more, often difficult to find elsewhere. Index of poets, titles, first lines. xxiii + 325pp. 5⅝ x 8¼. 27044-0

DUBLINERS, James Joyce. Fifteen stories offer vivid, tightly focused observations of the lives of Dublin's poorer classes. At least one, "The Dead," is considered a masterpiece. Reprinted complete and unabridged from standard edition. 160pp. 5$\frac{3}{16}$ x 8¼. 26870-5

GREAT WEIRD TALES: 14 Stories by Lovecraft, Blackwood, Machen and Others, S. T. Joshi (ed.). 14 spellbinding tales, including "The Sin Eater," by Fiona McLeod, "The Eye Above the Mantel," by Frank Belknap Long, as well as renowned works by R. H. Barlow, Lord Dunsany, Arthur Machen, W. C. Morrow and eight other masters of the genre. 256pp. 5⅜ x 8½. (Available in U.S. only.) 40436-6

THE BOOK OF THE SACRED MAGIC OF ABRAMELIN THE MAGE, translated by S. MacGregor Mathers. Medieval manuscript of ceremonial magic. Basic document in Aleister Crowley, Golden Dawn groups. 268pp. 5⅜ x 8½. 23211-5

NEW RUSSIAN-ENGLISH AND ENGLISH-RUSSIAN DICTIONARY, M. A. O'Brien. This is a remarkably handy Russian dictionary, containing a surprising amount of information, including over 70,000 entries. 366pp. 4½ x 6⅛. 20208-9

HISTORIC HOMES OF THE AMERICAN PRESIDENTS, Second, Revised Edition, Irvin Haas. A traveler's guide to American Presidential homes, most open to the public, depicting and describing homes occupied by every American President from George Washington to George Bush. With visiting hours, admission charges, travel routes. 175 photographs. Index. 160pp. 8¼ x 11. 26751-2

NEW YORK IN THE FORTIES, Andreas Feininger. 162 brilliant photographs by the well-known photographer, formerly with *Life* magazine. Commuters, shoppers, Times Square at night, much else from city at its peak. Captions by John von Hartz. 181pp. 9¼ x 10¾. 23585-8

INDIAN SIGN LANGUAGE, William Tomkins. Over 525 signs developed by Sioux and other tribes. Written instructions and diagrams. Also 290 pictographs. 111pp. 6⅛ x 9¼. 22029-X

ANATOMY: A Complete Guide for Artists, Joseph Sheppard. A master of figure drawing shows artists how to render human anatomy convincingly. Over 460 illustrations. 224pp. 8⅜ x 11¼. 27279-6

MEDIEVAL CALLIGRAPHY: Its History and Technique, Marc Drogin. Spirited history, comprehensive instruction manual covers 13 styles (ca. 4th century through 15th). Excellent photographs; directions for duplicating medieval techniques with modern tools. 224pp. 8⅜ x 11¼. 26142-5

DRIED FLOWERS: How to Prepare Them, Sarah Whitlock and Martha Rankin. Complete instructions on how to use silica gel, meal and borax, perlite aggregate, sand and borax, glycerine and water to create attractive permanent flower arrangements. 12 illustrations. 32pp. 5⅜ x 8½. 21802-3

EASY-TO-MAKE BIRD FEEDERS FOR WOODWORKERS, Scott D. Campbell. Detailed, simple-to-use guide for designing, constructing, caring for and using feeders. Text, illustrations for 12 classic and contemporary designs. 96pp. 5⅜ x 8½.
25847-5

SCOTTISH WONDER TALES FROM MYTH AND LEGEND, Donald A. Mackenzie. 16 lively tales tell of giants rumbling down mountainsides, of a magic wand that turns stone pillars into warriors, of gods and goddesses, evil hags, powerful forces and more. 240pp. 5⅜ x 8½. 29677-6

THE HISTORY OF UNDERCLOTHES, C. Willett Cunnington and Phyllis Cunnington. Fascinating, well-documented survey covering six centuries of English undergarments, enhanced with over 100 illustrations: 12th-century laced-up bodice, footed long drawers (1795), 19th-century bustles, 19th-century corsets for men, Victorian "bust improvers," much more. 272pp. 5⅜ x 8¼. 27124-2

ARTS AND CRAFTS FURNITURE: The Complete Brooks Catalog of 1912, Brooks Manufacturing Co. Photos and detailed descriptions of more than 150 now very collectible furniture designs from the Arts and Crafts movement depict davenports, settees, buffets, desks, tables, chairs, bedsteads, dressers and more, all built of solid, quarter-sawed oak. Invaluable for students and enthusiasts of antiques, Americana and the decorative arts. 80pp. 6½ x 9¼. 27471-3

WILBUR AND ORVILLE: A Biography of the Wright Brothers, Fred Howard. Definitive, crisply written study tells the full story of the brothers' lives and work. A vividly written biography, unparalleled in scope and color, that also captures the spirit of an extraordinary era. 560pp. 6⅛ x 9¼. 40297-5

THE ARTS OF THE SAILOR: Knotting, Splicing and Ropework, Hervey Garrett Smith. Indispensable shipboard reference covers tools, basic knots and useful hitches; handsewing and canvas work, more. Over 100 illustrations. Delightful reading for sea lovers. 256pp. 5⅜ x 8½. 26440-8

FRANK LLOYD WRIGHT'S FALLINGWATER: The House and Its History, Second, Revised Edition, Donald Hoffmann. A total revision–both in text and illustrations–of the standard document on Fallingwater, the boldest, most personal architectural statement of Wright's mature years, updated with valuable new material from the recently opened Frank Lloyd Wright Archives. "Fascinating"–*The New York Times*. 116 illustrations. 128pp. 9¼ x 10¾. 27430-6

PHOTOGRAPHIC SKETCHBOOK OF THE CIVIL WAR, Alexander Gardner. 100 photos taken on field during the Civil War. Famous shots of Manassas Harper's Ferry, Lincoln, Richmond, slave pens, etc. 244pp. 10⅝ x 8¼. 22731-6

FIVE ACRES AND INDEPENDENCE, Maurice G. Kains. Great back-to-the-land classic explains basics of self-sufficient farming. The one book to get. 95 illustrations. 397pp. 5⅜ x 8½. 20974-1

SONGS OF EASTERN BIRDS, Dr. Donald J. Borror. Songs and calls of 60 species most common to eastern U.S.: warblers, woodpeckers, flycatchers, thrushes, larks, many more in high-quality recording. Cassette and manual 99912-2

A MODERN HERBAL, Margaret Grieve. Much the fullest, most exact, most useful compilation of herbal material. Gigantic alphabetical encyclopedia, from aconite to zedoary, gives botanical information, medical properties, folklore, economic uses, much else. Indispensable to serious reader. 161 illustrations. 888pp. 6½ x 9¼. 2-vol. set. (Available in U.S. only.) Vol. I: 22798-7
Vol. II: 22799-5

HIDDEN TREASURE MAZE BOOK, Dave Phillips. Solve 34 challenging mazes accompanied by heroic tales of adventure. Evil dragons, people-eating plants, bloodthirsty giants, many more dangerous adversaries lurk at every twist and turn. 34 mazes, stories, solutions. 48pp. 8¼ x 11. 24566-7

LETTERS OF W. A. MOZART, Wolfgang A. Mozart. Remarkable letters show bawdy wit, humor, imagination, musical insights, contemporary musical world; includes some letters from Leopold Mozart. 276pp. 5⅜ x 8½. 22859-2

BASIC PRINCIPLES OF CLASSICAL BALLET, Agrippina Vaganova. Great Russian theoretician, teacher explains methods for teaching classical ballet. 118 illustrations. 175pp. 5⅜ x 8½. 22036-2

THE JUMPING FROG, Mark Twain. Revenge edition. The original story of The Celebrated Jumping Frog of Calaveras County, a hapless French translation, and Twain's hilarious "retranslation" from the French. 12 illustrations. 66pp. 5⅜ x 8½. 22686-7

BEST REMEMBERED POEMS, Martin Gardner (ed.). The 126 poems in this superb collection of 19th- and 20th-century British and American verse range from Shelley's "To a Skylark" to the impassioned "Renascence" of Edna St. Vincent Millay and to Edward Lear's whimsical "The Owl and the Pussycat." 224pp. 5⅜ x 8½. 27165-X

COMPLETE SONNETS, William Shakespeare. Over 150 exquisite poems deal with love, friendship, the tyranny of time, beauty's evanescence, death and other themes in language of remarkable power, precision and beauty. Glossary of archaic terms. 80pp. 5$\frac{3}{16}$ x 8¼. 26686-9

THE BATTLES THAT CHANGED HISTORY, Fletcher Pratt. Eminent historian profiles 16 crucial conflicts, ancient to modern, that changed the course of civilization. 352pp. 5⅜ x 8½. 41129-X

THE WIT AND HUMOR OF OSCAR WILDE, Alvin Redman (ed.). More than 1,000 ripostes, paradoxes, wisecracks: Work is the curse of the drinking classes; I can resist everything except temptation; etc. 258pp. 5⅜ x 8½. 20602-5

SHAKESPEARE LEXICON AND QUOTATION DICTIONARY, Alexander Schmidt. Full definitions, locations, shades of meaning in every word in plays and poems. More than 50,000 exact quotations. 1,485pp. 6½ x 9¼. 2-vol. set.
Vol. 1: 22726-X
Vol. 2: 22727-8

SELECTED POEMS, Emily Dickinson. Over 100 best-known, best-loved poems by one of America's foremost poets, reprinted from authoritative early editions. No comparable edition at this price. Index of first lines. 64pp. $5\frac{3}{16}$ x 8¼. 26466-1

THE INSIDIOUS DR. FU-MANCHU, Sax Rohmer. The first of the popular mystery series introduces a pair of English detectives to their archnemesis, the diabolical Dr. Fu-Manchu. Flavorful atmosphere, fast-paced action, and colorful characters enliven this classic of the genre. 208pp. $5\frac{3}{16}$ x 8¼. 29898-1

THE MALLEUS MALEFICARUM OF KRAMER AND SPRENGER, translated by Montague Summers. Full text of most important witchhunter's "bible," used by both Catholics and Protestants. 278pp. 6⅝ x 10. 22802-9

SPANISH STORIES/CUENTOS ESPAÑOLES: A Dual-Language Book, Angel Flores (ed.). Unique format offers 13 great stories in Spanish by Cervantes, Borges, others. Faithful English translations on facing pages. 352pp. 5⅜ x 8½. 25399-6

GARDEN CITY, LONG ISLAND, IN EARLY PHOTOGRAPHS, 1869–1919, Mildred H. Smith. Handsome treasury of 118 vintage pictures, accompanied by carefully researched captions, document the Garden City Hotel fire (1899), the Vanderbilt Cup Race (1908), the first airmail flight departing from the Nassau Boulevard Aerodrome (1911), and much more. 96pp. 8⅞ x 11¾. 40669-5

OLD QUEENS, N.Y., IN EARLY PHOTOGRAPHS, Vincent F. Seyfried and William Asadorian. Over 160 rare photographs of Maspeth, Jamaica, Jackson Heights, and other areas. Vintage views of DeWitt Clinton mansion, 1939 World's Fair and more. Captions. 192pp. 8⅞ x 11. 26358-4

CAPTURED BY THE INDIANS: 15 Firsthand Accounts, 1750-1870, Frederick Drimmer. Astounding true historical accounts of grisly torture, bloody conflicts, relentless pursuits, miraculous escapes and more, by people who lived to tell the tale. 384pp. 5⅜ x 8½. 24901-8

THE WORLD'S GREAT SPEECHES (Fourth Enlarged Edition), Lewis Copeland, Lawrence W. Lamm, and Stephen J. McKenna. Nearly 300 speeches provide public speakers with a wealth of updated quotes and inspiration–from Pericles' funeral oration and William Jennings Bryan's "Cross of Gold Speech" to Malcolm X's powerful words on the Black Revolution and Earl of Spenser's tribute to his sister, Diana, Princess of Wales. 944pp. 5⅜ x 8⅜. 40903-1

THE BOOK OF THE SWORD, Sir Richard F. Burton. Great Victorian scholar/adventurer's eloquent, erudite history of the "queen of weapons"–from prehistory to early Roman Empire. Evolution and development of early swords, variations (sabre, broadsword, cutlass, scimitar, etc.), much more. 336pp. 6⅛ x 9¼.
25434-8

AUTOBIOGRAPHY: The Story of My Experiments with Truth, Mohandas K. Gandhi. Boyhood, legal studies, purification, the growth of the Satyagraha (nonviolent protest) movement. Critical, inspiring work of the man responsible for the freedom of India. 480pp. 5⅜ x 8½. (Available in U.S. only.)   24593-4

CELTIC MYTHS AND LEGENDS, T. W. Rolleston. Masterful retelling of Irish and Welsh stories and tales. Cuchulain, King Arthur, Deirdre, the Grail, many more. First paperback edition. 58 full-page illustrations. 512pp. 5⅜ x 8½.   26507-2

THE PRINCIPLES OF PSYCHOLOGY, William James. Famous long course complete, unabridged. Stream of thought, time perception, memory, experimental methods; great work decades ahead of its time. 94 figures. 1,391pp. 5⅜ x 8½. 2-vol. set.
Vol. I: 20381-6   Vol. II: 20382-4

THE WORLD AS WILL AND REPRESENTATION, Arthur Schopenhauer. Definitive English translation of Schopenhauer's life work, correcting more than 1,000 errors, omissions in earlier translations. Translated by E. F. J. Payne. Total of 1,269pp. 5⅜ x 8½. 2-vol. set.   Vol. 1: 21761-2   Vol. 2: 21762-0

MAGIC AND MYSTERY IN TIBET, Madame Alexandra David-Neel. Experiences among lamas, magicians, sages, sorcerers, Bonpa wizards. A true psychic discovery. 32 illustrations. 321pp. 5⅜ x 8½. (Available in U.S. only.)   22682-4

THE EGYPTIAN BOOK OF THE DEAD, E. A. Wallis Budge. Complete reproduction of Ani's papyrus, finest ever found. Full hieroglyphic text, interlinear transliteration, word-for-word translation, smooth translation. 533pp. 6½ x 9¼.   21866-X

MATHEMATICS FOR THE NONMATHEMATICIAN, Morris Kline. Detailed, college-level treatment of mathematics in cultural and historical context, with numerous exercises. Recommended Reading Lists. Tables. Numerous figures. 641pp. 5⅜ x 8½.   24823-2

PROBABILISTIC METHODS IN THE THEORY OF STRUCTURES, Isaac Elishakoff. Well-written introduction covers the elements of the theory of probability from two or more random variables, the reliability of such multivariable structures, the theory of random function, Monte Carlo methods of treating problems incapable of exact solution, and more. Examples. 502pp. 5⅜ x 8½.   40691-1

THE RIME OF THE ANCIENT MARINER, Gustave Doré, S. T. Coleridge. Doré's finest work; 34 plates capture moods, subtleties of poem. Flawless full-size reproductions printed on facing pages with authoritative text of poem. "Beautiful. Simply beautiful."—Publisher's Weekly. 77pp. 9¼ x 12.   22305-1

NORTH AMERICAN INDIAN DESIGNS FOR ARTISTS AND CRAFTSPEOPLE, Eva Wilson. Over 360 authentic copyright-free designs adapted from Navajo blankets, Hopi pottery, Sioux buffalo hides, more. Geometrics, symbolic figures, plant and animal motifs, etc. 128pp. 8⅜ x 11. (Not for sale in the United Kingdom.)   25341-4

SCULPTURE: Principles and Practice, Louis Slobodkin. Step-by-step approach to clay, plaster, metals, stone; classical and modern. 253 drawings, photos. 255pp. 8⅛ x 11.   22960-2

THE INFLUENCE OF SEA POWER UPON HISTORY, 1660–1783, A. T. Mahan. Influential classic of naval history and tactics still used as text in war colleges. First paperback edition. 4 maps. 24 battle plans. 640pp. 5⅜ x 8½.   25509-3

CATALOG OF DOVER BOOKS

THE STORY OF THE TITANIC AS TOLD BY ITS SURVIVORS, Jack Winocour (ed.). What it was really like. Panic, despair, shocking inefficiency, and a little heroism. More thrilling than any fictional account. 26 illustrations. 320pp. 5⅜ x 8½. 20610-6

FAIRY AND FOLK TALES OF THE IRISH PEASANTRY, William Butler Yeats (ed.). Treasury of 64 tales from the twilight world of Celtic myth and legend: "The Soul Cages," "The Kildare Pooka," "King O'Toole and his Goose," many more. Introduction and Notes by W. B. Yeats. 352pp. 5⅜ x 8½. 26941-8

BUDDHIST MAHAYANA TEXTS, E. B. Cowell and others (eds.). Superb, accurate translations of basic documents in Mahayana Buddhism, highly important in history of religions. The Buddha-karita of Asvaghosha, Larger Sukhavativyuha, more. 448pp. 5⅜ x 8½. 25552-2

ONE TWO THREE . . . INFINITY: Facts and Speculations of Science, George Gamow. Great physicist's fascinating, readable overview of contemporary science: number theory, relativity, fourth dimension, entropy, genes, atomic structure, much more. 128 illustrations. Index. 352pp. 5⅜ x 8½. 25664-2

EXPERIMENTATION AND MEASUREMENT, W. J. Youden. Introductory manual explains laws of measurement in simple terms and offers tips for achieving accuracy and minimizing errors. Mathematics of measurement, use of instruments, experimenting with machines. 1994 edition. Foreword. Preface. Introduction. Epilogue. Selected Readings. Glossary. Index. Tables and figures. 128pp. 5⅜ x 8½. 40451-X

DALÍ ON MODERN ART: The Cuckolds of Antiquated Modern Art, Salvador Dalí. Influential painter skewers modern art and its practitioners. Outrageous evaluations of Picasso, Cézanne, Turner, more. 15 renderings of paintings discussed. 44 calligraphic decorations by Dalí. 96pp. 5⅜ x 8½. (Available in U.S. only.) 29220-7

ANTIQUE PLAYING CARDS: A Pictorial History, Henry René D'Allemagne. Over 900 elaborate, decorative images from rare playing cards (14th–20th centuries): Bacchus, death, dancing dogs, hunting scenes, royal coats of arms, players cheating, much more. 96pp. 9¼ x 12¼. 29265-7

MAKING FURNITURE MASTERPIECES: 30 Projects with Measured Drawings, Franklin H. Gottshall. Step-by-step instructions, illustrations for constructing handsome, useful pieces, among them a Sheraton desk, Chippendale chair, Spanish desk, Queen Anne table and a William and Mary dressing mirror. 224pp. 8⅛ x 11¼. 29338-6

THE FOSSIL BOOK: A Record of Prehistoric Life, Patricia V. Rich et al. Profusely illustrated definitive guide covers everything from single-celled organisms and dinosaurs to birds and mammals and the interplay between climate and man. Over 1,500 illustrations. 760pp. 7½ x 10⅛. 29371-8

Paperbound unless otherwise indicated. Available at your book dealer, online at **www.doverpublications.com**, or by writing to Dept. GI, Dover Publications, Inc., 31 East 2nd Street, Mineola, NY 11501. For current price information or for free catalogues (please indicate field of interest), write to Dover Publications or log on to **www.doverpublications.com** and see every Dover book in print. Dover publishes more than 500 books each year on science, elementary and advanced mathematics, biology, music, art, literary history, social sciences, and other areas.